Nancy S. Pyle
Cambridge
20 October 1976

15—

D1505955

Photographs by Christina Gascoigne

The Great Moghuls

Bamber Gascoigne

Harper & Row, Publishers

New York · Evanston · San Francisco · London

Text and illustrations copyright © 1971 by
Bamber and Christina Gascoigne

First U.S. edition 1971
All rights reserved under International and
Pan-American Copyright Conventions
Published in the United States by
Harper & Row, Publishers, Inc., New York

No part of this book may be used or reproduced in any
manner whatsoever without written permission except in
the case of brief quotations embodied in critical articles and
reviews. For information address Harper & Row, Publishers,
Inc., 49 East 33d Street, New York, N.Y. 10016

This book was designed and produced in Great Britain by
George Rainbird Ltd.
Marble Arch House, 44 Edgware Road, London W2

House Editor: Yorke Crompton
Designer: Michael Mendelsohn

Filmset in 11/12½ pt Apollo by Westerham Press Ltd
Printed and bound by
Dai Nippon Printing Company Ltd.
Tokyo, Japan

Library of Congress Catalog Card Number: 77–152348
ISBN: 06–011467–3

For the many friends in India and Pakistan
who helped us on our way

Authors' Note

It would be impossible to list here the many people who helped us on our travels with advice, facilities or hospitality—so to them we dedicate the book. For detailed assistance before our departure we would like to thank Mrs Vibha Pandhi, the Director of the Government of India Tourist Board in London, and Mr Abdul Qayyum, the Press Counsellor at the Pakistan High Commission in London; and we are grateful to their many colleagues who continued to provide us with every sort of official help throughout our journey in both countries. Among the many museums and libraries and private collections where we worked, we would like to thank for their help and cooperation the staffs of the Prince of Wales Museum in Bombay, the National Museum in Delhi, the Palace Museums at Jaipur and Alwar, the Raza Library at Rampur, the Khuda Bakhsh Library and the Jalan Collection at Patna, the Calico Museum at Ahmedabad, the Lahore Museum, the State Museum of Oriental Art in Moscow, the Hermitage in Leningrad, the Chester Beatty Library in Dublin, the Bodleian at Oxford, and the Victoria and Albert Museum, the British Museum, the London Library and the India Office Library in London. For detailed advice we are particularly grateful to Douglas Matthews at the London Library; to Peter Avery of King's College, Cambridge; to Dashrath Patel of the National Design Institute in Ahmedabad; and above all to Robert Skelton, of the Victoria and Albert Museum, who gave us invaluable help at every stage of planning and completing the work. For permission to photograph and to reproduce their material we thank all the museums and libraries credited in the notes to the illustrations (pp. 258–9). And finally our journey would have been impossible without the kind cooperation of Granada Television in rearranging recording dates.

B. and C.G.

Contents

Color Illustrations

Prologue

On September 22, 1398, an army of Mongols arrived at the bank of the River Indus, the first natural barrier protecting India after the mountain passes of Afghanistan. Two days later they had completed their bridge of boats and were continuing eastwards.

In normal circumstances this news would have caused no special alarm in Delhi. Mongol raiding parties had been descending on the Punjab every few years for almost two centuries. They were a continuous irritation, but when it came to a pitched battle they were usually defeated. As enemies they were regarded as mere savages, terrifying but ultimately inferior. The poet Amir Khusrau, who had for a while been their prisoner, brought back the information that their rough skin seemed suitable only for shoe leather, and that their bodies were covered with lice which looked like sesame growing on poor soil. In normal circumstances, then, the rulers in Delhi would not have felt unduly threatened.[1]

But in 1398 the circumstances were far from normal. First, it was not entirely clear who were the rulers in Delhi: since the death of Firuz Shah ten years before, the empire had been torn by rival claimants to the throne, and there were now two puppet kings, each manipulated by a more powerful noble. Secondly, the latest army of Mongols was led by none other than Timur, whose limp caused him to be known as Timur-i-Leng or Timur the Lame, a corruption of which provided the name by which he became known throughout the West—Tamburlaine.

Marlowe's 'scourge of God' was now sixty but even an extremely hostile Arab author, captured by Timur about this time, described him as still 'strong and robust in body, like a hard rock'.[2] Five years earlier he had taken Baghdad; three years earlier his hordes had ravaged Russia to within two hundred miles of Moscow. India had not been in such danger since 1221, when Jenghiz Khan himself had arrived at the same stretch of the Indus. But Jenghiz Khan had stopped there.

Timur progressed steadily south and east, delaying only to ransack the towns on his way. A few bought temporary reprieve with a large ransom, but invariably some argument during the collection of the money provided sufficient cause for a general massacre 'as a punishment for their past crimes'.[3] The truth was that in a medieval army so far from home the loyalty of the soldiers depended on whether their leader could find them enough to pillage. Timur could hardly afford good behaviour on the part of the towns he passed. If he did seem to hurry on towards Delhi, one of the reasons given by a contemporary chronicle was the 'multitude of dead carcasses which infected the air' just behind him.[4] Indeed almost the only people to survive his passage were those gathered together by the soldiers for present use or future sale as slaves. And of these there were soon a vast number.

Timur arrived near Delhi in early December. The capital was now held by Mallu Khan, a noble who had captured one of the two puppet kings, Mahmud Shah, and was ruling in his name. On December 12 there was a skirmish when a reconnaissance party, led by Timur himself, was attacked by Mallu Khan. The attack was easily beaten off, but the mere news of it cost fifty thousand Indian lives. The

Sources (see p. 252) [1]74, 84 [2]56, 84 [3]1, 86 [4]1, 45

11

prisoners in Timur's camp failed to conceal their excitement, and so branded themselves an unacceptable risk. Timur ordered each man to kill his adult male captives. Within the hour the work was done, even an old divine 'who could never consent so much as to kill a single sheep' being forced to participate.[1]

Timur's preparations for battle were mainly directed against the legendary Indian elephants, the mere prospect of which reduced his army to near panic—several of the learned men whom Timur liked to have around him even went so far as to say that during the battle they would prefer to be near the ladies.[2] He surrounded his position with a stout rampart and ditch, and made ready various devices to cripple the elephants or frighten them into turning and trampling their own army. He planted in the ground stakes armed with three-pronged metal spikes (a variant of the device used by Sultan Bayazid two years before at Nicopolis, and by Henry V at Agincourt seventeen years later), and for good measure he provided his cavalry with caltrops. These were metal objects consisting of four sharp prongs, angled so that at least one of the four must always point upwards; the riders could entice an elephant into pursuing them and then scatter these treacherous barbs in its path. Timur's technique for causing the elephants to panic was no less ingenious. Bundles of dried grass were tied to the backs of large numbers of camels and buffaloes, which would be driven towards the advancing elephants. At the last moment the bundles were to be set on fire. The terror of these unfortunate animals would, it was hoped, infect the elephants as they ran blazing and screaming among them.[3]

Both techniques worked. On December 17 the army of Mahmud Shah and Mallu Khan emerged from the gates of Delhi: ten thousand horse, forty thousand foot and a phalanx of the dreaded elephants, clanking forward in their armour and with long swords bound on their tusks. On their backs were fortified turrets bristling with archers and crossbowmen and even specialists using primitive rockets and devices for slinging hot pitch. But this straightforward Indian magnificence was no match for unorthodox cunning. By the end of the day Mahmud and Mallu had fled back into the city and straight out again the other side, and the victorious Timur was pitching his camp by a large reservoir outside the walls.[4]

The next day Timur made his triumphal entry into Delhi, and sat enthroned while prominent citizens threw themselves at his feet to beg for mercy and agree a price—as usual a high one. The captured elephants, a hundred and twenty of them, were paraded before him and made a most favourable impression by falling down in a humble posture and making a great moan, as if suing for quarter. There were rhinoceroses too, but being incapable of any such flattering tricks they were less well received. Then, having arranged for his own preachers to enter the great mosque and to read in his name the *khutba*, Friday's midday sermon, and for his treasury officials to set about collecting the ransom money, Timur retired to his lavish complex of tents outside the city walls for a prolonged bout of feasting.[5]

How the situation deteriorated from these orderly beginnings into mass pillage and the burning of Delhi is a matter on which the chronicles disagree. But the city was soon in flames; common soldiers were laden with jewellery, easier to loot in India than in any other country because then, as now, even the poorer women wore their gold and jewels every day; and hardly a man but drove before him twenty new slaves, while some were said to have gathered as many as a hundred and fifty. Timur continued to feast.[6]

When the thousands of prisoners were assembled outside the city, the craftsmen among them were handed over to Timur. He was particularly interested in Delhi's famous stonemasons, who, like the elephants, were destined for Samarkand. It was his invariable policy, after capturing any sophisticated town, to send the skilled men back to Samarkand, where they would provide the art and architecture to embellish his capital city.

Timur waited another ten days near Delhi, receiving tribute money from neighbouring princes whom he did not intend to waste time attacking, and then he set off homewards by a leisurely route which brought the maximum plunder. According to one account the army was now 'so laden with booty that they could scarce march four miles a day',[7] but this was an exaggeration since by March 19 Timur, having laid waste Lahore, was already recrossing the Indus. He had been in the country less than six months and he left behind him a carnage unprecedented in India's history. Famine was the inevitable result of the destruction caused by his troops; plague followed equally certainly from the corpses they left behind them. It was said that in Delhi nothing moved, not even a bird, for two months.[8]

The Indian elephants and stonemasons safely reached Samarkand, where the masons became part of a community which already included painters, calligraphers and architects from Persia, and which would soon be joined, after Timur's next expeditions, by silk-weavers and glass-blowers from Damascus and by silversmiths from Turkey. When Ruy Gonzales de Clavijo, the ambassador from Spain, reached Samarkand in 1404 he found so many of these skilled foreign captives that 'the city was not large enough to hold them, and it was wonderful what a number lived under trees, and in caves outside'.[9] Clavijo also came across those same obsequious elephants; they were now painted green and red, and guarded the entrance to the sumptuous garden where the nomadic Timur, even in his own capital, chose to live in a tent. These were the first elephants that Clavijo, like so many of Timur's troops at Delhi, had set eyes upon. But Clavijo could view them more calmly, and he provided his readers in Spain with a description which is as brilliantly straightforward as a child's painting: 'the animals were very large, and their bodies were quite shapeless, like a full sack; their legs were very thick, and the same size all the way down.'[10]

Both stonemasons and elephants must have worked in Samarkand on the emperor's magnificent tomb, the Gur-Amir (Plate 1, p. 17). Its beautiful turquoise dome, Persian in inspiration, can be seen as a foretaste of splendours to come. Where Timur brought Indian craftsmen to work on his Persian designs in Samarkand, his descendants would more profitably take Persian ideas to the craftsmen in India who, blending the two traditions, would raise domes of even greater style and fame.

Timur's departure in 1399 proved, thankfully, the last that Delhi would see of his family for over a century. When they returned they came to stay, but the family character had changed. Apart from the ability to win battles, the only quality they seemed to inherit from their gruesome ancestor was his liking for learned men and his passion for beautifying his capital city. Their form of patronage had less of slavery in it than his; and the desire to create, subsidiary in his life, became almost paramount in theirs. Where his ambition was to terrify the world, theirs seemed more to impress it. He brought Delhi a shattering disaster. They, instead, gave Muslim India her period of greatest splendour.

[1]1, 53–4; 15, I, 490–1 [2]1, 57 [3]2, 97–8 [4]3, 2–7; 1, 46–61 [5]1, 61–7 [6]1, 66 [7]1, 83 [8]56, 198–201; 74, 199–200 [9]28, 171 [10]28, 131, 154, 157

13

Babur

Babur's credentials as an oriental conqueror could hardly be improved upon: his father's descent from Timur was matched by his mother's from Jenghiz Khan. Of the two, Babur was much more proud of his connection with Timur, whom he thought of as a Turk. The name Mongol had by now become synonymous with barbarian, being reserved mainly for the wild tribes to the north and east of Transoxiana who were still nomadic.[1] By contrast the highly cultured courts which had been created by Timur's descendants in the areas which are now Afghanistan and Uzbekistan had given a lustre to the so-called Turks. Babur would therefore have been horrified to discover that the dynasty founded by him in India would become known throughout the world as Moghul—an adaptation of *mughul*, the Persian word for Mongol.

In fact Timur himself was probably a Mongol, though Turks and Mongols were so intermixed in his region that to try to separate them is meaningless. Both races had come from roughly the same area in Mongolia (as had also the Huns), but the Turks had moved west some centuries before the Mongols and had therefore settled earlier and become civilized earlier. The wilder Mongols, following in their tracks, first overwhelmed the Turks and then learnt from them.[2] Timur himself came from a tribe known as the Barlas Turks, but it is thought that they were originally Mongols who had adopted Turki[3]—the language which Babur spoke and wrote, and which was to remain a private language of the Moghul royal family in India, useful when secrecy was required, until as late as 1760.[4] As a measure of the impossibility of separating Turk and Mongol in Babur's ancestry, the Barlas Turks were a subdivision of the Chaghatai Turks, who were themselves a contradiction in terms since Chaghatai was a son of the Mongol Jenghiz Khan. And to add to the confusion people often claimed to be whichever was more fashionable at the time. Timur definitely wanted to be thought of as closely connected with the Mongols—he was most proud of his title *Gurgan*, son-in-law to the Mongol royal family, which he acquired by marrying a princess descended from Jenghiz Khan, and the genealogy carved on his tomb in Samarkand laboriously traces for him a common ancestor with Jenghiz Khan in one Buzanchar, himself descended from a legendary virgin who was ravished by a moonbeam.[5]

The events of the century after Timur's death had made Babur wish to be thought a Turk, but after a hundred years of his family's successful rule in India under the name Moghul it once again became highly fashionable to be thought a Mongol. European visitors in the first half of the seventeenth century believed the term Moghul merely meant circumcised; in other words they found it applied almost indiscriminately to the ruling class of Muslims.[6] Others in the second half of the century were under the impression it referred mainly to a white skin, and brought back tales of Indians rising in the emperor's service who married girls from Kashmir in the hope that their children would be light enough to pass as Moghuls.[7] Finally the wheel had come full circle when it could be reported in 1666 that the emperors had adopted the name Moghul in order to 'contribute much to

Babur enthroned in one of the gardens he made in India: late 16th century

Sources (*see* p. 252)
[1]4, I, 2, 4, 104–5, 140
[2]5, *Intro.,* 72–98 [3]56, 41
[4]109, 184 [5]56, 41, 50
[6]40, 274; 41, 346
[7]48, 3, 48, 209, 404

15

the Glory of their Family, because by taking it they would more easily perswade men, that they are of the Race of *Ginguis Can*'.[1] All in all, and in spite of Babur's objections, Europe was justified in referring to the dynasty as Moghul and to its ruler, rich it seemed beyond the wildest dreams of bourgeois London or Amsterdam, as the Great Moghul.

Babur was born on February 14, 1483. His father, Umar Shaikh, was the ruler of Ferghana, a small but fertile province to the east of Samarkand, and at the age of eleven, in 1494, the young prince was suddenly catapulted into his inheritance by a strange accident. His father, whom he describes as a 'short and stout, round-bearded and fleshy-faced person'[2] was also an enthusiastic fancier of pigeons. One day in the rugged fort of Akshi the portly king was tending his birds in a pigeon house on the outer wall of the palace when the precipice below began to crumble, and 'Umar Shaikh Mirza flew, with his pigeons and their house, and became a falcon.'[3]

ABOVE *A dovecote on a palace roof: detail, late 16th century*

OPPOSITE *The tomb of Timur at Samarkand, known as the Gur-Amir, completed in 1404*

Babur now found himself one among many petty rulers in a conglomeration of provinces governed by his uncles, or by cousins of varying degrees of remoteness. All these princes were descended from Timur. Each felt that he had the same right as any other to the territories which over the past century had been governed by members of the family. Their ferocious common ancestor had conquered from Delhi to the Mediterranean, from the Persian Gulf to the Volga, but the area over which his sons had consolidated the family hold was much smaller. His capital, Samarkand, was at the very north of this area. A hundred and fifty miles to the west of Samarkand was Bukhara, and about two hundred miles to the east was Babur's green and pleasant valley of Ferghana, 'abounding in grain and fruits', as he himself wrote, and where 'the pheasants grow so surprisingly fat that rumour has it four people could not finish one they were eating with its rice and vegetable stew'.[4] This northern section of the Timurid territories was the area known as Transoxiana, because to the south of it flows the River Oxus which is today the boundary between the Soviet Union and Afghanistan. And to the south of the Oxus stretched the remainder of the family inheritance, larger but less hospitable than Transoxiana. Down through the rugged passes of the range known as the Hindu Kush one came after two hundred miles to Kabul, and to the west the mountains gradually gave place to parched plains in which rested the large and pleasant oasis of Herat. This territory, small compared to Timur's conquests but still the size of Spain and Portugal, the Timurid princes of the sixteenth century regarded as their own. But they were united only in the convinction that in each of its many small and fluctuating kingdoms a Timurid prince should occupy the throne. The question of which prince should sit on which thrones was a matter of constant warfare among themselves. Birth gave each a general claim; only possession could establish it.

Within these Timurid territories there were a few walled cities of considerable strength and importance, containing beautiful tiled buildings and a prosperous merchant class, of which Samarkand, Bukhara and Herat were the three greatest. And throughout the whole area there was a profusion of small forts and fortified villages, with high mud walls baked hard in the sun, any of which could be used as a base in extremities. The families occupying Samarkand, Bukhara and Herat were able to live in considerable style, supported by agriculture and artisans; and having once established even a hint of permanence they would begin to in-

[1]50, 5 [2]4, I, 14 [3]4, I, 13; 10, I, 220 [4]4, I, 2–4

*Fourteenth-century tile-work
on one of the tombs in the
Shah-i-Zindah at Samarkand*

dulge the Timurid love of painting and poetry, of architecture and gardens. Of the latter two, the garden tended to be where the prince lived, either in pavilions or tents. Architecture was more part of his patronage of religion and learning. Timur's buildings at Samarkand had been tombs, mosques and magnificent colleges, but apparently no palace. There was a building for his use within the citadel, the central walled enclosure of the city, but when home between campaigns he and his court preferred to take up residence in one of his splendid gardens. The same was true at Herat, which after his death became the real centre of Timurid culture. Timurid princes were still, essentially, the most cultivated of nomads. To be at home was to be camping in one's favourite surroundings.

With such an attitude it was surprisingly easy to move. A prince's wealth lay in the very objects which it was most desirable to take with him—elaborate tents, warm and richly patterned carpets for the floor, bolsters to loll against covered in silk and braid, dishes and goblets of silver and gold, and above all good horses, good pack animals, good armour and swords and bows. His luxuries, such as manuscripts, jewels, small *objets d'art* and paintings (almost always designed to be bound into books) were essentially portable in kind. His strength consisted only in the groups of freelance soldiers, most of them smaller tribal chieftains with their own bands of followers, who were attracted to his leadership by his royal blood and to his cause by the hope of reward and loot; they owned their own horses and weapons, their loyalty depended on results, and they were unusually prone to change sides because the arrival of new followers was an occasion for celebration and present-giving second only to a victory. If the prince happened to be settled in a prosperous area, the everyday necessities for himself and his men, such as food and warm fur clothing, might be derived from the dues levied from the local peasants. Just as often they depended on the sheep and goats rustled from other neighbourhoods and kept on the hoof till needed. It was a world in which fortunes could change surprisingly far and surprisingly fast. Babur at various times captured and lived in great Samarkand, at others wandered for months on end, homeless, with a handful of followers. In another context the abrupt change seems almost inconceivable, or at the very least irreversible. But within the nomadic framework the two extremes were merely the best and the worst examples of the same type of life.

Of all the cities and forts within this family inheritance Samarkand, the capital of Timur himself, had always seemed to his many descendants the most glittering of prizes. Babur in his kingdom of Ferghana was a neighbour of Samarkand, and he was dominated during his 'teens and twenties by a longing to possess it. Early in his reign he was given his first exciting opportunity. Two successive rulers of Samarkand died within a space of six months, civil war broke out, and in 1496 Babur marched west to lay siege to the famous city. He was still only thirteen. True to the times, he found beneath the walls of Samarkand two of his cousins already engaged in the same pursuit, though it turned out that one of them had only come to try to carry off a girl in the city with whom he was in love. They pooled their resources, but winter came with Samarkand intact and they had to retire. Only the lover had attained his end. But the following spring Babur returned and after a siege of seven months was able to enter in triumph, in November 1497 and at the age of fourteen, the city so richly embellished by his famous ancestor.[1]

[1] 4, I, 64–74

He immediately went sightseeing and had the ramparts of his new possession paced out. They measured ten thousand yards. He visited Timur's tomb; he was conducted round the elaborately tiled group of colleges for Islamic study which had been erected on three sides of an open square by Timur and his grandson Ulugh Beg; and he inspected the famous observatory, where Ulugh Beg had constructed a gigantic quadrant, with which he had compiled the most complete catalogue of stars then known. All these buildings survive today in varying degrees of collapse and restoration, but predictably the bulk of Babur's sightseeing was in the enchanting gardens which in those times surrounded the walled town. He mentions no fewer than nine, several of them with delightful pavilions forming the centre-piece; one such building was decorated with murals showing Timur's victories, another with panels of porcelain brought from China. Offering so many civilized delights, together with bustling bazaars and 'orthodox and law-abiding' citizens, it is not surprising that the place lived up to Babur's expectations. 'Few towns in the whole habitable world', he decided, 'are so pleasant as Samarkand.'[1]

But the prize was his for only three exciting months. A typical series of events now deprived him of Samarkand almost as soon as he had won it. His supporters, finding disappointingly few rewards in a city which had been impoverished by civil war and siege, soon drifted away—including even, to Babur's great surprise and distress, some of those whom he had most trusted. At the same time the nobles in Ferghana, hearing that Babur was installed in Samarkand, judged it an opportune moment to please another prince by handing over the greater part of the province to Babur's younger half-brother, Jahangir, now aged twelve. Babur marched back in February 1498 to retrieve the situation, but his departure lost him Samarkand and he arrived too late to save Ferghana. He had to spend the rest of the winter in the only place he had been able to rescue, the tiny fort of Khujand. 'It came very hard on me', he later wrote, far away in his new empire of India, remembering the fourteen-year-old boy whose fortunes seemed already to have come to an end in Transoxiana; 'I could not help crying a good deal.'[2]

Babur's remarkable autobiography, based on notes taken throughout his life but for the most part written in his last years in India, gives a vivid account of what he calls these 'throneless times' with his small band of adventurers in search of food, wealth and a kingdom. Rarely can such a sophisticated mind have recorded so wild an existence, which combined to an extraordinary degree the romantic and the sordid. He tells of how he and his followers, reduced now to two or three hundred, used Khujand as a base for night raids on neighbouring forts and villages—and every village in this particular region, he says, had its own fortifications. Leaving in the middle of the day they would ride up to forty miles in any direction, timing their arrival for after dark. Then they would assemble ladders and place them quietly against the walls in the hope of entering unobserved. Usually they were noticed, and rode back exhausted with nothing achieved. But sometimes they found their way in, and then they would fight in the lanes with sword and bow and arrow until the village acknowledged its new masters, a capitulation not often long delayed. It was a freebooting existence in which death was a commonplace. A chance encounter with a rival group when out foraging would end almost invariably in bloodshed, and heads were severed and carried away on the saddle for trophies. A remark of Babur's conveys well the

The Shah-i-Zindah, a comple of 14th- and 15th-century tombs at Samarkand

[1] 4, I, 74 [2] 4, I, 86–91

very casualness of the brutality. 'Aughan-Birdi came back at breakfast time', he reports; 'he had got the better of an Afghan and had cut his head off, but had dropped it on the road.'[1]

But as he steadily won back territory in Ferghana from his younger brother, the gentler side of life became possible again. His mother and other female members of the family joined him—protected by purdah the women could move invisible and in comparative safety between the warring factions, and after each upheaval it was customary for the ladies of the harem to wait until their prince was newly settled and then to join him. Now too, when he was sixteen, his first wife arrived to introduce herself. Like almost everyone else she was his cousin, and the marriage had been arranged several years previously by their two fathers. Babur found himself 'not ill-disposed towards her', and claims that it was only his virgin modesty which made him visit her in her tent only once every ten or fifteen days. But later on, 'when even my first inclination did not last', the frequency of his attentions fell to once every forty days, and this only after his mother had driven and pestered him to visit the girl.[2]

The truth was that his affections were engaged elsewhere. In later life he strongly disapproved of any practice of homosexuality among his followers, but his own first love-affair, unconsummated, was for a boy in the camp bazaar and he describes it with an almost Proustian subtlety of self-analysis. He mooned about the orchards and gardens, bare-headed, barefoot, dreaming and composing couplets, but whenever he actually met his love, as when with a crowd of companions he turned the corner of a lane and came face to face with the boy, he was covered in confusion and unable to look at him. On the rare occasions when the boy was sent for into his presence, the situation was even worse; 'in my joy and agitation I could not thank him for coming; how was it possible for me to reproach him for going away?' Babur claimed it to be his intention in his journal 'that the truth should be reached in every matter, and that every act should be recorded precisely as it occurred', and he seems to live up to his ideal.[3]

By February 1500, two years after he had left Samarkand, Babur had recovered so much of Ferghana from his brother that Jahangir was willing to make a treaty. The two princes were each to rule half of Ferghana for the moment, but they would pool their resources to recapture Samarkand; once Babur was re-established there, the whole of Ferghana should be Jahangir's.[4] In any case honour had by now been added to ambition as an incentive for combining to recapture Samarkand. During the past century the city had changed hands many times, but always from one member of Timur's dynasty to another. Now, in this very year, 1500, it was taken by a dangerous intruder into the nest of Timurid principalities. His name, Shaibani Khan, was one which would increasingly dominate Babur's world for the next ten years. He had begun life much like Babur, as a small prince turned adventurer in the country north of Transoxiana among the Mongol and Turkish tribes known as the Uzbegs, but his own aggressive genius combined with the ferocity of his tribesmen had proved too much for his neighbours, and his territories had extended steadily southwards.

Babur calculated that the citizens of Samarkand were unlikely to be enthusiastic about their new and primitive masters, and that if he could once get into the city the townspeople would support him. And, amazingly, in the autumn of 1500 one of his sudden midnight dashes from far away proved successful. Shaibani Khan was encamped outside the walled town in one of the gardens, since he expected no immediate danger, and under cover of darkness seventy or eighty of Babur's men were able to place their ladders against the city wall opposite the so-called Lovers' Cave and climb in unobserved. They hurried round to the Turquoise Gate, killed those who were guarding it, broke the lock with an axe and opened the door to Babur and the rest of his men, numbering fewer than two hundred. The people were still asleep. A few traders in the bazaar peeped out of their shops, recognized Babur and gave him a welcoming sign that their prayers were for him. He went straight to Ulugh Beg's college in the centre of the city and established his headquarters on its roof. Here the leading townspeople hurried to pay their respects—wisely recognizing at one and the same time both a true Timurid prince and a *fait accompli*—while Babur's men and the rabble of the town joined forces to butcher any Uzbegs about in the streets, accounting in this manner for some five hundred. By the time news of this unexpected disaster had reached Shaibani Khan in his camp, the city was safely closed against him.[5]

Through the winter of 1500 Babur was secure in Samarkand, but the following spring Shaibani Khan returned to besiege him. Babur again pitched his tents on the roof of the college, from which vantage point he directed operations—and he claims even to have done effective work from there with a cross-bow when a party of Uzbegs had slipped into the city and were trying to storm his headquarters—but Shaibani Khan was more interested in starving out the garrison. Babur's men were soon reduced to eating the flesh of asses and, particularly repugnant to a Muslim, even of dogs, and the horses had to make do with a diet of elm leaves and wood pulp. More and more soldiers and officers, including again some of Babur's trusted friends, were found each morning to have let themselves down from the ramparts during the night in twos and threes and so vanished. Finally Babur was forced to arrange 'a sort of peace' with Shaibani Khan, which included the surrender of Babur's elder sister Khanzada as a wife for the Uzbeg. And one evening around midnight Babur and his mother and a few followers themselves slipped out of the town and away.[6]

Already twice conqueror of Samarkand, Babur was still only eighteen. But now his fortunes seemed to reach their lowest ebb. He went to visit some of his relations, particularly his Mongol uncles living to the north around Tashkent—a prince was always welcome to visit his relatives in this family of kingdoms as long as he showed no signs of wanting or being able to displace them—but Babur disliked the ambiguous position of an impoverished guest. With his uncles' help he made some progress in recovering parts of Ferghana once again, but any success was rapidly outweighed by the ever expanding power of Shaibani Khan. By 1504 the Uzbegs were firmly established in Ferghana as well as retaining Samarkand, and Babur, retreating before them, was more destitute than ever before. His number of followers was down again to some two or three hundred. He had in the past achieved considerable successes with even fewer men but now, a great indignity, they were nearly all on foot, wearing peasant clothes and armed only with staves. The party had only two tents between them. Babur's own may still have been tolerably weather-proof, but he reserved it for the use of his mother. For himself they pitched an open tent of felt under which he could hold court. 'It passed through my mind', he later wrote, 'that to wander from mountain to mountain, homeless and houseless, had nothing to recommend it.'[7]

[1] 4, I, 376–7 [2] 4, I, 120
[3] 4, I, 120–1, 318 [4] 4, I, 118–9
[5] 4, I, 131–7 [6] 4, I, 141–7
[7] 4, I, 155

But once again the number of his followers grew, gradually and almost inevitably—a talented prince of authentic Timurid blood, even if wintering among goatherds, would sooner or later be sought out by discontented warriors eager for somewhere new to pin their hopes. And Babur was a more popular leader than most because he had long ago discovered—and noted in his diary—that in this world of shifting allegiances the long-term benefits of a reputation for justice and fair-dealing were worth more than the instant disciplines of terror and cruelty.[1] But even though by this natural process his strength was growing anew, he was wise enough not to chance it further against Shaibani. It was clearly time for him to seek his fortune elsewhere.

By a stroke of luck Kabul was, so to speak, vacant. Three hundred miles south of Ferghana, through the difficult passes of the Hindu Kush, it had always seemed a remote kingdom. It had been ruled until 1501 by one of Babur's uncles, but in the confusion which had followed his death, leaving only an infant son as an heir, a non-Timurid ruler from Kandahar had stepped in. Kabul had the advantage of being not only far from Shaibani's territories but separated from them by mountains, and Babur, indignant that yet another Timurid territory had been lost to an outsider, could press a strong legal claim—so strong, when combined with the forces which he was gathering up on his way south in 1504, that the usurper withdrew to Kandahar after only a token resistance.[2]

So nearly the most significant move of Babur's life had proved also one of the easiest. For the rest of his days Kabul was his base. It stands surrounded by rocky ridges rising from the plain like the scaly backs of huge fossil dinosaurs. The ridge nearest the walled town had been fortified along its summit to provide a citadel, and at its feet Babur was delighted to discover pleasant gardens well watered by springs and a canal. There was excellent fruit and honey, good grazing and a climate which suited his constitution. And for the first time he found himself in a truly international world, for Kabul, like Kandahar to the south of it, was an important trading post on the caravan routes linking India with Persia, Iraq and Turkey to the west—and to the north, through Samarkand, even with China. In Andizhan, the largest town of his native Ferghana, everyone had spoken Turki; in Kabul he found at least twelve languages in use, Arabic and Persian from the west, Hindi from the east, Turki and Mongol from the north and several other more local tongues. Babur reported in some awe that as many as ten thousand horses came down through Kabul on the way to India every year, and in the opposite direction there was a constant flow of cloth, sugar, spices and slaves. The traders expected a profit of up to four hundred per cent on what they sold, which—in view of the goods lost to thieves on the road and the bribes and dues required for a safe passage—was probably not excessive. Even so the district around Kabul was far from rich and was in itself incapable of supporting all Babur's followers, but he supplemented the revenue by regular raids into the surrounding areas, on one occasion returning with no fewer than a hundred thousand sheep.[3]

Even in India, when he was preparing to leave his empire to his sons, Babur still regarded Kabul as the home province.[4] Here at last he led a stable existence and was able to establish the cultured court life which was such an important part of the Timurid ideal. Relaxing for the first time after eight years of almost constant alarms and excursions, he busied himself with agriculture, introduced bananas

Babur, enthroned in Kabul, receiving tribute: detail, late 16th century

and sugar-cane to the district, and developed a passion for gardening which was to last him through his life.[5] But of all the many gardens which he created the one on the hillside at Kabul remained his favourite, and it was here at his own wish that his body was finally brought back to be buried.

As a point of unexpected stability in an unsettled world his court also became something of a haven for persecuted Timurid princes retreating before Shaibani. One such refugee, his cousin Sultan Said Khan, described it as the 'island of Kabul which Babar Padshah had contrived to save from the violent shocks of the billows of events', and said that the two and a half years which he spent there were the 'most free from care or sorrow of any that I have ever experienced. . . . I never suffered even a headache, unless from the effects of wine; and never felt distressed or sad, except on account of the ringlets of some beloved one.'[6] A much younger cousin, Haidar, who escaped to Kabul at the age of nine, was also highly impressed by the state which Babur kept here; he was presented with rich gifts suitable for a schoolboy, a jewelled inkstand, a stool inlaid with mother-of-pearl, and an alphabet;[7] and he later recorded his gratitude that Babur had been 'for ever, either by promises of kindness or by threats of severity encouraging me to study'.[8]

Haidar describes his education as having consisted in the 'arts of calligraphy, reading, making verses, epistolary style, painting and illumination . . . such crafts as seal-engraving, jeweller's and goldsmith's work, saddlery and armour-making, also in the construction of arrows, spear-heads and knives . . . in the affairs of the State, in important transactions, in planning campaigns and forays, in archery, in hunting, in the training of falcons and in everything that is useful in the government of a kingdom'.[9]

The curriculum gives a good idea of the pleasures and activities at a Timurid court, and Babur himself now had leisure to indulge his considerable talent for poetry, a talent which gave him a reputation second only to one other, says Haidar, among poets using Turki.[10] The Turki language is such that versification seems to have come nearer to the pleasures of the crossword than of conventional poetry; Babur, for example, amused himself during an illness by writing a couplet and then somehow reorganizing it in five hundred and four different ways.[11] Short poems of Babur's are scattered through his memoirs but they are for the most part meaningless in translation since they depend on verbal conceits, made possible by the Turki habit of building up compound words which make the most elaborate of German conglomerations look as simple as two plus two. To give one example, *biril* is 'to be given', *birilish* is 'to be given to one another', *birilishtur* is 'to cause to be given to one another', *mai* is the negative, *dur* is the present tense, and *man* indicates the first person singular; so *birilishturalmaidurman* means 'I am unable to cause them to be given to one another.'[12]

By now there was only one Timurid court more important than Babur's at Kabul. This was Herat, which had become a city of artistic importance under Timur's favourite son, Shah Rukh, and which had reached a peak of achievement during Babur's lifetime when the studio there was headed by the great Bihzad, the most influential single painter of both the Timurid and Persian schools. But in 1507 even Herat fell to Shaibani Khan, only a few months after Babur had paid his first visit to his illustrious relations and had spent a happy forty days sightseeing among their splendid buildings. The first that he mentions is the Gazurgah, where

[1]4, I, 104–5
[2]4, I, 198–9; [1]5, II, 24
[3]4, I, 199–206, 228, 324–5
[4]4, II, 627, 645; [6], 147
[5]4, I, 208, 216–17 [6]5, 226
[7]6, 16 [8]5, 229–30 [9]5, 3–4
[10]5, 173–4 [11]4, II, 585–6
[12]JASB, XLVI(1877), 300

he would certainly have been greatly moved to see the elegant marble tombs of many of his Timurid relations in a large alcove at one end of a most peaceful courtyard (Plate 3, opposite). The capture of Herat by Shaibani left Babur in the distinguished but alarming position of being the only Timurid prince still with a respectable throne, and he now conferred on himself the title of Padshah, thus claiming with some justification the position of chief of the Timurid clans.[1]

It seemed more than likely that Shaibani would wish to expand further and would sooner or later sweep round below the mountains through Kandahar to Kabul, but fortunately he now made the mistake of antagonizing the powerful Shah Ismail, the founder of the Safavid dynasty in Persia. An insulting exchange of diplomatic gifts, reminiscent of the Dauphin's tennis balls, in which Shaibani sent a begging bowl and the Shah replied with a spinning wheel, led predictably to war.[2] But Shaibani had met his match, both in resources and tactics. By a series of ruses he was led, in 1510, into an ambush and was cornered in a cattle compound. His body was dismembered and was sent to different parts of the Persian empire for display purposes, and his skull, set in gold, was turned into a drinking cup which the Shah himself much enjoyed using.[3]

The good news was soon followed by the return of Babur's sister Khanzada, the widow of Shaibani, whom the Shah had rescued and whom he now most courteously sent under escort with costly gifts to Babur in Kabul.[4] This was Babur's first diplomatic contact with Persia and it was to lead to a new and finally unsatisfactory episode in his life. His thoughts were still turned towards Samarkand, and it soon became evident that the Shah would be willing to help him recover the capital of his ancestors, but on one rather crucial condition—that he should adopt the dress and customs of the Shia sect of Islam. Ever since the first century of Islam there had been a deep rivalry between the Shia sect and the Sunnis, or orthodox Muslims, among whom Babur and all the Timurids numbered themselves. The doctrinal split related back to disagreements in the years after Mohammed's death about who was his legitimate successor as Imam, and whether the office was an elected one or should be restricted, as the Shias believed, to the descendants of the prophet through his son-in-law Ali. In later centuries the Shia faith was specially identified with Persia, with the result that the spreading of it became a matter of nationalistic as well as religious pride—and one which the new Safavid dynasty was inclined to press with more than usual zeal since the family claimed descent from Musa al-Kazim, the seventh of the twelve Shia Imams.[5] Its founder, Shah Ismail, whose bigotry was matched only by his territorial ambitions, planned to use Babur's legitimate claim to Samarkand as a way of bringing that area within his own empire. In return for military assistance Babur was to strike coins and read the *khutba* in Ismail's name, and as these were the two conventional symbols of sovereignty he would in effect be a vassal holding Samarkand for the Persian Shah. But he was still to be allowed to strike his own coin and read the *khutba* in his own name in Kabul, so Babur, far from a bigot himself, seems to have reasoned that there was nothing to lose by this devious route back to his beloved Samarkand and he accepted, unwisely in the event, Ismail's terms.[6]

Babur marched north again and with the help of his new allies drove the Uzbegs first from Bukhara. To the people of Transoxiana this was a movement of liberation. A popular Timurid prince was returning to his inheritance. Town and

OVERLEAF *The remains of the citadel at Kandahar, taken by Babur in 1522*

[1] 4, I, 305–6, 344 [2] 5, 232 [3] 76, I, 303–4 [4] 5, 239 [5] 133, II, 563 [6] 4, I, 354

غرابتی دارد دیگر که هند وستان متناهی کو بین از عکه

جزویی خورد تر باشد عکه ابلق سیاه و سفید است متا
ابلق ماده و سیاه است یک جانورک دیگر است کلای نی او
برابر ساند و لاج مموله بوده باشد سرخ و خوش رنگ است در بال های خود

که سیاهی دارد یک دیگر که حراست بمار لو عاج سفید است از
لو عاج خیلی کلان تر است یک رنگ سیاه است دیگر

A page of birds, illustrating the section in Babur's memoirs on the fauna of Hindustan: late 16th century

countryside alike rose to greet him and at Bukhara he was able, tactfully, to dismiss his Persian forces before making a triumphal entry into Samarkand, in October 1511, after an absence of ten years. The bazaars were draped with gold brocades and hung with paintings, and people of all classes crowded the streets to shout their welcome. There was only one disturbing anomaly—it was Babur himself, in the middle of all these excited Sunni citizens, wearing the costume of a Shia. But in the enthusiasm of the day even this was overlooked. The people assumed that once he was safely enthroned he would drop these hated impieties, but they were to be disappointed. Babur's cousin Haidar, who was with him at the time, explains that Babur thought the Uzbegs still too strong for him to do without the support of the Shah.[1] But he had placed himself in an impossible position. He refused to go so far as to persecute Sunnis, which was all that would have really pleased the Shah; and yet by maintaining an outward show of collaboration with the Shias he rapidly lost the support of the people of Samarkand. The result, eight months later, was that the Uzbegs captured the city once again.

To the court historians of Babur's descendants in India his triple failure to hold Samarkand appeared the greatest of God's blessings,[2] and this last adventure with the Persians does seem finally to have turned his ambitions away from the north and towards the east. He had already made brief attempts to expand through the Khyber Pass into India, in order to strengthen himself against Shaibani Khan; moreover Hindustan, and in particular the Punjab, was an area which he regarded, like Samarkand, as his by right. His claim went all the way back to Timur's rapid conquest of northern India in 1399. Khizr Khan, the man whom Timur left as his vassal in control of the Punjab, had later become the Sultan of Delhi, founding the Sayyid dynasty, but even as such he had still professed allegiance to the house of Timur, refusing to call himself Shah and claiming only to be the viceroy in India of Timur's son, Shah Rukh.[3] This fact was particularly important to Babur and at one stage, while actively engaged in preparations to take Hindustan, he sent an envoy 'for the sake of peace' to Sultan Ibrahim of Delhi proposing perhaps the most optimistic exchange ever suggested; 'I sent him a goshawk', Babur wrote in his memoirs, 'and asked for the countries which from old had depended on the Turk'.[4]

Babur was in no great hurry to launch his invasion. He continued steadily to build up his power in Kabul and busied himself, no doubt with at least as much energy as he had devoted to his young cousin Haidar, in educating his sons; Humayun had been born in 1508, the two brothers Kamran and Askari in 1509 and 1516, and finally in 1519 his youngest, news of whose birth reached Babur during one of his preliminary expeditions into Hindustan, and who was therefore called Hindal.

His preparations for India also involved the capture of Kandahar, a strong fortress which was essential to him if he was to defend Kabul from the west while himself advancing deep into Hindustan, but it took three successive summers of siege before the powerful citadel, backed by a high rocky ridge, fell to him in 1522 (Plate 4, pp. 28–9). And another important part of Babur's preparations was to prove a decisive one. At some time between 1508 and 1519, a long gap during which his memoirs are lost, he acquired his first supply of guns and a Turkish artilleryman, Ustad Ali, to work them. In this he was benefiting from a bitter defeat experienced by his neighbour Shah Ismail, whose magnificent cavalry had

[1] 5, 246 [2] 10, I, 277 [3] 74, 204–10 [4] 4, I, 384–5

galloped bravely against the Turks in 1514 only to be slaughtered by this new weapon.[1] The Shah rapidly imported artillery and Turkish gunners for his own army, and Babur thought it wise to follow suit. When his memoirs resume in 1519, Ustad Ali is already in action on his behalf in a small local engagement, and Babur gives a pathetic picture of the opposing tribesmen, who had never seen a gun before, laughing at the noise of this weapon which seemed to shoot no arrow and confronting it with obscene gestures.[2] In India at this time guns were in regular use down the west coast owing to contact by sea with both Turks and Portuguese, but they do not seem to have spread north into the plains of Hindustan to any effective degree until Babur brought them with him through the passes from Kabul. The assistance of Ustad Ali and his machines was therefore crucial.

Babur's fifth and final expedition into Hindustan began in October 1525, when he marched south and east with twelve thousand men. Recently the empire of Delhi had been in some chaos, with increasingly powerful factions forming against Sultan Ibrahim, and it was not until late February 1526, when Babur had already advanced far into the Punjab, that he met any serious opposition in the form of an advance party sent against him by Ibrahim. Babur detached his right wing under the seventeen-year-old Humayun to deal with it, and the prince scored a complete success, bringing in a hundred prisoners and seven or eight elephants; 'Ustad Ali-quli and the matchlockmen were ordered to shoot all the prisoners, by way of example', recorded Babur; 'this had been Humayun's first affair, his first experience of battle; it was an excellent omen!'[3] The example intended by the execution of the prisoners was probably not one of ferocity, since

Babur's great-great-grandson, Shah Jahan, using a matchlock: mid-17th century

Babur was usually careful to pacify his defeated enemies. The oddity of this early firing squad, using expensive powder where a sword was so much easier, suggests instead that it was meant to be a demoralizing demonstration, word of which would certainly get back to Ibrahim's army, of the magical power of the new weapons.[4]

The two armies came face to face at Panipat in the middle of April. Babur's forces may have grown to as many as twenty-five thousand with reinforcements collected on the way, but Ibrahim's army was said to number a hundred thousand men and a thousand elephants. Babur dug himself in using a formation which was to become standard in the following years in India, but which he says he had adapted from Turkish practice—this was, incidentally, the very year in which Turkish guns under Suleiman the Magnificent were blasting their way far west into Europe with the defeat of Hungary at the Battle of Mohács. Babur ordered his men to gather as many carts as they could find. They rustled up seven hundred and these were joined together with ropes of raw hide. From behind this barricade of carts Ustad Ali and his matchlockmen would fire on the enemy's charging cavalry, much as the Turks had against the Persians in 1514 or as pioneers in North America would against the American Indians more than three centuries later. It took several days before Babur could provoke Ibrahim into attacking his prepared position, but when he finally succeeded in doing so on April 20 Ibrahim's army did, as planned, grind to a halt before the musket fire from the barricades while Babur's cavalry wheeled to rain arrows on them from both flanks. The battle continued fiercely till noon, but then the field was Babur's. About twenty thousand men of the Indian army were dead, including their leader. Babur made arrangements for Ibrahim, as a mark of respect, to be buried where he fell and his tomb still stands at Panipat. But it was typical of Babur that to celebrate his own victory he created at Panipat not another monument but a pleasant garden.[5]

That very afternoon Babur ordered Humayun to ride fast and light with a small detachment to secure the treasure at Agra, which had been used as the capital of the Lodi dynasty since 1502. The next morning Babur and the rest of the army marched on towards Delhi, reaching it three days later. He, as usual, immediately went sightseeing and celebrated the occasion by drinking arrack with his friends in a boat on the River Jumna. He remained in Delhi long enough for the *khutba* to be read in his name in the mosque the following Friday, thus proclaiming himself emperor of Hindustan, since to listen peacefully to the *khutba* in a ruler's name was regarded as tacit acceptance of that ruler by the people. He then marched on to join Humayun at Agra, and on his arrival was presented by his son with a magnificent diamond which had been given to Humayun by the family of the Raja of Gwalior, whom he had found sheltering in the Agra fort and had protected from harm; the Raja himself had died with Ibrahim at Panipat. It has always been a matter of some dispute, but it seems almost certain that this splendid stone was the Koh-i-Nur, now making its first appearance in history. 'Humayun offered it to me when I arrived at Agra', wrote Babur. 'I just gave it him back', he adds casually, though he did calculate that its value would provide 'two and a half days' food for the whole world'.[6] Humayun later gave it to Shah Tahmasp of Persia, the Shah sent it as a present to Nizam Shah in the Deccan, and from there it somehow found its way back during the seventeenth century into the treasury of the

[1]57, 110–11 [2]4, I, 368–9
[3]4, II, 466 [4]4, II, 445–66
[5]4, II, 403–74; 75, 12; 97, 113
[6]4, II, 475–7

33

Moghul emperor Shah Jahan; it was seized with all the other Moghul jewels by Nadir Shah of Persia when he sacked Delhi in 1739, and it was he who first gave it the name Koh-i-Nur, meaning 'mountain of light'; it passed from his grandson to the reigning family in Kabul, from them to Ranjit Singh, the famous Sikh ruler of the Punjab, and when the Punjab was annexed by the British in 1849 it was given to the chief commissioner, Sir John Lawrence, who was apparently so disinterested in the spoils of empire that he left it for six weeks, forgotten, in a waistcoat pocket; by him it was finally forwarded to Queen Victoria, arriving in time to become the prize exhibit in the Great Exhibition of 1851, and so into the Tower of London from which nothing escapes.[1]

The collapse of the Lodi dynasty seemed for the moment complete—so much so that Ibrahim's mother was willing to accept from Babur the large pension which he graciously offered her, though she later nearly succeeded in killing him after bribing a cook to poison his food[2]—but Babur's immediate difficulties were far from over. A majority of his troops, appalled by the onset of the hot season in India, were eager to get back to the pleasant summer of Kabul, hoping to treat the expedition as an extended raid comparable to Timur's. Even Alexander the Great, admittedly further from home, had been forced by the dissatisfaction of his troops to turn back after crossing the Indus. But Babur, after summoning a council, delivered an oration which brilliantly combined encouragement with mockery and which had the desired effect.[3]

The immediate danger against which he needed all possible support was the Rajput confederacy under Rana Sanga of Chitor. During the previous ten years the Hindu princes of Rajasthan had combined in an increasingly powerful group and had been on the verge of attacking Ibrahim, to wrest from him the control of Delhi and Hindustan, when Babur had forestalled them. They now, therefore, were preparing to march on him. He would find himself outnumbered once again, in roughly the same proportion as at Panipat, and his men—already gloomy about their extended stay in India—were further demoralized by the Rajput reputation for valour. But Babur made maximum use of the fact that this was to be a battle, the first in his thirty years of warfare, against infidels. In a dramatic gesture he ceremonially abjured the use of wine, pouring on to the ground a mouth-watering new consignment that had arrived from Ghazni and breaking up his gold and silver goblets for distribution to the poor; the rank and file, fired by this example, were persuaded to swear on the Koran that no man would 'think of turning his face from this foe, or withdraw from this deadly encounter so long as life is not rent from his body'.[4] The armies met at Khanua, about forty miles to the west of Agra, on March 16, 1527, and after a battle considerably more closely fought than at Panipat Babur finally won the day, claiming for himself after his success the proud title of *ghazi*, a warrior for Islam.[5]

This victory left him in undisputed control of the centre of Hindustan, and he now extended his boundaries by the simple device of granting to his nobles tracts of land which were not yet conquered, and sending them off to claim their own. His sons were put in charge of the provinces furthest away from the new centre of operations at Agra. Kandahar had been left in the hands of Kamran; Askari was sent towards Bengal; and Humayun set out to govern the extremely remote province of Badakhshan, tucked away among the mountains to the north east of Kabul.[6] Babur himself was longing as much as any of his followers for the climate and the famous fruits of Kabul—one of his happiest moments was his return to Agra after a campaign to find waiting for him the first grapes and melons from stock which he had imported and planted in Hindustan—but he remained in his new provinces and spent his time moving round to quell local disturbances.[7]

Babur took enormous pleasure in his developing artillery, particularly in the vast mortars which Ustad Ali was now beginning to cast for him, and he leaves a delightful description of the first casting operation, which he hurried to watch. Ustad Ali had built a circle of eight furnaces, from each of which molten metal was to dribble into the central mould, but by an unfortunate miscalculation the furnaces all ran dry before the mould was full. Ustad Ali was so distressed that he suggested throwing himself into the liquid metal, 'but we comforted him, put a robe of honour on him, and so brought him out of his shame'.[8] Babur's typically generous response to this apparent disaster proved also to be justified. Two days later, when the cast could be opened, the stone-chamber or barrel of the mortar was found to be perfect, and Ustad Ali happily announced that it was an easy matter to make the powder-chamber separately and attach it. When this mortar was first tested three months later, Babur was delighted to discover that it would throw a large stone nearly a mile.[9] To build up sufficient pressure for such a shot in a barrel so haphazardly cast was an undertaking at least as dangerous to those behind the gun as to those in front of it, as was shown by another mortar which exploded on its first trial and killed eight bystanders. It was also an extremely slow weapon, and Ustad Ali was very pleased if he could fire off an average of twelve stones a day. But in spite of the dangers and delays, Babur loved to be present whenever the exciting business of shooting was going on, whether against a fort such as Chanderi or trying to pot enemy boats on the Ganges. A typical entry in the memoirs reads: 'At the Mid-day prayer a person came from Usta, saying "The stone is ready; what is the order?" The order was, "Fire this stone off; keep the next till I come."'[10]

As he travelled the country Babur was also taking an active interest in the physical details of his new territories. At Chanderi, which he stormed and captured in 1528 because it was held by a strong lieutenant of Rana Sanga's, he was much impressed to find all the houses in the town built of stone, 'those of the chiefs being elaborately carved'; and at Gwalior later in the same year he greatly admired the palace completed by Raja Man Singh some twenty years before, which he found to consist of 'wonderful buildings, entirely of hewn stone', with coloured tile-work on the outer walls and cupolas above covered in gilded copper (Plate 7, p. 40).[11] The only parts of Gwalior which Babur disliked were the huge Jain figures which had been carved in the rock face below the fort during the previous century. 'These idols', wrote the emperor, 'are shown quite naked without covering for the privities. . . . I, for my part, ordered them to be destroyed.'[12] In fact only the faces and the offending privities were mutilated, and modern restorers seem to have partially agreed with Babur; the faces alone have been reconstructed. But Babur was certainly right to be impressed with what he saw in the fort, and his descendants were to agree with him. In this Hindu architecture at Gwalior was prefigured the style of Akbar's Fatehpur Sikri, with its heavily ornamented beams and brackets of red sandstone; and, half a century later in the reign of Shah Jahan, the exquisite tile-work on the outside of the Lahore fort and the gilded cupolas of Agra.

One of the 15th-century Jain figures in the cliff face at Gwalior, with naked 'privities' mutilated by Babur

[1]12, 200–14; **47**, II, 343–6
[2]4, II, 478, 541–3 [3]4, II, 524–5
[4]4, II, 550–7 [5]4, II, 574–5
[6]4, II, 699, 628, 538
[7]4, II, 645–6, 686 [8]4, II, 536
[9]4, II, 547 [10]4, II, 588–99, 670–2
[11]4, II, 597, 608–9 [12]4, II, 612

ABOVE *Elaborate stone brackets in the palace of Man Singh at Gwalior: c. 1510*

OPPOSITE *A courtyard of carved stone at Chanderi, of the type which impressed Babur: 15th century*

Babur also found time now to record his impressions. In the gardens which he was creating, largely to remind himself of the pleasures of Kabul and to find shelter from the summer heat, he worked away at his memoirs. His daughter Gulbadan, then only about six years old, has described him busy with his papers in a garden he had built at Sikri and he himself leaves a most evocative account of an occasion when a storm blew up and the tent in which he was writing came down on his head; 'sections and book were drenched under water and gathered together with much difficulty. We laid them in the folds of a woollen throne-carpet, put this on the throne and on it piled blankets;' in spite of the wet a fire was kindled, and Babur was 'busy till shoot of day drying folios and sections'.[1]

He was occupied at this time in linking in narrative form the jottings which he had made throughout his life as a rough diary, but he also found time for a magnificent and very detailed forty-page account of his new acquisition, Hindustan. In it he explains the social structure and the caste system, the geographical outlines and the recent history; he marvels at such details as the Indian method of counting and time-keeping, the inadequacy of the lighting arrangements, the profusion of Indian craftsmen, or the want of good manners, decent trousers and cool streams; but his main emphasis is on the fauna and flora of the country, which he notes with the care of a born naturalist and describes with the eye of a painter—an interest and a talent which would be very precisely inherited by his great-grandson, Jahangir. He separates and describes, for example, five types of parrots; he explains how the plantain produces bananas; and with astonishing scientific observation he announces that the rhinoceros 'resembles the horse

[1]6, 102–3; 4, II, 581, 678–9

more than any other animal' (according to modern zoologists, the order Peris-sodactyla has only two surviving sub-orders; one includes the rhinoceros, the other the horse).[1] In other parts of his book too he goes into raptures over such images as the changing colours of a flock of geese on the horizon, or of some beautiful leaves on an apple-tree.[2] The sensitivity with which he observed his own reactions in love extends also to his observations of nature.

The precious manuscript, saved and dried out from the storm, was brought virtually up to date by 1530 and now took an honoured place in the already fast growing family library. The collection and care of manuscripts was something of a Timurid tradition. Babur had brought many with him into India, and when he entered the fort in Lahore one of his first actions was to go in some excitement to Ghazi Khan's library and choose precious books to send to his sons.[3] Humayun, who himself annotated his father's memoirs twenty-five years later, carried the family library round with him, even on occasion taking his favourite books into battle, and it was probably during his wanderings that various long sections of the memoirs were lost.[4] And under Akbar's energetic patronage the manuscript collection would become one of the finest in the world. Babur's own manuscript of his memoirs is now lost, but although last recorded as being in the royal library during Shah Jahan's reign, it almost certainly remained there until the looting in the sack of Delhi by Nadir Shah in 1739 or the Indian Mutiny in 1857, during which the great collection was finally dispersed.[5]

The position of Padshah, which Babur had claimed at Kabul when he alone of the Timurid princes still had a throne, was now more fully justified than ever and he took the opportunity of publicly celebrating his supremacy. Soon after the victory at Panipat word was sent out that all descendants of Timur and Jenghiz Khan, and all who had served Babur in the past, should now come to Agra and 'receive fitting benefits'.[6] By the end of 1528 sufficient people seem to have answered this summons for a magnificent feast to be held. The more important guests sat in a semi-circle stretching a hundred yards, with Babur at the centre in a pavilion erected for the occasion, and the two main activities of such an event—eating and the giving of presents—went on to the constant accompaniment of animal fights, wrestling, dancing and acrobatics. Gold and silver was poured by Babur's guests on to a carpet specially placed for the purpose, and he in return gave the type of royal presents most favoured on such occasions, sword-belts and

LEFT *A rhinoceros, in an illustration to a manuscript of Babur's memoirs: late 16th century*

OPPOSITE *'In that charmless and disorderly Hindustan plots of garden were laid out with order and symmetry,' wrote Babur, seen here supervising the work: detail, late 16th century*

[1] 4, II, 480–521 [2] 4, I, 240, 418
[3] 4, I, 460
[4] 4, I, xxxv; 10, I, 309–10
[5] 4, I, xl; 89, 27–8 [6] 6, 97

The tiled wall of Man Singh's palace at Gwalior: c. 1510

dresses of honour—the most popular of gifts, because being articles of dress they became a visible mark of the emperor's favour. Important visitors from distant places included envoys from his old enemies the Uzbegs, whose presence must rather have gratified the new emperor, but it was not only the distinguished who were rewarded; a raftsman, some matchlockmen, a keeper of cheetahs and even some peasants from Transoxiana, who had befriended Babur during his 'throne-less times' and who had now come for their reward, all received honour and gifts. [1] This great feast was the climax of a period of spectacular generosity, an indulgence which Babur clearly enjoyed in his new dominions, so rich after sparse little Kabul. 'The treasures of five kings fell into his hands', wrote Gulbadan later; 'he gave everything away.'[2] He had coolly returned the Koh-i-Nur to Humayun. He had sent a collection of most magnificent gifts back to the ladies of his family in Kabul.[3] It was all most gratifying but short-sighted, and even before the feast the reserves had fallen so low that officers were ordered to return a third of their salary to the treasury.[4] The empire which Humayun inherited had very little to back it up.

Although still only forty-five, Babur was remarkably often ill. His health had never been good—the memoirs are scattered with alarming illnesses and even more alarming cures—and like many of his family he was a hard drinker. His brother Jahangir and several of his own descendants died of drink, and indeed the Koran's prohibition on alcohol seems to have had precisely the same effect in their case as the eighteenth amendment in America.[5] Babur even explains at one point that having decided to renounce wine when he was forty he was 'drinking to excess now that less than a year was left',[6] and his pages are full of attempts by himself or by others to coax or trick people into taking alcohol. For many the subject even seems to have exercised the peculiar fascination that sex holds for certain puritans; a favourite type of titillating story tells of the wicked amir who tortured his pious sister by locking her up in a room with no food or drink except a glass of wine, and who finally, when she was beyond recall on the way to a martyr's death, forced it through her lips to add revulsion to her suffering.[7] If anything, Babur himself preferred to alcohol a drug which he calls *majun* and he is very modern in his expression of its pleasures; 'while under its influence wonderful fields of flowers were enjoyed . . . we sat on a mound near the camp to enjoy the sight'.[8] But it is certainly an exaggeration to brand him, as he has been, an addict of either alcohol or drugs—apart from anything else his approach was far too orderly, Saturday, Sunday, Tuesday and Wednesday being allotted to wine and the remaining three days to *majun*.[9] His illnesses—frequent boils, sciatica, discharge from the ears or the spitting of blood—were far more the result of his hard life as a young man.

But it was noticeable that his periods of sickness had become much more frequent since his arrival in Hindustan, perhaps because of his age, perhaps because of the climate, and this fact certainly contributed to Humayun's decision to hurry back from Badakhshan to Agra in direct disobedience to orders in 1529. The more immediate reason was the news that some of Babur's closest advisers were planning to bypass Humayun and all his brothers and to win the succession for Mahdi Khwaja, a mere uncle of theirs by marriage. In the event the uncle dissipated any support for his cause by his own arrogant behaviour[10] and it was Humayun, rather than his father, who soon fell grievously ill. Tradition provides

[1] 4, II, 630–4 [2] 6, 94 [3] 6, 95–6 [4] 4, II, 617 [5] 5, 199, 202 [6] 4, I, 422 [7] 5, 258 [8] 4, I, 393 [9] 4, II, 447, n.2; 16, II, vi [10] 14, II, 41–4

a moving tale of Babur's response to the crisis. It was suggested to him, sitting in despair with wise men by the Jumna, that the prince's life might be saved if Babur gave away his most precious possession in return for it. The wise men meant the Koh-i-Nur (legend overlooked the fact that this belonged to Humayun), but Babur understood the necessary sacrifice to be his own life. He walked three times round the patient's bed crying aloud this offer to God, and on that very day Humayun began to recover while Babur fell ill of the fever from which he soon after died.[1] It may well be that Babur did practise this rite, which is apparently a familiar one in eastern tradition, but the instant transference of the illness, essential to the appeal of the story, is not borne out by the facts. There were several months between Humayun's recovery and the onset of Babur's final illness, which when it came was fairly brief.[2]

Humayun, who had been posted to Sambhal, was the only one of Babur's sons who was near enough to reach his bedside. The emperor in his final distraction called repeatedly for Hindal, still only eleven and now on his way from Lahore; but the reason was apparently nothing more political than a last wish to see once more the Benjamin of his family, since he asked again and again how tall the boy had grown and studied intently a garment of the prince's which was produced.[3] The evidence seems to be clear that even if Babur may have shared the doubts of some of his advisers about Humayun's fitness to rule, he nevertheless had every intention that his eldest son should succeed.

The emperor died on December 26, 1530. His progression with all its ups and downs from tiny Ferghana to Hindustan would in itself ensure him a minor place in the league of his great ancestors, Timur and Jenghiz Khan; but the sensitivity and integrity with which he recorded this personal odyssey, from buccaneer with royal blood in his veins revelling in each adventure to emperor eyeing in fascinated amazement every detail of his prize, gives him an added distinction which very few such men of action achieve. And his book itself became a powerful and most beneficial source of inspiration to his descendants. Avid readers of family history, they found here the most personal expression of their own tradition. In certain respects they consciously imitated Babur; Jahangir wrote a very similar book about his own life, Shah Jahan deliberately copied Babur's gesture of pouring away his wine before a decisive campaign.[4] Even more important, for several generations the Great Moghuls instinctively followed Babur's concept of a ruler, which by the standards of the time was decidedly liberal. Again and again in his memoirs he demonstrates a belief that defeated enemies must be conciliated rather than antagonized if they are to be ruled effectively afterwards, and that one's own followers must be prevented by rigid discipline from victimizing the local population. It was a belief which would play an important part in the great days of the Moghul empire.

Babur was buried at first in his garden on the banks of the Jumna at Agra, but he had left a wish that his final resting place should be in his favourite garden at Kabul. The body remained at Agra for at least nine years, but at some time between 1540 and 1544 it was escorted to Kabul from a Hindustan now governed by Sher Shah, the conqueror of Humayun. The grave at Kabul is on a high terrace in the steeply sloping garden where he loved to sit and admire the view, in the small kingdom which he certainly regarded as home. Two of his children, Hindal and Khanzada, are buried nearby on the same terrace and various Great Moghuls

[1] 10, I, 275–6; 6, 105 [2] 83, 158–63 [3] 6, 106 [4] 65, 27

among his descendants made pious additions to his tomb; Jahangir added to the simple flat grave a marble headstone and Shah Jahan contributed an elegant marble railing and, on the terrace below, a mosque, also in white marble. The whole ensemble would make a delightful open air memorial, but unfortunately some modern civil servant has thought it necessary to protect this durable marble with a ludicrously incongruous superstructure, looking much like an expensive bus stop, with red-tiled sloping roof and dormer window—in direct opposition, as it happens, to the emperor's own expressed wish that no roof should cover his tomb.[1] And Babur, who together with Jahangir was the keenest gardener among the Great Moghuls, would be highly disappointed in the present state of his terraces, almost totally uncared for and given over in part to a barracks and a huge concrete swimming-pool. At the present time, and probably for the last two centuries, Babur's romantic notion of a grave in his favourite garden has misfired. But no doubt sooner or later, with the steady increase of tourism to all the territories of the Great Moghuls, Kabul will think it wise to do him justice again.

The 15th-century Jahaz Mahal, the so-called Ship Palace, in the fort at Mandu, captured by Humayun in 153

[1] 4, II, lxxx

his own valet, who later wrote a book about him—but his charm was of a rather childish nature and verged at times on the embarrassingly sentimental. His sister Gulbadan describes a most revealing scene after Humayun's youngest brother, Hindal, had murdered one of the emperor's favourite advisers, a venerable old shaikh, and had then marched away from Agra. Humayun's response was to visit Hindal's mother, in whose company he found Gulbadan and four ladies-in-waiting. To the intense embarrassment of the assembled ladies he began to swear on the Koran that he bore no grudge against young Hindal but would merely like him to return to Agra, and he would not cease from his protestations until Hindal's mother had agreed to go and fetch him back.[1]

Humayun enthroned: a late painting in the Moghul tradition, c. 1800

Immediately after his accession Humayun set about reorganizing the court to his own fancy, and his new regulations turned the business of administration into an elaborate astrological game. Public offices were divided into four departments according to the four elements. The Earth department looked after agriculture and architecture, Water supervised canals and the wine-cellar, Fire was in charge of military matters; these were at least symbolically apt, but as symbolism rarely dovetails perfectly with the facts, Air was left with a rag-bag of misfits, such as the 'wardrobe, the kitchen, the stables, and the necessary management of the mules and camels'.[2] Each day of the week was reserved for an appropriate type of business or pleasure according to the relevant planet, which also governed the colour of the clothes Humayun wore on that day. So on Sunday he appeared in yellow and dealt with state affairs, on Monday in green and was merry.[3] Among those who suffered more than inconvenience and delay from this system were a group of miscreants who had the misfortune to come before Humayun on a Tuesday 'when his Majesty wore the red vesture of Mars and sat on the throne of wrath and vengeance' and who therefore received punishments out of all proportion to their crimes.[4] The superstition and childishness inherent in these ideas seem to have reached their peak in Humayun's 'carpet of mirth', a huge round carpet painted with all the paraphernalia of astrology. Humayun sat on the sun surrounded by his officers and courtiers, who rolled dice showing figures of people either standing, sitting or lying down. They were expected to do what they threw, and this, says the account, 'was a means of increasing mirth'.[5]

But the emperor also had in hand more serious plans for his capital, in keeping with the cultured and liberal traditions of his Timurid inheritance. In 1533 Humayun personally laid the foundation stone for a new city at Delhi—an area rivalled only by Troy in the spawning of cities, the present New Delhi by Lutyens being at least the twelfth. It was to be called Din-panah, 'Asylum of Faith', and its foundation gave notice to the entire Muslim world that here was the capital of a liberal empire where philosophers and poets of no matter what Islamic sect would be welcome, in deliberate contrast to the bigotry and persecution practised by the present ruling dynasties in Persia and Turkey. Learned refugees did indeed begin to arrive from those countries and Humayun must have felt that he was set fair to establish a cultural centre worthy of the traditions of Samarkand and Herat. But he was not to be allowed time for this to happen, though his descendants would fulfil his hopes later in Fatehpur Sikri and Agra. All that remains today of Humayun's Din-panah at Delhi are the high walls of the citadel, known now as the Purana Qila, or old fort. Ironically, the only two buildings still standing within those walls were put up ten years later by his great enemy, Sher Khan.[6]

[1] 6, 137–40   [2] 10, I, 647
[3] 10, I, 640, 650–1   [4] 10, I, 314
[5] 10, I, 650   [6] 59, 62–4
[7] 58, 157–223; 59, I, 118–68;
60, 68–9

During the first five years of the reign two dangerous opponents had been steadily extending their power. They were Sultan Bahadur of Gujarat to the south-west; and to the east Sher Khan, who later called himself Sher Shah and who had established himself as the leader of the many Afghans who over the years had settled along the Ganges in Bihar. In the event Sultan Bahadur was surprisingly easily disposed of, though not by the Moghul army alone. In 1535 Humayun at last decided to march against him and made rapid progress, taking the two famous forts of Mandu and Champaner and driving Sultan Bahadur down to the coast, where he took refuge with the Portuguese who were establishing themselves on the island of Diu. But Humayun then settled down to enjoy himself for a long spell in his two new forts, until the details of Sher Khan's activities in the east became so alarming that he was forced to march back to Agra—whereupon Sultan Bahadur calmly returned to occupy his territory once more. However, only a few months later his new allies, the Portuguese, succeeded where Humayun had failed. At a diplomatic parley, during which Bahadur intended to kidnap the Portuguese viceroy and the viceroy had laid plans to seize Bahadur, a fight not surprisingly broke out and Bahadur was killed. The Europeans were proving themselves more than able to master local customs.[7]

Humayun's main task in the east was to prevent Sher Khan from overwhelming Bengal, the possession of which would add greatly to his wealth and power, but it was not until the rainy season of 1537 that the emperor was ready to set off in boats down the Jumna and so into the Ganges, accompanied by two of his brothers, Askari and Hindal, and by most of his harem. The party was delayed for six months at Chunar, a strong fort perched high above the bank of the Ganges which was held by Sher Khan's son and which Humayun felt he must capture to protect his rear. The delay meant that Humayun reached Bengal too late. When he

BELOW *The Ganges at Chunar*

arrived at its capital, Gaur, a city famous for its wealth and great stores of grain, he found the streets strewn with corpses and the granaries empty. Sher Khan had been there before him, had carted away the city's wealth, and was now consolidating his position behind Humayun and across his line of communication with Delhi. In spite of these obvious dangers Humayun once again, according to one of his personal servants, 'very unaccountably shut himself up for a considerable time in his Harem, and abandoned himself to every kind of luxury'.[1]

But this time the news that reached him from the centre was even more alarming than the situation which had brought him back from Mandu. His brother Hindal, now aged nineteen, had been stationed half way along the Ganges precisely for the purpose of securing Humayun's rear, but he had deserted his post and had returned to Agra, where he was now living in the royal palace and behaving, albeit rather tentatively, as emperor. Humayun sent the venerable Shaikh Buhlul to reason with him, but Hindal murdered the old man and proclaimed definite rebellion by having the *khutba* read in his own name and marching on Delhi. Meanwhile another brother, Kamran, older and more subtle than Hindal, was also converging on Delhi from his territories in the Punjab—ostensibly to help Humayun but in reality, as his subsequent actions proved, to stake his own claim to his brother's crumbling empire. He dissuaded Hindal from further open disloyalty, but his real intentions were clear from the way the two brothers now disregarded Humayun's urgent appeals for help on his dangerous journey back through the territory which had been relinquished by Hindal to Sher Khan. To make matters more ominous, it was at this point that Sher Khan decided to start calling himself Sher Shah, as if claiming already an imperial status.[2]

The armies of Humayun and Sher Shah converged on the banks of the Ganges at Chausa, to the east of Benares. In the tactics of the time it was almost invariably a disadvantage to attack, the reason being that artillery, easily the most powerful weapon in the field since its introduction by the Moghuls, was also virtually immobile and therefore was only useful in defence. An army's first task, therefore, was to dig itself in with carts lashed together around the position as Babur had at Panipat. So now at Chausa the two armies sat side by side for three months improving their defences and engaging in leisurely diplomacy. A vivid account survives of how Humayun's ambassador, a mullah called Mohammed Aziz, found Sher Shah with his sleeves rolled up and a spade in his hand, helping to strengthen a barricade.[3] Ambassador and general sat together on the ground for an informal discussion, and their negotiations led eventually to an agreement whereby Sher Shah was to be allowed Bengal and Bihar, but only as provinces granted to him by his acknowledged emperor, Humayun. It was typical of Humayun that he should now insist on a childish but ostensibly face-saving device whereby his army was to be allowed to advance towards Sher Shah's forces, who would then turn and retreat in evident fear and subservience; and it was equally typical of Sher Shah that he should accept his role in this sad charade and then use it to surprise and demolish Humayun in ruthless betrayal of their recent treaty. Humayun's brief advance brought his army out of its prepared defensive position, and Sher Shah, having withdrawn a few miles, returned at night to find the Moghul camp asleep and unprepared.[4]

Those of Humayun's troops who were not massacred were driven back into the Ganges, where most of them drowned. The emperor himself escaped only because

Crossing a river on inflated skins: detail, c. 1590

one of his water-bearers inflated his water-skin with air for Humayun to hold in his arms and float. The use of the inflated skin as a float was not quite as novel as the accounts of the emperor's escape suggest—it was, for example, the normal way for the peasants of Ahmedabad to cross the river after the rains[5]—but Humayun was sufficiently impressed to promise the water-bearer, whose name was Nizam, that he would seat him on the throne of Delhi. One of the most distressing details of Humayun's shame was that several distinguished ladies of the harem and one of Humayun's young daughters were lost in the chaos, presumably drowned. Others, captured by Sher Shah, were treated extremely well and were sent with an escort back to Humayun in Agra. There was something of a tradition among Muslim princes of respecting their enemy's family—just as Babur had taken care of Ibrahim's women after Panipat—but they could not be relied on to extend the courtesy to non-Muslims. When Sher Shah captured the children of a raja he gave the daughter 'to some itinerant minstrels that they might make her dance in the bazaars' and had the young sons castrated 'that the race of the opressor might not increase'.[6]

Humayun crept back to Agra, where, for the first time since his succession, all four brothers were now gathered together. Hindal's rebellion was formally and publicly discussed in the garden where their father lay buried, and Humayun pardoned him. The affair of the water-carrier provides at this point an insight into the tensions within the family. Humayun insisted on keeping his word to the humble Nizam and at this supreme moment of family crisis allowed him to sit on the throne and give orders, for a period which in the different sources varies from two days to two hours. Humayun's sister Gulbadan, normally very well disposed to him, grumbles that 'for as much as two days the Emperor gave royal power to that menial' and records a curt but certainly justified message from their brother Kamran; 'at a time when Sher Khan is near, what kind of affair is this to engage your majesty?'[7]

Clearly another battle was imminent against Sher Shah, who was continuing a leisurely advance westwards, and it was one which—fought so near to the centre—would decide the immediate fate of the empire. Yet even in the face of this threat the two eldest sons of Babur failed to unite. Kamran had arrived from Lahore with a force of twelve thousand whose loyalty was to him personally. He was eager to use them against Sher Shah, but more it seemed on his own behalf than Humayun's. Recognizing the threat to his own position Humayun, partly through pride and partly through caution, opposed Kamran's plans for immediate action and tried to persuade him to help in building up a larger army under Humayun's leadership. After some months of ill-feeling between the two, Kamran withdrew to his own base in Lahore. Those of his forces who stayed with Humayun soon deserted, and it was with a demoralized though fairly large army that Humayun again marched east to confront Sher Shah, who by now was only a hundred and fifty miles east of Agra. The armies met at Kanauj on May 17, 1540. Once again Humayun contrived to station himself with the Ganges at his rear; once again after a severe defeat he had to flee with considerable difficulty across the river, this time on an elephant. His brothers Askari and Hindal had remained with him for the engagement, and the three of them limped together back to Agra. News of defeat travels fast, and mere villagers began to harass the royal party as they hurried by. They delayed in Agra only long enough to gather up

[1]7, 3; **58**, 224–90; **60**, 115–22
[2]**59**, I, 215–21; **60**, 134, n.1
[3]**13**, I, 460
[4]**58**, 317–47; **60**, 123–31
[5]**47**, I, 60
[6]**9**, IV, 370–5, 402–3; **7**, 18; **6**, 136–7 [7]**6**, 140; **7**, 19–20

their families and the treasure, and then continued westwards as fast as possible, not stopping until they reached Lahore. Sher Shah continued calmly behind them. By the middle of June he had reached Delhi and there was a new dynasty in Hindustan—the Sur dynasty, from the name of Sher Shah's tribe.[1]

In Lahore all was confusion. Humayun's sister Gulbadan records that every day news arrived that Sher Shah had advanced another few miles, not fast but relentlessly, until he reached Sirhind. At this point Humayun sent an ambassador to him saying 'I have left you the whole of Hindustan. Leave Lahore alone, and let Sirhind be a boundary between you and me'; to which Sher Shah sent the curt reply 'I have left you Kabul. You should go there.'[2] Unfortunately this was precisely what Humayun was unable to do. Kabul was Kamran's province, and Kamran had no wish to make good Humayun's loss of the centre of the empire by handing over his own carefully nursed territory at its western extremity. 'The King remained inactive in the palace of Lahore, not knowing what to do, or where to go', wrote the ewer-bearer Jauhar, who, in charge of Humayun's washing and dressing, can best be described in modern terms as his valet.[3] To add to Humayun's danger, Kamran now made a secret and treacherous approach to Sher Shah, offering his support in return for the Punjab, but Sher Shah had no need of help and the offer was declined. It is at this stage that the histories first mention Humayun's being urged by his followers to kill Kamran, and his quoting Babur's words of mercy in reply.[4]

Finally Humayun decided to move down the Indus, hoping to gather forces in the province of Sind in order to strike back eastwards into Gujarat, while Kamran withdrew to the comparative safety of Kabul. At this parting of the ways the deepest family ties regrouped the brothers, two against two, in a pattern which would last throughout the remaining ten years of their struggles. Askari was full brother to Kamran, and accompanied him now to Kabul. Humayun and Hindal were only half-brothers, but Hindal had been brought up by Humayun's mother.[5] From now on, with occasional lapses by Hindal, their interests would combine against Kamran and Askari.

Humayun hoped for assistance from the ruler of Sind, Husain, who technically owed him allegiance, but Husain was too wise to offend Sher Shah and he parried Humayun's demands on him with a string of diplomatic evasions. Humayun's attempts at force were no more successful, and he failed to take either of Husain's two powerful forts on the Indus at Bhakkar and Sehwan. Eighteen months, from early 1541 to mid-1542, were frittered away in Sind and the only happy event was Humayun's marriage to Hamida, the future mother of Akbar. Even this Humayun almost failed to achieve. He saw the fourteen-year-old girl, daughter of Hindal's teacher and adviser Shaikh Ali Akbar, at a lavish party given in Hindal's camp—a measure of the luxuries still enjoyed by the fugitives compared to the horrors to come, but then Humayun was said to have left Lahore with a camp-following that numbered some two hundred thousand. But it took Humayun a month to persuade the girl to marry him. Her opposition seemed incredible fifty years later, when she was the grand old lady of her son's magnificent court at Agra, but Humayun may well not have seemed much of a catch at the time; nineteen years older than her, frequently befuddled with opium, he had an aura of failure about him. Indeed in their first two years of marriage he was able to offer her nothing but a series of exhausting and dangerous treks across desert and

[1] 14, II, 75; 60, 140–1; 7, 22–3
[2] 6, 144 [3] 7, 26
[4] 7, 26; 10, I, 318–19 [5] 4, I, 374

Hamida crossing the deserts of Rajasthan: 18th century

mountain. Perhaps too she had hopes of Hindal; he certainly, for reasons equally unclear, was so angry at the marriage that he deserted Humayun once again and set off with his troops for Kandahar. Finally the girl did allow herself to be persuaded. Humayun took up the astrolabe himself to work out the most propitious moment for their marriage. It turned to be at midday on Monday, August 21, 1541.[1]

Humayun left Sind in May 1542 in response to an invitation from Maldeo, the Raja of Marwar (now known as Jodhpur), who was at that moment the most powerful prince in Rajasthan and who clearly was contemplating an alliance against Sher Shah. But a diplomatic approach from Sher Shah, combined with a first glimpse of the feebleness of Humayun's forces, seems to have changed the raja's mind. As Humayun drew near to Marwar, messages began to reach him that he should fly for his own safety. His party had to retrace their steps across two hundred miles of desert, at the hottest season of the year, and to make matters worse the son of the Raja of Jaisalmer was moving ahead of them filling the already infrequent wells with sand because Humayun's men had been unwise enough to kill some cows in this Hindu province. Fierce fights broke out whenever water was found and the soldiers were reduced to eating berries. Only one tiny miracle occurred, but it was precisely the sort of omen to encourage a man of Humayun's disposition. Hamida was now nearly eight months pregnant, and she suddenly felt the famous arbitrary longing for some particular type of food; in her case, in the middle of the desert, it had to be a pomegranate; but soon they crossed paths with a merchant who was found to have in his bag one large juicy pomegranate.[2]

A particularly scandalous incident later became famous as exemplifying how desperate conditions had become. Hamida was one day without a horse and, in spite of her condition, nobody would lend her one. Humayun gave her his and climbed on top of one of the camels belonging to Jauhar's department, which was regarded by all as a most undignified mount. He had gone three or four miles in this unroyal manner before an officer, Khaled Beg, offered his horse.[3]

On this borrowed animal the emperor approached Umarkot, a small town in the desert, where things unexpectedly and briefly changed for the better. The raja and his sons rode out to meet the Moghul party, welcomed them with every courtesy and offered to provide seven thousand horsemen with whom Humayun could move against Husain. The reason for this unexpected new alliance was that Husain had killed the raja's father. But Umarkot was to become famous in Moghul history for its connection with a much greater and more long-term change in the family fortunes. It was here, on October 15, 1542, that the fifteen-year-old Hamida gave birth to Akbar.[4]

The future emperor's own friend and biographer, Abul Fazl, should be allowed to announce such an important event in his own inimitable words—his style being one which has brought him the scorn of many western readers, but which was the conventional manner of Persian prose of the time and was used with far greater vividness by him than by most. He tells us that 'the pains of travail came upon her Majesty and in that auspicious moment the unique pearl of the vice-regency of God came forth in his glory'; then the royal infant was 'bathed and composed by the hands of shade-loving, radiance-darting, chaste, rare-bodied nymphs', after which 'even-tempered, spiritually-minded nurses swathed the divine form and heavenly body in auspicious swaddling-bands and then his

The grave of Humayun's aunt Khanzada, which stands near Babur's in Kabul

[1] 7, 30–1; 6, 149–52 [2] 10, I, 375
[3] 7, 36, 42–3
[4] 13, I, 566; 134, I, 316

honied lips, being brought in contact with the benign breasts, his mouth was sweetened by the life-giving fluid'.[1]

Only for a short while were the benign breasts Hamida's. The position of wet-nurse was a political appointment of considerable importance, since the nurse's own sons became foster-brothers of the future monarch, and here was an admirably cheap way in which Humayun, who had recently had to borrow money at twenty per cent from one of his nobles to pay the soldiers,[2] could reward some of his followers. Abul Fazl lists nine noble ladies who received the honour of suckling the royal babe before he was finally weaned, and adds that there were many others, but the lady who had been chosen for the special honour of heading the queue had mismanaged things so badly that she was still pregnant when her opportunity occurred, and she only came in again at number five.[3] The birth was an event which Humayun's entourage had been awaiting for years. He was thirty-

four already and the need for an heir had become so pressing, and the attention paid to any of his women who were pregnant so flattering, that Gulbadan tells of one concubine who managed to eke out a false pregnancy for twelve full months (on the grounds that a relative of hers had once given birth three months late) before her pretensions were finally deflated.[4] This shortage of heirs, a problem which would plague Akbar too until his twenty-seventh year, seems surprising in a context where the royal harem could number several hundred young women, the son of any of whom would become an acceptable future emperor. Infant mortality played a certain part but the deaths of royal babies seem usually to be mentioned in the chronicles and journals, and their number is not sufficient to explain the whole case. It seems clear that in the hectic life of a Moghul emperor sex played less of a part than conventional images and dreams of harem life would lead one to suppose. Humayun, needless to say, took a personal hand in casting the infant's horoscope, which runs to sixty pages in the printed text of Abul Fazl, every detail proving most auspicious—and rightly so, as it turned out.[5]

Humayun made some small progress with his new allies from Umarkot against Husain, but Husain was now sufficiently irritated by Humayun's continuing presence in Sind to be willing to bribe him to leave. For two thousand loads of grain and three hundred camels (most of which proved so wild that 'one might say they had not known city, or load, or man for seven, or rather seventy, genera-

[1] 10, I, 57, 129 [2] 6, 157
[3] 10, I, 130–1 [4] 6, 112–13
[5] 10, I, 64, 69–128

tions'[1]), Humayun crossed the Indus on July 11, 1543, and set off north-west towards Kandahar—and towards the biggest affront which he had yet received from his brothers.[2]

A painting by Mir Sayyid Ali c. 1540, just before Humayun met him in Persia

Kamran had removed Hindal from Kandahar when he refused to read the *khutba* there in Kamran's name, and Hindal was now living a life of forced retirement, virtually under house arrest, in Kabul. Kandahar was held on Kamran's behalf by Askari, who now received instructions from his elder brother to seize Humayun.[3] In early December the emperor was approaching the province of Kandahar when news came that Askari was close at hand with a large force and in a hostile mood. Humayun decided that the only course open to him was to move on into Persia, in the hope of assistance from the Shah, and he hurriedly rode away from his camp with his forty closest supporters and Hamida, with only one other lady to accompany her. As it was December, and the journey would take them through snow-covered mountain passes, the young Akbar, now aged fourteen months, was left in the camp with all the domestic servants; and when Askari arrived a few hours later, Jauhar himself presented the child to its uncle, who 'took the babe in his arms and embraced it'.[4] In European history of the early sixteenth century it would have been a fatal error to allow one's heir to fall into the hands of a rival claimant to the throne, but the Timurid princes seem to have been able to rely on clear though unspoken rules by which they were fighting for supremacy —rules which safeguarded the infant Akbar and which also, no doubt, governed Humayun's treatment of his brothers. Askari put the child in the care of his own wife, who, it was generally agreed, treated him with the greatest kindness.[5]

Humayun's party was ill-equipped to cope with the rigours of the journey—on the first night, without domestic servants or even a cooking-pot, they were reduced to boiling horse meat in a helmet[6]—but by early January 1544 they had struggled through to Persia, where they must have been relieved to discover that Shah Tahmasp welcomed their visit. He had sent his local governor detailed instructions, which still survive, about the lavish clothes, food, travelling arrangements, lodging and bathing facilities which were to be provided for his royal guests. Even the roads were to be swept and watered in front of them.[7]

Humayun was now able to move on in a style to which he had grown unaccustomed, but first he spent a month sightseeing in Herat. Like Babur before him, he was here exposed to the cultural traditions of his Timurid inheritance in their most refined form and it was this aspect of his stay in Persia which was to have the most significance for future Indian history. The painter Bihzad had moved his studio from Herat to Tabriz some forty years before, and it was while he was a guest of the Shah that Humayun met two distinguished pupils of Bihzad's, Khwaja Abdus Samad and Mir Sayyid Ali. Humayun invited them to join him when—or perhaps with his usual lack of self-confidence he said if—he recovered a throne for himself. They did so. It was from them that Humayun and the young Akbar later took lessons in drawing (a subject which his present host, the Shah, also studied), and it was under the guidance of these two Persians that Indian artists undertook the *Dastan-i-Amir-Hamzah*, the first great series of paintings in what is now known as the Moghul or Mughal school.[8]

A further forty days were spent at Meshed, visiting the shrine of the Imam Riza and meeting the local divines, and it was not until July that the visitors reached Shah Tahmasp in his summer residence west of Qazvin at Surliq. The meeting of

[1] 6, 163 [2] 7, 47–9; 14, II, 93–4
[3] 6, 160–2 [4] 7, 52 [5] 10, I, 396
[6] 6, 166–7 [7] 10, I, 418–33
[8] 89, 53–4, 119–20; 10, II, 67;
87, I, xix; 92, 204

the monarchs—'two eyes of the world in companionship/ Joining in courtesy like two eye-brows', as a Persian poet promptly put it[1]—led to a long series of festivities and hunting parties. Gifts were heaped on Humayun and he in return dipped into his secret reserve of portable wealth, the jewels which he carried under his clothing in a green-flowered purse. During his three years of wandering he had handed out jewels to local chieftains who needed to be bribed or rewarded, but there were still enough in the purse to meet the demands of this most important occasion. He took a mother-of-pearl box and placed in it, with a selection of lesser diamonds and rubies, the Koh-i-Nur. And Abul Fazl is quick to emphasize that this gift repaid the Shah for all his expenditure on Humayun 'more than four times over'.[2]

But behind the festivities there were severe tensions. Tahmasp, like his father Ismail before him, was fanatically eager to spread the Shia doctrine. There could hardly have been a less provocative Sunni guest than Humayun, since his wife Hamida was a Shia, as also was Bairam Khan, who had become one of Humayun's most important followers and who was sent ahead as ambassador to Tahmasp. But the Shah wanted nothing less than Humayun's outward acceptance of Shiism, just as his father had with Babur, and Humayun was coaxed, tricked and threatened into wearing the pointed Shia cap and having his hair cut in the approved Shia fashion. Finally he was presented with the Shia doctrine written out on a piece of paper; he expressed polite interest and said he would very much like to copy it out. But this was not enough. He was expected to sign the document. Much to the distress of Jauhar, who had escaped from Kandahar to rejoin Humayun in Herat, he did so.[3]

In addition to these religious tribulations there were envoys from Kamran at Tahmasp's court offering the city of Kandahar in exchange for Humayun. But it seems that the Shah's favourite sister, Sultanam, was very enthusiastically on Humayun's side; and in the end the Shah decided to support Humayun in an attack on Kamran's territories, on condition that Kandahar should be handed over to him when captured. He announced this decision to his new friend by a device medieval in its splendour and romanticism. He invited Humayun to a party for which three hundred tents had been set up on an area covered with imperial carpets, with twelve military bands providing music, and he mentioned in a lull that all this, together with twelve thousand chosen horsemen, was his for his return to his own dominions. The Shah's son Murad, an infant not yet weaned, was to accompany the expedition and would represent his father in Kandahar.[4]

Humayun took a roundabout route eastwards sightseeing as he went, rather to the impatient Shah's annoyance. But he particularly wanted to see the Caspian, although Jauhar was convinced that it was always hidden in thick fog; and a visit to Tabriz, a splendid city torn again and again by earthquakes, set him dreaming on the wheel of fortune.[5] By about February 1545 he had joined up with the infant Murad and his army in eastern Persia, and together they advanced on Kandahar. A century later to have entertained a destitute Great Moghul seemed sufficiently surprising for the scene to be painted, as one of the proud moments of Persian history, on a wall in the throne-room of Shah Abbas in his Chehel Sotoun, or Palace of Forty Pillars, at Isfahan. In the way of such paintings, a large Tahmasp, bristling with jewelled weapons, offers food to a smaller and unarmed Humayun, but in one crucial respect historical memory was mercifully short—Humayun

A shaikh: painted by Bichitr c. 1620, at the peak of the Moghul School of painting, some sixty-five years after Humayun brought Persian artists to India

[1] 10, I, 437
[2] 7, 66–8; 6, 167–8; 10, I, 439
[3] 7, 65–6; 13, I, 572
[4] 7, 72–5; 14, II, 99–100
[5] 7, 75; 10, I, 444

عمل باد در العصر استاد منصور نقاش

OPPOSITE *A Himalayan blue-throated barbet: by Mansur, c. 1615*

wears the familiar Moghul turban in marked contrast to Tahmasp's pointed Shia cap.

Kandahar, which was held by Askari, fell to Humayun on September 3, 1545, and it was duly given to the Persians. By the familiar ebb and flow of power this initial success meant that nobles began to come over to Humayun—'in very truth the greater part of the inhabitants of the world are like a flock of sheep, wherever one goes the others immediately follow', wrote a contemporary historian describing precisely this process[1]—and when the young prince Murad suddenly died, Humayun was strong enough to step in and take Kandahar from its Persian garrison. The very principle which had made it worth Tahmasp's sending a suckling child to head the expedition meant also, when the child died, that a royal vacuum was created which Humayun, abhorring such a thing as much as anyone else, rushed in to fill.

Humayun now set out to take Kabul, and was able to do so without even a fight —largely because the unpopularity of Kamran's harsh rule led to more and more desertions from his camp as Humayun approached, until Kamran himself decided

RIGHT *Humayun and Hamida reunited with Akbar: late 16th century*

to flee from the city. So, in November 1545, Humayun and Hamida were reunited with the three-year-old Akbar. The festivities provided a perfect setting and occasion for the circumcision of the child, an important public ceremony after which the nobles indulged in wrestling matches, even Humayun himself taking a part.[2] Wrestling was a skill required in these circles from a very early age. A few months before, when not yet three, Akbar had won his first bout against his slightly older cousin, Ibrahim, a son of Kamran's. The two infants were quarrelling over a painted drum and so Kamran set them to wrestle for it. Abul Fazl explains that Akbar 'despite his tender years, by Divine inspiration and celestial teaching, without hesitation girt up his loins, rolled up his sleeves, grappled with Ibrahim Mirza according to the canons of the skilful and so lifted him up and flung him on the ground that a cry burst forth from the assemblage'. Kamran took it as a bad omen.[3]

The wider struggle between Humayun and Kamran continued for the next eight years. Humayun had the upper hand but was as careless as ever about defending his rear when away on expeditions, with the result that Kamran twice recaptured Kabul and Humayun had twice more to win it back. But Kamran's

[1] 13, I, 578–9 [2] 10, I, 486
[3] 10, I, 456

periods of possession were more and more marked by atrocities against the inhabitants, and Humayun emerged clearly as the prince by whom the majority wished to be ruled. And the nobles in his immediate entourage were now persuading him to act more decisively, although a mysterious ceremony—in which they appear solemnly to have sworn allegiance to him in return for his virtual promise of obedience to them on matters of policy—suggests that many of the decisions he was being decisive about were in fact theirs.[1] He still seemed to enjoy the tearful reconciliations and long reunion feasts with his brothers,[2] but they could no longer rely on his mercy. Hindal, ever since Humayun's return, had remained loyally on his side and died fighting for him in 1551. But Askari now spent a long period in chains, being moved around with Humayun's camp, until he was sent on pilgrimage to Mecca. He died on the journey somewhere beyond Damascus.[3]

Kamran had betrayed Humayun's trust so many times that the pressure to have him killed had been mounting for years. Finally, in 1552, he tried to make a treacherous alliance with Islam Shah, son of Sher Shah and now emperor of Hindustan; but the emperor, though impressed by Kamran's knowledge of poetry (he identified each of the first three quotations that Islam Shah threw at him), offered him a present of only a thousand rupees, a derisively small sum which clearly implied that no serious help was forthcoming.[4] Kamran escaped from Islam Shah's court and made his way, disguised at one point as a woman, to

The two-year-old Akbar wrestling with his cousin for a painted drum: 17th century

the territory of Sultan Adam Ghakkar, a ruler in the Punjab. But Adam handed the fugitive over to Humayun.

This time Humayun had to concede that his brother should at least be blinded, but there were the usual days of feasting together before this was finally decided —perhaps the previous feasts had been more nerve-racking for the supplicants than they seem in retrospect. Kamran had forebodings that this was to be the last time. Jauhar was sent to attend him in his tent and he recalls a 'melancholy discourse', while he was massaging the prince, on the subject of death. The next day he was also present when soldiers arrived to blind Kamran and he gives an eyewitness account of a scene which would seem gruesome in a Jacobean tragedy, with men sitting on the prince to hold him down while they made repeated stabs into the sockets of his eyes and filled them with salt and lemon juice. Humayun then provided funds for Kamran to journey to Mecca. Unlike Askari he completed the pilgrimage and died in Arabia in 1557.[5]

From the point of view of the official Moghul historians Kamran was an unmitigated traitor and villain, and he was certainly a far less attractive character than his gentle elder brother. But it is likely that in his own mind he was behaving within his rights. The tradition among the descendants of both Jenghiz Khan and Timur had been for the sons to divide their inheritance and then, within certain agreed limits such as those which probably prevented Kamran from killing Akbar, to struggle to increase their share. On this basis Kamran, who had originally been given the province of Kabul, would have felt every justification in keeping his dispossessed brother out; and Humayun would have found it unthinkable, as he evidently did, to execute Kamran for treachery. But Kamran was following an older nomadic tradition of the Mongols and Turks, whereas Humayun was being forced into the ways of strong centralized kingdoms, such as existed in India and Persia, where the inheritance of the whole by one ruler was the established system. Without the accompanying principle of primogeniture this leads almost inevitably to fratricide in the struggle after each king's death: so, for example, Humayun's enemy, Sultan Bahadur of Gujarat, had systematically set about exterminating his brothers after winning the throne in 1526; and Sultan Mohammed of Turkey murdered no fewer than nineteen of his brothers on his accession in 1595, a simple fact of history which astounded Akbar when he heard it.[6] In centralized kingdoms such ruthlessness was the norm. It was Humayun's misfortune that he grew up in one system but needed to operate another, though it is doubtful whether he would by nature have been capable of the cold-blooded murder of his brothers. Fortunately for his family's future empire in India, his son and grandson inherited the throne with no brothers capable of making a strong rival claim. But after them the fraternal struggles for the Moghul empire were to prove as ruthless as any.

Since Humayun's departure in 1543 there had been virtually no communication with India, except for Kamran's final journey in search of help and Sher Shah's quasi-symbolic gesture in providing safe passage for Babur's body from Agra to Kabul, as if finally sweeping his dynasty from the land. But in 1554 Islam Shah died and his empire immediately fell to pieces. Three rival claimants to the throne of Delhi marched against each other, minor rulers set about establishing their independence; and in precisely the same way as the disorders in the Tughluq empire had enticed Timur through the Khyber Pass, so these suicidal squabbles

[1] 7, 99; 6, 195, n.3
[2] e.g. 7, 92; 10, I, 536–8
[3] 10, I, 536; 60, 302
[4] 8, 498; 6, 200
[5] 7, 105–6; 10, I, 608
[6] 10, III, 1016

within the Sur dynasty unexpectedly left the door open for Humayun's return to India—and left it open so wide that his army, under the immediate generalship of Bairam Khan, advanced right through the Punjab without meeting serious resistance and had reached Sirhind before it was opposed by Sikandar Shah, the most powerful of the three pretenders. Even Rohtas, the magnificent fort constructed on the Jhelum only a few years previously by Sher Shah precisely to prevent an invasion from this side, was surrendered without a struggle. Sikandar's army at Sirhind was larger than Humayun's but superior Moghul tactics, for which the credit should go to Bairam Khan, gave the invaders a resounding victory on June 22, 1555. Bairam's chief subtlety, since it was no longer possible to persuade an enemy to attack an established defensive position after the lesson of Panipat in 1526, had been to pull his army back from an open battle through previously prepared fortifications, which came in effect to the same thing. Sikandar himself escaped, but the victory was sufficiently complete to leave Delhi open to Humayun. On July 23 he remounted his father's throne.[1]

His remaining period on the throne was unusually restful. He was still sur-

Sher Shah's fort at Rohtas: c. 1545

rounded by Afghan enemies, the supporters of the Sur dynasty, but he could now afford to send out armies under trusted generals to deal with threats from all sides simultaneously. One of his main disadvantages during his earlier ten years of rule in India had been that only when he himself marched in any one direction did that particular enemy withdraw. In those days he had no commanders whom he could sufficiently trust. Now, with his brothers dead or banished, there was nowhere for the loyalty of his followers to swerve.

It was a time for rewarding the faithful few who had followed him through so many dangers. Bairam Khan was now created Khan-Khanan, the lord of lords; and Jauhar, the humble ewer-bearer, rose rapidly through several minor administrative appointments to become the treasurer of Lahore and a man of sufficient substance to be chosen to entertain an ambassador in his own house. He ended his life as loyal as ever, and his book with the prayer that 'the whole habitable world may be subjected to the descendants of the great Emperor Timur, and be dependent on the kingdom of Delhi for ever'.[2]

During this period there reached Delhi the earliest of the many foreign travellers who have left first-hand reports of the Moghul emperors. He was a Turkish admiral, Sidi Ali Reïs, and he found Humayun busy with his favourite pursuits. The emperor had selected the sites for several observatories, and was gathering together the necessary instruments. Poetry was almost the *lingua franca* of court life, and certainly of diplomacy. Even the Imperial Archer—a 'superb youth', says Sidi Ali, and a special confidant of Humayun's—was a regular contributor to the literary discussions. When Sidi Ali was first presented to Humayun he made more of an impression with two poems and a chronogram on the reconquest of India than with the gift which they accompanied. And he soon consolidated his reputation with two further poems in praise of the beautiful Archer. 'My God', cried the monarch, 'this is truly sublime!', or so claims the unbashful Turk.[3]

The poetry discussions probably took place in Sher Shah's elegant octagonal building, the Sher Mandal, which Humayun was fitting up as a library. Here Humayun's precious manuscripts at last found a safe home. Babur had brought many of them from beyond the Khyber and they had been with Humayun on his dangerous travels. One of his greatest joys after a victory over Kamran had been to discover that two captured camels were laden with the very books which Kamran had seized during an earlier encounter—a measure of how much a prince's treasure had to accompany him everywhere, and how to a Timurid in particular manuscripts were rated high among his valuables. It was in this same library building that Akbar was now taught drawing by Mir Sayyid Ali.[4]

Humayun also had schemes for reorganizing the administration of the empire, along more sensible lines now than his previous astrological fantasies. The difference was that this time he had an excellent example to follow. Sher Shah, known to Humayun only as a brilliant but unscrupulous opponent in the field, had proved himself during his five years as emperor to be an inspired administrator. He had set up a greatly improved system of provincial government and revenue collection, and although this had collapsed in the recent chaos, the concept survived. Humayun was preparing to recreate the system and make it his own, when an accident brought his life to a sudden end; it was left to his son to fulfil his intention and build an enduring administrative edifice on Sher Shah's foundations.

[1]10, I, 634; 59, II, 229–45; 60, 331–46 [2]7, 112–21 [3]29, 47–54; 10, I, 665 [4]10, I, 571, and II, 67

Humayun's death was as unlucky as anything in his unfortunate life, but it occurred in a context which perfectly fitted the man. On Friday January 24, 1556, he was sitting on the roof of his library, where there is a pleasant little open pavilion, hearing news of Mecca from some pilgrims who had recently returned and discussing with his astrologers the hour at which they expected Venus to rise, for he intended to hold a propitious assembly at that precise moment and to make appointments. He then rose and began to descend the steps which tumble almost sheer from a rectangular opening in the flat roof. His foot was on the second step when he heard the muezzin cry the summons to prayer from Sher Shah's nearby mosque. He was turning to bow the knee in respect when his foot caught in his robe. He slipped, fell headlong down the steps, and struck his right temple on a sharp edge. Three days later he died. A messenger hurried to inform Akbar, now

OPPOSITE The steps down which Humayun fell to his death

LEFT The Sher Mandal, used by Humayun as his library

thirteen years old, who was campaigning three hundred miles to the north at Kalanaur, and until such time as he should be safely proclaimed the usual devices were employed to calm the populace. A mullah named Bekasi, who happened to resemble the late emperor, was presented on a distant platform to the anxious crowds gathered by the river.[1]

Among the first six Great Moghuls the image of Humayun is inevitably that of the nonentity, the one obvious failure. Certainly he was a much less powerful character than his father or his immediate descendants. He could be impetuous as well as indecisive, but usually chose the wrong moment for each. In a family always threatened by addiction, his own need for opium was rivalled among the emperors only by his grandson Jahangir's for alcohol. He also inclined alarmingly to modesty. After listening to Sidi Ali Reïs boasting about how the Turkish empire

[1]10, I, 656; **29, 57**

covered all the land conquered by Alexander and more, Humayun replied—or so Sidi Ali reported—'Surely the only man worthy to bear the title of Padishah is the ruler of Turkey, he alone and no one else in all the world.'[1] No other member of Humayun's dynasty would have allowed such subversive matter to be discussed in his presence. With his air of civilized lethargy, his excessive superstition, his sentimentality, his lack of self-confidence, Humayun gives the overall impression of a man childish but endearing—not perhaps the best qualifications for an emperor. But it is worth adding that his life, which looks like a failure, ran a course remarkably parallel to his father's, which certainly looked a success. Each inherited a kingdom; each lost it, largely because a more powerful military leader appeared on the scene; each in the very last years of his life conquered Hindustan. Admittedly Humayun began with more, admittedly he was confronted by a much weaker Hindustan, but the parallel puts his failures in perspective. And even he left India a highly productive legacy—Akbar.

[1] 29, 57

A shield inscribed with Akbar's name, and said to have belonged to him, though possibly of a later date

OVERLEAF *Akbar receiving the submission of a rebel, Bahadur Khan, and a harvest of heads:* c. 1590

Akbar

One of Humayun's last recorded decisions had been an unusually wise one. Only two months before his death he had appointed Bairam Khan, whose generalship had already recovered the empire for the Moghuls, to be the guardian of Akbar. When the news of Humayun's fatal fall from his library roof reached them, Akbar and Bairam were together in the Punjab campaigning against Sikandar Shah, who had been defeated but not destroyed at Sirhind in the previous year. In a garden at Kalanaur, on February 14, 1556, the thirteen-year-old boy was enthroned as emperor. He wore a golden robe and a dark tiara, and sat on a large platform specially constructed for the occasion which still stands isolated in the middle of rich Punjabi farmland.[1]

The three Afghan rivals for the throne of Delhi had between them a claim which was equal with absolutely mathematical precision to Akbar's. Babur and his son Humayun had ruled for fifteen years; Sher Shah and his son Islam Shah had ruled for fifteen years. There was no balance of legitimacy to tip support to one side or the other, and the strength of the Afghans, if they could have combined, would have been too great for Akbar. Luckily they remained divided. Bairam Khan and Akbar decided that Sikandar was still the most dangerous of the three and so concentrated on reducing him in the Punjab, while entrusting the defence of Delhi to its Moghul governor, Tardi Beg Khan.

In the event the main threat to Akbar's future came not from one of the three Afghan princes but from a Hindu who, without even the advantages of belonging to a high caste, made at this time a brief but dramatic incursion into the Muslim centres of power. His name was Hemu and he had started life selling saltpetre in the streets of Rewari. Having achieved the position of weighman in the market, his abilities attracted the notice of the ruling Afghans and he rose in their service until he became the chief minister of Adil Shah, one of the three rival princes. Although himself tiny and of feeble physique, Hemu proved a magnificent leader and won twenty-two battles in succession for his Afghan master—a sequence which not surprisingly gave him the idea of setting up on his own. Now, in October 1556, he advanced with a large force on Delhi; and by concealing three hundred elephants for a last-minute surprise attack he was able to panic the Moghul forces under Tardi Beg Khan into a sudden and ignominious flight. Hemu then entered Delhi and set himself up as an independent ruler under the Hindu title of Raja Vikramaditya.[2]

On the news of the fall of Delhi most of the nobles in the army in the Punjab urged withdrawal to the safety of Kabul, but Bairam and Akbar took the courageous decision to press forward against Hemu's undoubtedly superior forces. To bolster the morale of their followers, the prince and his guardian indulged in some expensive showmanship. The master of ordnance was given instructions to 'prepare fireworks as a treat for the soldiers' and to 'make an image of Hemu, fill it with gunpowder, and set it on fire'.[3] When they were joined by the Moghuls retreating under Tardi Beg Khan from Delhi, the pressure to withdraw once again

Akbar's sandstone wall round the fort at Agra, surmounted by the marble buildings of Shah Jahan

Sources (*see* p. 252)
[1] 10, II, 5; 62, 29
[2] 10, II, 48; 62, 34; 63, 24–6
[3] 10, II, 69

mounted until Bairam took the high-handed step, probably without Akbar's knowledge, of executing Tardi Beg on a charge of cowardice for his hurried flight from the capital. Abul Fazl and Jahangir later wrote that Bairam used the retreat from Delhi as an excuse to get rid of a rival.[1] Possibly, but his action had the necessary effect of bracing the reluctant Moghuls for an unequal battle ahead. And in many ways Tardi Beg's death reads as a fitting conclusion to his life. Like Bairam he had been one of Humayun's small band of close followers during the long flight from Sher Shah. But it was always Tardi Beg who had refused his horse to Hamida, who had charged his emperor twenty per cent for a loan, who had deserted at a moment of crisis.[2] If his death was a cold-blooded murder between old rivals from Humayun's days in the wilderness, it was fortunate that it was the better man who did his rival the greater wrong.

On November 5, 1556, the Moghuls met the army of Hemu at Panipat, the very same field of battle where Babur had won the victory which took him to Delhi thirty years before. This was not mere coincidence. Armies about to fight each other in the plains of Hindustan tended to move towards the nearest area where it was known from experience that an advantage could be derived from the lie of the land. In this, only one of three famous battles at Panipat (1526, 1556 and 1761), the Moghuls were saved by a lucky accident after a hard fight which looked more than likely to go against them: an arrow hit Hemu in the eye, and although it did not immediately kill him it made him unconscious. In any battle at this period the death of the leader meant the end of the fight, and the sight of the tiny Hemu slumped in the howdah of his famous elephant Hawai was enough to make his army turn tail. He was brought unconscious before Akbar and Bairam, and in that condition was decapitated amongst much self-congratulation about the holy duty of slaying the infidel. His head was then sent to Kabul, and his torso to Delhi for exposure on a gibbet. There was great slaughter of those who had been captured from his army, and in keeping with the custom of Jenghiz Khan and Timur a victory pillar was built with their heads.[3] Peter Mundy, an Englishman travelling in the Moghul empire some seventy-five years later, found such towers still being made of the heads of 'rebbells and theeves' and made a drawing of one 'with heads mortered and plaistered in, leaveinge out nothing but their verie face'.[4] Most of Hemu's fifteen hundred elephants had been captured, and with such an access of power and wealth Delhi was securely Akbar's, at the very least for a while. An advance guard was sent straight on from the battle to occupy the city, and Akbar and the rest of the army followed the next day.[5]

The arrival of Hemu's head in Kabul came as a gory but welcome relief to the ladies of the harem. Humayun had learnt his lesson when he lost some of his female relations in the Ganges after his defeat by Sher Shah at Chausa, and when he departed for India he left the harem in the comparative safety of Kabul. Hindustan after his death had seemed too unsettled for them to make the journey, but now the arrival of this bloodstained souvenir brought the news that they could set out. For Gulbadan, Akbar's aunt, history must have seemed to be repeating itself; as a small girl of five or six she had made precisely this journey in the company of the other ladies when her father, Babur, had captured Delhi after another battle of Panipat.[6] By the time the harem reached Hindustan, Akbar and Bairam had come west again into the Punjab to continue the pursuit of Sikandar Shah, whom they were now besieging in the fort of Mankot. Akbar rode out a

ABOVE *Peter Mundy's drawing of a tower of heads: 1632*

OPPOSITE *A Moghul version of the same: c. 1590*

[1]10, II, 51–2; 16, I, 39
[2]7, 52; 10, I, 391–3; 13, I, 568
[3]10, II, 65; 13, II, 10; 14, II, 220
[4]45, II, 90 [5]63, 31 [6]6, 20,100

day's journey from Mankot to meet his mother and the rest of the family, and Hamida's 'wishful eyes were gratified by the world-adorning beauty of H.M. the Shahinshah'.[1] Sikandar soon surrendered in return for a promise of his life and a grant of land—he caused no more trouble and died peacefully on this land two years later—and in the same year of 1557 Adil Shah, another of the Afghan claimants to the throne, was killed in a battle against the ruler of Bengal. Within eighteen months of his accession, and before he was yet fifteen, the three most serious threats to Akbar's throne—Hemu, Sikandar Shah and Adil Shah, had all been removed.

The credit remained largely Bairam Khan's, and those close to the royal circle could not fail to notice that the regent's young charge seemed remarkably uninterested in his responsibilities as emperor. The most disturbing aspect was his apparent refusal to learn anything of any possible use, apart from the purely physical accomplishments required for doing battle. Abul Fazl, for whom every action of Akbar's has to be given at least a gloss of perfection, struggles again and again to explain that his apparently frivolous activities were only 'impenetrable by the superficial of this age' and that even if he 'wore the guise of one who did not attend to affairs, in reality he was deeply interested, and was testing the loyal'.[2] Nevertheless, the picture that comes through is a familiar one of a high-spirited but idle schoolboy. After the astrologers had computed the perfect hour for the prince's very first formal lesson back in the years at Kabul, 'when the master-moment arrived that scholar of God's school had attired himself for sport and had disappeared'.[3] Sport, as usual, was what the schoolmasters were up against, and in particular hunting or any sport that involved animals. Akbar's first tutor had been dismissed for having addicted the boy to pigeon-flying, but it seems just as likely that the pupil corrupted the unfortunate master. Any teacher who has had to write a school report for an influential child will surely admire the skill with which Abul Fazl blends the real with the desired when he announces that the young scholar 'carried off the ball of excellence with the polo stick of divine help'.[4]

The apparent and now notorious result was that Akbar, alone in a royal family which prized learning and culture more than most, was illiterate. There has been much argument about how precisely this categorical statement by several of Akbar's contemporaries can be taken. Abul Fazl says that the emperor himself used to mark with a line the place which the servant reading to him had reached; and there is in a manuscript of the *Zafar-nama* the name of a month written in childish and unformed characters, and a note beneath it by Jahangir saying that it is in his father's hand.[5] The truth seems to be that Akbar as a boy had learnt the rudiments of reading and writing, but preferred not to use them—perhaps originally from choice, and later because to read and write badly was worse than not doing so at all. For a ruler of Akbar's time not to read was no great disadvantage and might in some respects even be an advantage. It meant that he must acquire all his facts from other people and must test his opinions publicly against theirs; in doing so he would inevitably learn how to delegate authority and to assess the merit of those to whom he delegated it; and he would be likely to develop a prodigious memory, as Akbar certainly did.[6] Timur—ancestor, conqueror, and patron of art whose life Akbar liked to have read to him—was illiterate.[7] There was nothing much to make the boy or the man change his ways.

A Moghul book-rest, of a type visible in many paintings of the period: 17th century

He had had an unsettled childhood, shuttled like a pawn between his father and his uncles, and from a very early age he had taken an active part in military affairs; at ten he was beside his father in battle, and was given the leadership of his dead uncle Hindal's followers; at twelve he was with the advance guard, and nominally in command of it, during the victory at Sirhind; as a boy in Kabul he had terrified everyone by his passion for riding fierce camels, and later in India he loved nothing more than to be on top of a male elephant fighting another.[8] The very activities which took Akbar away from his books were, in their way, a good preparation for being a soldier king, the only sort of king that it was possible to be in such times. Even his passion for hunting he turned later to a very effective purpose. As his empire grew in strength it became impolitic for him to march in battle array against minor disturbances or rebellions, but the Moghul style of hunting involved the use of the army as beaters and for years Akbar's routine pattern of life was to move on hunting expeditions wherever there was trouble, whereupon his mere presence in pursuit of deer or tigers would calm things down. In retrospect Akbar's failures as a schoolboy must have looked more sensible than in fact they were.

While the young emperor was thus, in Abul Fazl's phrase, 'behind the veil', Bairam Khan continued very efficiently to run the affairs of state, keeping firm control in the centre and continually sending out expeditions to enlarge the frontiers of the kingdom. But pressures were building up against him. For one thing he was a Shia and most of the nobles were Sunni—a sore spot into which he recklessly rubbed salt by appointing an insignificant Shia divine, Shaikh Gadai, to the office of Chief Sadr, one of the two highest ecclesiastical positions in the land. But religious hostility was also a respectable peg on which to hang deeper resentment of Bairam's overwhelming personal power and prestige. He was arrogant, and sufficiently confident of his own power to make no effort to conceal it. He lived a life of ostentatious magnificence, so much so that even Akbar was able to complain that his own servants were impoverished compared to Bairam Khan's.[9]

The most powerful opposition to Bairam came from the fringes of Akbar's family and harem, being headed by Maham Anga, a shrewd and ambitious woman whose power derived from her former position as Akbar's chief nurse. Her ambition centred on the advancement of her son Adham Khan, who, as Akbar's foster brother, was regarded almost as one of the family. Though brave in battle, he was impetuous, cruel and totally unfitted for any sort of command. Between them, mother and son tricked Akbar into coming to Delhi in March 1560 without Bairam, who remained at Agra, and they were then easily able to persuade him to write dismissing Bairam from his post as chief minister—easily because Akbar himself, now seventeen, felt ready to take a more personal control of affairs. He suggested that Bairam should make the pilgrimage to Mecca—the Moghul version of ostracism—and offered to put money at his disposal for the journey. Bairam, though obviously pained at Akbar's refusal even to meet him, was too loyal to accept the suggestion of some of his followers that he should march on Delhi and forcibly rescue the young emperor from his new advisers. He did indeed set off for Mecca, but Akbar unwisely sent an army to chase his guardian out of the kingdom. This was too much for Bairam, who turned and fought but was captured and brought before the emperor as a rebel. But now Akbar's good sense prevailed. The

[1]10, II, 86 [2]10, II, 26, 96
[3]10, I, 519 [4]10, I, 588–9
[5]11, I, 103; **87**, I, xxi
[6]10, I, 32 [7]56, 3
[8]10, I, 582, 587, and II, 111–16;
14, II, 134; **16**, I, 38
[9]10, II, 162; **13**, II, 30

interview was a touching one; the emperor showed every honour to the man who in the past four years had laid down the firm foundations of the empire, and sent him on his way again to Mecca. Unfortunately on January 31, 1561, when Bairam was sightseeing in Patan, the ancient capital of Gujarat and not far from the pilgrimage port of Cambay, he was murdered in vendetta by an Afghan whose father had died in a battle against Bairam's forces five years before.[1]

Much of the power enjoyed by Bairam Khan now passed to Maham Anga, but she and her son were soon to discover that they could no longer use it in a manner nearly as absolute. In February 1561 Adham Khan was sent to invade Malwa, a province ruled by a voluptuary called Baz Bahadur who was a household name both for the quality of his harem and for his talents as a musician—indeed his love songs in Hindi to the most famous and beautiful of his women, Rupmati, were so popular that they could be heard throughout the bazaars of Hindustan. But Baz Bahadur was less impressive as a general than as a lover, and when a battle against Adham Khan near his city of Sarangpur seemed irretrievably lost he made his own escape, callously leaving his harem behind, with instructions that the women should be killed rather than fall into the hands of the Moghuls. But many of them were able to hide long enough to be captured. Even the great Rupmati, though she had been slashed several times with a sword by the eunuch left to guard her, was taken alive; but when Adham Khan insisted on an assignation and came to her house, he found that she had taken poison.[2]

Adham Khan's behaviour after the victory at Sarangpur was outrageous both in itself and in relation to Akbar. Instead of sending the captives and treasure back to Agra he forwarded only a few elephants and kept the rest for himself.[3] Those captives who were not young girls from the harem were brought in droves before his fellow commander, Pir Mohammed, and himself, and were butchered while the two generals sat jesting. The historian Badauni was present and a friend of his had the courage to protest, but to no avail. The real offence, in the eyes of the orthodox mullah Badauni and no doubt many others like him, was that many of the victims were Muslims; 'Sayyids and Shaikhs came out to meet him with their Qurans in their hands, but Pir Mohammed Khan put them all to death and burnt them.'[4] In these early days of Akbar's reign such a massacre still seemed normal if it was largely of Hindus, as after the defeat of Hemu at Panipat.

When the news from Malwa reached Akbar he showed that he was now very much his own master, capable of moving fast and decisively. He was so outraged at what he heard—though more, it would seem, at the loss of the treasure and women than at the details of the massacre—that he set off with a small band without consulting his advisers, and moved so fast that he arrived in Malwa before fast couriers from Maham Anga could reach her son and bring him warning. Adham Khan was therefore appalled to find himself suddenly confronted by his emperor. After some alarming days of uncertainty, and after handing over the booty, he was officially forgiven, but even now he secretly kept two of the most special beauties for himself. When this was discovered by Akbar, Maham Anga coolly had the girls murdered for fear of what they could tell about her son.[5]

It should have been becoming every day more clear to Maham Anga and her faction that the young emperor was not someone lightly to be crossed. His new decisiveness was more than matched by his physical daring, which he now demonstrated in feats even more alarming than his boyhood escapades with wild

Akbar having Adham Khan thrown to his death: c. 1590

camels and elephants. On the way back from Malwa he faced a tigress on foot and killed her with his sword;[6] on another occasion he terrified his followers by driving his elephant through the wall of a house which was sheltering armed local bandits, receiving five arrows on his shield as he approached.[7]

The unscrupulous cruelties of Adham Khan and his mother were soon to come up against this physical impulsiveness of Akbar's in a dramatic confrontation which brought their days of ambition to an abrupt end. A new sign of their fading power had been his appointment of Atkah Khan, a man outside their sphere of influence whom Akbar summoned from Kabul in November 1561 to become chief minister. A few months later, in May, Atkah Khan was sitting one day dealing with affairs of state in a public hall which adjoined Akbar's private quarters and the harem, when Adham Khan burst in with some followers, went straight up to the chief minister and gave a sign to one of his men to stab him. Adham then tried to get into the harem, but the eunuch on guard locked the door from inside while Akbar emerged from another door to confront the assassin. Adham laid his hand on Akbar's arm in an ambiguous gesture, which might have been either of supplication or assault, whereupon Akbar punched him in the face. It was boasted later that the mark looked as though it had been a blow from a mace; at any rate it knocked him unconscious. Akbar then ordered him to be thrown over the parapet. The first fall failed to kill him, so the mangled body was heaved up again for a final drop to his death. Akbar himself broke the news to Maham Anga, and within a short while she too died. The emperor, aged nineteen, was now his own master.[8]

Around this time Akbar was already laying the foundations of the policy of religious toleration, which was to become one of the most significant aspects of his reign. It would be wrong to suggest that there had been no fruitful collaboration between Muslims and Hindus during the previous centuries; the tide of bigotry had ebbed and flowed much as it did within the Moghul period itself. But Akbar undoubtedly made a more far-reaching attempt than any other emperor to represent all the major religious groups within the nation. Although earlier Muslim rulers had married Hindu wives, only Akbar allowed them to practise their Hindu rites within the walls of the royal harem.[9] During his reign more Hindus than ever before were employed in the civil service.[10] Above all, it was only under Akbar that cooperation was a deliberate and passionate policy of state.

The first great event in putting this policy into practice was Akbar's marriage with a Rajput princess, the daughter of the Raja of Amber (now known as Jaipur), in 1562. She was to become the mother of the next emperor, Jahangir, and he in his turn would marry further Rajput princesses, thus binding more securely the Moghul link with the most important and powerful of the Hindu provinces in northern India, Rajputana or Rajasthan. The Rajputs were famed as the greatest warriors in India. They went into battle drugged with opium, to remarkably good effect, a device which they shared with the Afghans, who once had to give up a season's campaigning because the harvest of poppies had failed.[11] For the next century Rajput armies would always be at the service of the Moghuls. Even more important, the rajas themselves would lend their considerable talents, as administrators and governors as well as generals, to the needs of the empire. The succession of distinguished Hindu counsellors in the Moghul service begins now with Bhagwan Das and Man Singh, members of the royal house of Amber into which Akbar had

[1]10, II, 138–203; 13, II, 33–5;
14, II, 241
[2]0, II, 213–14; 14, II, 252; 63, 56
[3]10, II, 214 [4]13, II, 43
[5]10, II, 219–20
[6]10, II, 222–3; 14, II, 255
[7]10, II, 251–4 [8]10, II, 269–75
[9]126, 16 [10]120, 45–9
[11]148, 39–40; 42, 78; 120, 97

married, and each in turn destined to become the Raja of Amber and Akbar's leading general.

The remission of two obnoxious taxes reflected the same policy of conciliation. When hunting in 1563 near Mathura, a sacred place of Hindu pilgrimage, Akbar discovered that his officers were levying a tax on every pilgrim, in keeping with the custom of previous Muslim rulers. He forbad the practice throughout the kingdom on the grounds that the Hindus should not be penalized because 'they had no conviction that they were on the wrong path'.[1] More boldly, and at even greater expense to the treasury, he abolished in the following year the much hated *jizya*, a tax stipulated in the Koran to be paid by *dhimmis* or unbelievers. The removal of this symbolic and hallowed piece of fiscal discrimination effectively gave notice that from now on everyone was equally a citizen of the empire, a modern concept to which previous Muslim rulers had not even paid lip-service.[2] As his reign progressed Akbar continued to make deliberate concessions to Hindu customs— introducing their festivals at court and having newly washed and painted cows brought into his presence after Diwali, letting his hair grow long in a Hindu fashion and adopting a Rajput style of turban, even on occasions wearing the *tilak,* the Hindu sectarial or ornamental mark made on the forehead[3]—until the more orthodox Muslims became convinced that the emperor had abandoned their faith.

There were, of course, sound political reasons for all this. Akbar could look back on nine successive Muslim dynasties in India before his, which had lasted on average less than forty years each,[4] and he was shrewd enough to see that any stable rule in India must enjoy the consent of both religious groups. But Akbar was also by nature inclined to such reforms. He was, it has been pointed out, 'the child of a Sunni father and a Shia mother born in Hindustan in the land of Sufism at the house of a Hindu',[5] and he had been much impressed by one, even if by only one, aspect of his education—the obsession of his teacher Mir Abdul Latif with the principle of *sulh-i-kull* or religious toleration. (It was typical of Mir Abdul Latif's gentle freethinking that he should have been persecuted in Persia for being a Sunni and distrusted in India for seeming a Shia.[6]) Finally, Akbar himself seems to have had in him a mystical streak which made him hunger for some expansion of conventional religious beliefs. There were various incidents in his life—a sudden 'internal bitterness' and sense of 'exceeding sorrow' when he was twenty, an occasion when he galloped alone far into the desert to meditate and deliberately allowed his horse to escape, an unexpected revulsion from killing at the climax of a most elaborate hunt[7]—which may seem to others not particularly unusual, but which clearly acquired for Akbar himself the significance of some sort of revelation and which can be seen as anticipating the unorthodoxy of the experiments with religion which formed an important part of his later life.

Akbar continued the policy, set up by Bairam Khan, of steady and ceaseless expeditions to extend the area of empire. One of his so-called Happy Sayings, as recorded by Abul Fazl, was that 'a monarch should be ever intent on conquest, otherwise his neighbours rise in arms against him'.[8] He could have added that otherwise the exchequer runs dry, for expansion is an economic necessity in a predominantly military society. Each of Akbar's three favourite ways of enlarging his empire—through conquest, treaty or the harem—involved a handsome contribution to the imperial treasury. Like Jenghiz Khan or Timur he was con-

82

[1] 10, II, 295 [2] 10, II, 316–17
[3] 113, 83–4, 99; 10, III, 348;
13, II, 269 [4] 111, 160 [5] 124, 93
[6] 10, II, 35 [7] 11, III, 386;
10, II, 92–3, and III, 346–8
[8] 11, III, 399

stantly on the move, resisting the temptation to which Humayun had succumbed of relaxing in one place after an initial success. The nature of Akbar's life is well suggested by Abul Fazl when he uses a routine phrase to introduce a routine expedition into Rajasthan in 1570; he says that Akbar 'for political reasons, and for subduing oppressors, etc. etc., and under the veil of indulging in hunting, proceeded towards Nagaur'.[1]

The main events during this particular and brief expedition were three, again typical in kind. First, Akbar finally received the homage of Baz Bahadur, who had been defeated at Sarangpur nine years before and had been on the run ever since; he was given a pension and was allowed to join the Moghul court, where he was appreciated mainly for his musical skill and where he became a colleague of the great Tansen, India's foremost musician of the period who had been summoned by Akbar into his service in 1562 to become his Master of Music. Secondly, the Raja of Jaisalmer asked to be allowed to present a daughter to the imperial harem; she was graciously accepted and Bhagwan Das was sent to collect her. Thirdly, the Raja of Bikaner offered a niece; she too was accepted, and so 'that occupant of the howdah of chastity was brought within the screens of purity'.[2]

The screens of purity were already bursting at the seams—Akbar finally had more than three hundred wives—but the political advantages of this stream of presentation princesses, one of whom later came from as far away as Tibet,[3] were incalculable. It was as though Henry VIII had been allowed to enjoy all his wives simultaneously and forty times over. The actual number of women in the harem was nearer to five thousand. Many of these were older women, but there were also young servant girls, or Amazons from Russia or Abyssinia as armed guards, all with the status only of slaves.[4] It was these who, if so required, were the emperor's concubines. The three hundred were technically wives, even though the Koran limits the number to four. But in one rather ambiguous verse in the Koran there is an implicit permission for a lower form of marriage, known as *muta* —as opposed to *nikah* for the orthodox marriage ceremony—and Mohammed seems historically to have condoned *muta* marriages among his own followers. A *nikah* marriage could only be with a free Muslim woman and had to be, at any rate in intention, for life. A *muta* marriage could be with free women of other religions and involved no ceremony, but was a private pact between the man and the woman for, officially, a limited period of time to be agreed between them. It is thought to have been an earlier Arabian custom which Mohammed was not able to suppress and it became, particularly in Persia, the conventional cloak for prostitution, with the managers of caravansarais offering *muta* wives to travellers for the night.[5] The Shia interpretation of the Koran was that such an arrangement constituted a legal Muslim marriage. The Sunnis disagreed, and Badauni records fascinating discussions between Akbar and his *ulama*, or group of learned divines, as to whether his superfluity of wives could be said to have legal marriage status under the *muta* principle. The arguments raged back and forth, precedents were provided and refuted, until—completing the parallel with Henry VIII—Akbar dismissed the Sunni *qazi* or expert on divine law who would not see his point of view, and replaced him with a Shia who did. Later, Akbar had the effrontery to decree that it was best for ordinary men to have only one wife.[6] Or perhaps he was speaking from experience.

When Akbar set out on an expedition 'under the veil of engaging in hunting',

[1] 10, II, 517 [2] 10, II, 518–19
[3] 10, III, 921
[4] 11, I, 44–5; 10, III, 994
[5] 133, III, 774–6, 912–14
[6] 13, II, 211–13, 367

Akbar hunting with cheetah. c. 1590

the sight was usually alarming enough to deter most opponents. The Moghuls' favourite style of hunting was the *qamargah*, or enclosure, which involved the use of a large army and had been favoured by both Jenghiz Khan and Timur precisely for its value as military training.[1] The soldiers acted as beaters, forming a huge circle and driving the game slowly towards the centre. On one occasion in 1567 an area sixty miles in diameter was surrounded by fifty thousand beaters who over the space of a month closed slowly in until all the animals, on this occasion mainly deer, were gathered in an area less than four miles wide. At this point Akbar rode into the circle. He was accompanied by several courtiers but he alone hunted, using at various times a bow and arrow, a sword, a lance, a musket and even a lasso. The circle was still being tightened, and this was the stage when it was hardest to prevent the animals from breaking out—Jauhar and his friends accidentally let some through at their part of the line during a hunt organized by Shah Tahmasp for Humayun, and they were fined a horse and a coin for each escaped deer.[2] At a certain moment wattle screens were put up in place of the human chain. Akbar hunted in the *qamargah* for five days on this occasion in 1567, after which the nobles were allowed to take their turn, and after them the servants of the court, and finally the troopers and soldiers. By then this crowded sport must have been highly dangerous, and Abul Fazl records at least two occasions when people used the confusion to settle private scores.[3] When the common soldiers had killed their fill, it was traditional for holy men to ask mercy for the remaining animals. It was just before one of these scenes of carnage that Akbar had a mystic experience and suddenly ordered the accumulated animals to be released unharmed—a moment of revulsion hardly surprising now, but most unusual to Akbar's fellow warriors.[4]

Another form of hunting, and Akbar's personal favourite, was with the Indian 'leopard' known as the cheetah. His first cheetah had been presented to him soon after he and his father entered Hindustan in 1555 and he became extremely fond of 'this strange animal'.[5] Cheetahs were captured in pits or wicker cages and within a month or two could be trained to obey their keepers, being released to stalk and kill deer and then to return after the kill much like a hawk. Akbar took his cheetahs very seriously. They were divided into eight classes, their rations of meat being graded accordingly. They wore coats studded with jewels, and were taken to the hunt sitting blindfold on beautiful carpets. Bets could be placed on which cheetah would kill most deer during the day, and a cheetah which in 1572 leapt a huge ravine to catch a deer was raised to the rank of chief cheetah and had a drum beaten before it in procession.[6]

Hunting was a substitute for war, both for those taking part in it and for those whom it was designed to frighten, and what with roping wild elephants, facing tigers on foot, laying bets surrounded by loose cheetahs and taking part in the scrum at the end of a *qamargah*, it could often be as dangerous as war. Even at the age of fifty-four Akbar was foolhardy enough to seize a stag by the horns one moonlit night. He was knocked to the ground and gored in a testicle. He was ill for two months and Abul Fazl received the supreme honour of being allowed to apply the balm to this most intimate of wounds.[7]

The main trouble spots in Akbar's growing empire were to the east in Bihar and Bengal and to the west in Kabul. Bihar and Bengal had been ruled by Suleiman Karrani, an Afghan who until his death in 1572 professed a loose kind of obedience

[1] 56, 66–7 [2] 7, 66
[3] 10, I, 440, and II, 416–18
[4] 10, II, 416–18; 13, I, 93
[5] 10, I, 629–30
[6] 11, I, 285–9; 10, II, 539
[7] 10, III, 1061–3

which Akbar accepted. In the rivalries which followed his death Akbar interfered in the usual manner, and in 1575 the provinces were formally conquered and made part of the empire—though Bengal in particular had to be reconquered on several later occasions, being full of Afghans naturally resentful of the Moghuls who had supplanted the brief Afghan dynasty of Sher Shah in Delhi. Around Kabul there was an unending family struggle, reminiscent of Babur's early days, between Akbar's half-brother Hakim and his cousins Suleiman and Shahrukh. This was not in itself particularly important but Hakim, as Akbar's brother, was the only possible pretender to the throne and there was always the danger that disaffected elements would gather round him for a more serious rebellion. To both east and west Akbar's armies had to be ready to move decisively to preserve the status quo. The climax came in 1580 when both flanks combined against the centre. Hakim invaded the Punjab and besieged Lahore, and was at the same time proclaimed emperor in Bengal. Together the two uprisings represented the greatest threat to the Moghul empire since the early days after Humayun's death, but Akbar was able to put down the rebellion on each side. Then, in keeping with his consistent policy, he treated the rebels with sufficient leniency for their supporters to be able to accept a peaceful place again within the empire.[1]

Akbar was also expanding towards the south. He gradually made more secure his control over Malwa. In 1564 he seized Gondwana from its magnificently courageous warrior-queen, Rani Durgawati. He conquered Gujarat in 1573. And, probably the most important single aspect of his policy, he steadily extended his control over Rajasthan. Akbar rightly saw the special importance of Rajasthan in his scheme to weld both religious communities of Hindustan into one nation. Rajasthan could be said to represent, both then and now, the very spirit of ancient and Hindu India. It was the only part of the subcontinent, except for the very southern tip, which was still almost entirely Hindu after five centuries of Muslim occupation. Either the harsh deserts of the province or the famous warrior spirit of the Rajputs had discouraged successive Muslim sultans and emperors from overrunning Rajasthan.

Akbar had, more subtly, infiltrated the area by marrying into its ruling houses, and his armies had steadily been seizing various forts on the eastern fringes of the territory. But there stood in his way the proud refusal of the Rana of Mewar, head of the senior house of all Rajasthan, to have anything to do with him. The Rana's family had held their capital, the great fort of Chitor, almost uninterruptedly for over eight centuries; history proves their descent from Bappa, who seized it in A.D. 728, and legend projected their line further back to the god Rama and through him to the sun.[2] The Rana, who at present was Udai Singh, was the real figurehead of the Hindus in northern India, just as Akbar himself could by now be said to be the figurehead of the Muslims. To make matters worse, it was known that the Rana openly despised the Raja of Amber for having so demeaned himself as to give a daughter to the Moghul's harem. A clash was inevitable, and Akbar decided to attack Chitor.

At this point Udai Singh behaved in a manner rather different from the traditional image of the Rajput, famous throughout history for a positively impetuous inclination towards death rather than dishonour. Hearing of Akbar's plans he left Chitor to be defended by eight thousand Rajputs under an excellent commander, Jaimal, and took himself and his family to the safety of the hills. This action has

The fort of Chitor since brought on his head the vilification of romantic historians, in phrases such as craven prince, the unworthy son of a noble sire, eternal shame, disgrace to his race,[3] and even an 'anomaly' in the annals of Rajasthan, a 'coward succeeding a bastard to guide the destinies of the Sesodias'.[4] But it was a tactical withdrawal which any modern general would have made in the circumstances. Chitor, usually referred to as impregnable, was in fact not so. It had been taken by Ala-ud-din in 1303, and by Sultan Bahadur of Gujarat as recently as 1535. It may be argued that Udai Singh cannot have looked—or should not have looked?—at the problem with the eyes of a modern general, and that he was in effect only leaving eight thousand Rajputs to die with the traditional brave abandon. But he had stored enough provisions in Chitor to feed the garrison for several years, and had laid waste the countryside for miles around to prevent the Moghuls from gathering local food.[5] It was therefore not certain that Chitor would fall, and if it did Akbar would now in effect be capturing nothing more than a strong outpost of the Rana's vast and cactus-ridden territory. The long-term result of Udai Singh's action was certainly most beneficial. He had already created an artificial lake some seventy

[1]63, 294–5 [2]63, 84
[3]63, 85; 75, 98 [4]86, I, 371
[5]10, II, 464; 63, 116

89

miles south-west of Chitor in one of the most pleasant defensive positions in the world, a fertile valley surrounded by a ring of high hills, a natural fort many miles in diameter. Here Udai Singh now built himself a palace and here, named after him, grew up one of India's most beautiful cities—Udaipur, which became from this time onwards the capital of Mewar.

Akbar arrived on October 24, 1567, below the fort of Chitor, which occupies the whole of a rock measuring three and a quarter miles in length and some twelve hundred yards at its point of greatest width, and which rises so steeply from the surrounding plain that it reminded a writer in the early years of our own century of a 'vast ironclad in a sea'.[1] Akbar's own camp extended some ten miles, so the confrontation was on a massive scale as befitted a clash between the leading Hindu and Muslim powers in northern India. But, although the Muslim chronicles make a great deal of how this was a holy war and those who fought in it acquired the title *ghazi*, the reality was a power struggle along less simple lines. Akbar had under his command such prominent Hindu leaders as Bhagwan Das and Todar Mal, and their presence in an army against the Rana of Mewar was less surprising than it might seem in retrospect. Only thirty years previously an earlier Rana of Mewar had marched from Chitor in alliance with his Muslim neighbour, Sultan Bahadur of Gujarat, to carve up between them the nearby kingdom of Malwa. Among so many long-established principalities, some Hindu and some Muslim but all jostling for space, most alliances were made along lines of political self-interest. And the local rivalries helped the Moghul power to expand just as they would later help the British.

Akbar planned to use two main methods of assault—mining and a device known as the *sabat* or covered way. He also attempted bombardment of the inside of the fort, but bombardment was not very effective unless either the important buildings were very crowded within the fort or it was possible to occupy a position high enough to see over the walls and to aim each shot with some accuracy. Neither condition held at Chitor.

Mining was a very laborious process. The sappers, given as much surface cover as possible from a battery of guns in their rear, burrowed under the rock until they reached a position beneath the walls. They would then excavate a chamber, pack it with gunpowder and retire. Those defending a fort could see where the tunnel began but they could not be certain of its course under the surface and so would often listen, ear to the ground, for tell-tale scratchings in order to start their own tunnel down to the point of contact.[2] There were even occasions where the besieged had been able to remove the sacks of gunpowder from the back as fast as the sappers piled them up in front, thus at the same time protecting the wall and replenishing their store of ammunition.[3] At Chitor two mines, close to each other, were successfully completed within a month but unfortunately the fuses were less efficient than the gunpowder. Though intended to blow simultaneously, there was a considerable time lag between the two explosions. The assault troops, expecting only one explosion, surged forward and were in the breach when the second charge went up. Two hundred Moghuls were killed, among them several of Akbar's favourite officers.[4]

After this disaster Akbar decided to concentrate his efforts on the *sabat*, a structure even more elaborate than the mines and therefore not yet completed. In concept it was a steadily growing fortification designed to provide the attackers

Workmen building the sabat, *shielded only by leather screens; and* RIGHT *gunners firing from the top: details, c. 1590*

with defensive cover almost identical with that enjoyed by the defenders, while moving them slowly nearer their prey. It consisted of a covered way—at Chitor wide enough for ten horsemen to ride abreast and high enough for a man on an elephant with raised spear to pass along[5]—with side walls of rubble and mud which could resist cannon balls, and a wooden roof held together with hides. On the roof and in the side walls there were chambers with loop-holes, just like any fort, to house cannon and musketeers. At Chitor the *sabat* followed a 'sinuous' course, presumably along the easiest line up the steep hill but also, Abul Fazl implies, so that no section of the wall ahead could remain a blind spot for the Moghul cannon hidden inside.[6] The front end was under permanent construction, and was, needless to say, an extremely dangerous place to work; although the craftsmen and labourers were protected by movable screens made of raw hides (an indication of the low muzzle velocity of the time), about two hundred of them died every day.[7] But as the perilous work progressed nearer and nearer the wall of the fort, the advantage steadily shifted to the attackers. It is much easier to fire guns at a sharp angle upwards than downwards while remaining effectively under cover, quite apart from the special gravity problems attendant on muzzle-loading. Moreover as the cannon concealed in the *sabat* slowly advanced they could do much more harm to the chosen length of wall, partly by the greater

[1]75, 97 [2]13, I, 599
[3]71, IV, 375–83 [4]10, II, 469
[5]13, II, 105–7 [6]10, II, 468
[7]10, II, 467

91

impact of the shot but also through being able to aim more precisely for the areas already damaged. And as soon as the broad mouth of the *sabat* reached the wall, men and elephants would pick and heave at the fabric under perfect cover until a hole had been forced. Akbar's *sabat* was a treacherous armoured snake writhing with infinite slowness towards the point where it would latch its jaws on to Chitor's walls and nibble.

A ruined palace in the fort at Chitor

Akbar took a close interest in the *sabat* and spent a considerable amount of time on its roof, sniping at the garrison above. Indeed it is claimed by some of the chroniclers that it was a bullet fired by Akbar himself from his favourite gun, Sangram, which killed the commander of the fort when he came down to help in defending the breach which was finally made on February 23, 1568. It is perfectly possible that Akbar did achieve this—he took his marksmanship very seriously and had a hundred and five muskets kept for his personal use in strict rotation, of which Sangram alone was later shown in the emperor's game book to have accounted for one thousand and nineteen animals in the chase, and he was known to enjoy himself in the palace workshops supervising the manufacture of guns.[1] But it should also be added that it is a custom of Abul Fazl's, and through him of other historians, to attribute every invention, whether mechanical, medical or cultural for the entire second half of the sixteenth century, to the fertile brain of the emperor. Whether or not the crucial bullet was traced only by courtesy to Akbar himself, the predictable result of the death of the governor was the immediate fall of the fort. At first no one among the Moghuls knew who the distinguished-looking Hindu was who had died, but soon fires appeared at several points in the fort and Bhagwan Das was able to explain to Akbar that the bullet must have found Jaimal and that this was the *jauhar*, the Rajput custom of burning their women before coming out to fight to the death. The Rajput warriors duly died in the ensuing battle, but Akbar later sullied his victory by a massacre of most of the forty thousand peasants who had also lived in the fort. Akbar was particularly keen to avenge himself on the thousand musketeers who had done such damage to his troops, but they escaped by the boldest of tricks. Binding their own women and children, and shoving them roughly along like new captives, they successfully passed themselves off as a detachment of the victorious Moghuls and so made their way out of the fort.[2]

Sir Thomas Roe, an Englishman who visited Chitor some fifty years later, found the fort deserted and in ruins and was led to believe that the Moghuls desolated in this way every ancient place which they captured; 'I know not out of what reason', he commented, 'unless they would have nothing remembred of greatnes beyond theyr beginnings, as if theyr family and the world were coevalls'.[3] In fact he was misinformed. The brutal massacre of Chitor was at odds with Akbar's general policy. When a neighbouring Rajput fort, Ranthambhor, was taken a year later, the inhabitants were treated much more leniently.[4] The difference may partly have been that they capitulated sooner. But also Chitor, the strongest fort of the senior Rajput prince, was a symbol which provoked Akbar beyond reason and it remained a firm tenet of Moghul policy throughout the next century that the fortifications of Chitor should remain unrepaired.[5] Even so, Akbar's campaign had failed in its main purpose. By 1570 all the prominent Rajput princes had recognized Akbar's sovereignty except one—the Rana of Mewar, though he would henceforth be better known as the Rana of Udaipur.

[1] 11, I, 115–16; 10, III, 744
[2] 10, II, 474–6 [3] 40, 82–3
[4] 10, II, 490–5 [5] 18, 103–4

To celebrate the fall of Chitor Akbar made a pilgrimage, partly on foot, to the tomb of Khwaja Muin-ud-din Chishti at Ajmer. He had made an annual pilgrimage here for the past six years, ever since hearing some village minstrels singing the praise of the saint,[1] and the road which he normally took from Agra to Ajmer had been suitably embellished with a series of *kos minar*, elegant brick towers at regular intervals to serve as milestones, each of them decorated with antlers of stags killed personally by Akbar on his almost continuous hunt.[2] But now a living member of the Chishti order of holy men began to dominate Akbar's religious enthusiasm. In spite of his ample supply of wives the twenty-six-year-old emperor still had no living heir; the several children born to him had all died in infancy. It was his habit to visit holy men to enlist their prayers for an heir, and Shaikh Salim Chishti living at Sikri had told the emperor that he would have three sons. Soon after these comforting words the daughter of the Raja of Amber became pregnant and Akbar, to give every pious chance of fulfilment to the holy man's optimistic prophecy, sent her to live in the house of Shaikh Salim. The child was born there on August 30, 1569. He would later, when emperor, become known as Jahangir but he was given the name of the holy man, Salim, and he recorded in his autobiography that his father never called him anything but Shaikhu Baba, a special nickname deriving again from the shaikh.[3] After a prudent delay of five months, presumably to establish a reasonable probability that this child too was not going to die an infant, Akbar again set out on foot to Ajmer to give thanks for the miracle. And Shaikh Salim's prophecy was fulfilled in its entirety. Another pregnant wife was sent to him at Sikri and safely gave birth to Akbar's second son, Murad, in 1570. And in 1572, when the court was at

Outside the tomb of Khwaja Muin-ud-din Chishti at Ajm[

Ajmer, a third son was delivered in the hermitage of a local Chishti saint called Daniyal, after whom he was named.[4]

Akbar was so impressed by this sequence of events that he resolved to build an entirely new capital city at Sikri in honour of Shaikh Salim. He had already put in hand an impressive amount of architecture. From the start of his reign he had made Agra rather than Delhi his capital (it remained so until Shah Jahan brought the administration back to Delhi in 1648), and in 1565 he had pulled down the old brick fort of Sikandar Lodi at Agra and had started building the magnificent wall of dressed red sandstone, seventy feet high, which encloses and gives its name to the Red Fort at Agra. It runs in the shape of a bow, with the straight side facing the River Jumna. Akbar's palaces were along the top of this wall, and from them he could watch his beloved elephant fights in the flat open space between fort and river—a site deliberately chosen so that the enraged elephants could at any time be run into the water to cool off.[5] Of Akbar's sandstone palaces in the fort only one, the so-called Jahangiri Mahal, remains; the rest were demolished, mainly by Shah Jahan, to make way for more refined marble dwellings along this same river front (Plate 16, p. 74). The building of the wall and of some of the palaces took not much more than five years, but during the noisy period of construction Akbar also built a temporary pleasure city seven miles south of Agra, where he enjoyed himself 'sometimes racing Arabian dogs, sometimes flying birds of various kinds', and sometimes playing polo with a new invention which caused a great stir—a luminescent ball of smouldering *palas* wood, making it possible to play the game at night.[6] (Polo with Akbar could be dangerous; one player was sent on pilgrimage to Mecca for not showing the right sporting spirit.[7]) This temporary city was called Nagarcin and today nothing of it remains, but already by the time the work at Agra fort was nearing completion Akbar's thoughts had moved on to an even more impressive project, and in 1571 his masons were moved to Sikri, the village of Shaikh Salim Chishti. By a fortunate chance the shaikh had set up his hermitage on a low hill consisting of hard red sandstone, a perfect material for building, easy to work and yet very durable. Over the next fourteen years a new city would appear on this hill, literally raised from the rock beneath. For its name the word Fatehpur, denoting victory, was added to that of the existing village, Sikri.

Fatehpur Sikri is today the world's most perfectly preserved ghost town. India's climate is gentle to stone if not to people, and a modern visitor could well be persuaded that these intricate casket-like buildings, with their elaborately carved stone ornamentation still crisp and unweathered, had been completed only yesterday. But to call the present Fatehpur Sikri a town or city, as is usually done, is slightly misleading. What remains in such perfect state is in fact the palace, though its unique arrangement of vast paved areas dotted with free-standing houses, some of them private dwellings and some assembly rooms, suggests more some architect's image of a small Utopian town for a select community of aesthetes. The real town occupied a large area round the foot of the hill with the palace and great mosque at its summit. Here the courtiers and the vast legions of camp followers—a capital city in these times was still essentially the imperial camp at home—built themselves dwellings of varying degrees of impermanence while Akbar and his thousands of craftsmen were creating their masterpiece up the hill. Today nothing remains of the town itself except the outer wall which Akbar provided to protect it.

[1]63, 61–2 [2]13, II, 176 [3]16, I, 2 [4]10, II, 542; 63, 133 [5]47, I, 68 [6]13, II, 74, 69; 10, II, 372–3; 11, I, 298 [7]10, II, 534–5

The view from the roof of the diwan-i-khas *at Fatehpur Sikri*

Unlike later Moghul architecture, which combined Persian influences with the Indian, Akbar's buildings in the fort at Agra and at Fatehpur Sikri are wholly Indian in style. Their immediate source of inspiration is the exquisite little palace built in the early years of the sixteenth century by the Hindu raja Man Singh inside the fort at Gwalior, the very palace so much admired by Babur in 1528 together with the similarly carved houses in Chanderi. The feature which most strongly strikes a western visitor about Akbar's buildings and their immediate predecessors is that they appear to be wooden houses made of stone, in that their techniques of construction and ornamentation are precisely those of craftsmen in wood in other countries. The Indian mason quarried doorways, lintels, screens, bannisters, beams and even floor-boards from his native sandstone just as the Tudor carpenter cleft them from the oak. He then carved their exposed surfaces with very similar fanciful elaboration, and fitted them together for his final building in precisely the same manner, except that gravity enabled him to do away with any system of pegs—the mere weight of the stones would hold them in place. The palace buildings of Fatehpur Sikri consist of nothing but perfectly tailored chunks and slabs of stone resting on each other; indeed the slabs were mostly brought to the site in a finished state, which greatly speeded the work of construction by making it more one of compilation.[1]

Fatehpur Sikri contains many fanciful individual buildings, such as the Panj Mahal, a palace for members of the harem consisting of five pillared floors, provided originally with delicate stone screens through which the ladies could see but not be seen, each floor diminishing in size up to a small pavilion at the top (Plate 18, p. 84); or the house of Birbal, a gadfly who was Akbar's favourite courtier, with its huge and elaborate brackets under the eaves. The interiors were delightful too. A room in the so-called palace of Jodh Bai suggests the gentle elegance which must have been possible within these carved sandstone walls, when the floor was covered with rich carpets and elaborate silken bolsters to lean against, and the alcoves were full of coloured bottles of perfume or feminine keepsakes (Plate 19, p. 101). The inside of Akbar's *diwan-i-khas* or 'hall of private audience' is rightly famous both for its architectural ingenuity and for its concept, which very accurately reflects Akbar's character and idea of himself; from the outside the building appears to have two storeys but within it consists of one high room, in the middle of which stands a sturdy swelling pillar, joined to balconies half way up the wall by four delicate bridges (Plate 20, p. 102). When Akbar was in conference, he would sit on the circular platform at the top of the pillar; those involved in the discussion would sit on the balconies on all four sides, and if they needed to bring anything to the emperor they could approach him along one of the bridges; those in attendance but not expected to participate could stand on the floor below, where they could easily hear whatever was said.

But in spite of the impressiveness of Akbar's buildings—and one could add during his reign forts and palaces at Ajmer, at Lahore, at Attock on the Indus, at Allahabad on the junction of the Jumna and the Ganges, and at Srinagar in Kashmir—the architecture of his period is far from being the peak of Moghul achievement in this field and his buildings at Agra and Fatehpur Sikri, splendid though they are, are in some ways less attractive than their model at Gwalior. The reason is partly that the ornamentation at Gwalior seems more free, but the raw materials also make a crucial difference; the sandstone at Gwalior is a pale honey colour and the light falling on the reliefs carved in the stone can create beautiful gradations of tone within the pattern. The darker sandstone of Fatehpur Sikri is much less sensitive to differences of light and shade and gives a rather sombre and flat feeling to many of the buildings.

The real Moghul achievement in architecture belongs to a later reign, but something of it can be glimpsed in the courtyard of the great mosque where Shah Jahan added marble facing and ornamentation to the tomb which Akbar had built for Shaikh Salim Chishti, who had died in 1572. And, oddly enough, a monument was completed just before the earliest buildings at Fatehpur Sikri, though not under Akbar's immediate auspices, which was later to prove much more influential in the development of Moghul architecture. This is the tomb of Humayun at Delhi, and its construction was an act of piety and affection by his senior widow,

[1]MASB III, 560, 642

97

*The contrast between the
architecture of Shah Jahan and
of Akbar—the courtyard of
the mosque at Fatehpur Sikri
seen from the tomb of Shaikh
Salim Chishti*

Haji Begam. The architect whom she chose, Mirak Mirza Ghiyas, was almost certainly a Persian and he provided India with her first dome in the Persian tradition—the same tradition as Timur's tomb in Samarkand. The dome is exclusively a characteristic of Muslim architecture in India (Hindu temples make no use of the principle, relying on horizontal stone beams), but the Indian Muslim dome had until now been of a flatter shape, much like half a grapefruit, as opposed to the tall Persian dome rising as if on a slender neck. To reconcile a pleasing exterior line with a not too lofty inner chamber, the Persian domes usually had two skins with a considerable space between them, and Humayun's tomb followed this pattern. Work began in 1564 and Haji Begam, after a pilgrimage to Mecca, took up her residence in a camp on the actual site and saw the building completed by 1573. But her design was before its time. It was used immediately afterwards in the much smaller tomb of Atkah Khan, which is near Humayun's and which was possibly built by the same workmen, but then it was neglected in India until reappearing in perfected form sixty years later in the Taj Mahal.[1]

Fatehpur Sikri was only fully inhabited for some fourteen years. In 1585 Akbar moved his court to the Punjab, from which over the following years he made three separate visits to Kashmir, and when he finally returned to the centre, in 1598, he went not to Fatehpur Sikri but to Agra. Although a small part of the town below the palace remained inhabited, and still is so today, never again did Fatehpur Sikri recover its brief magnificence. Even so, the years there had been the richest and most creative of Akbar's reign. It was there that he established the style of life and culture which would last his family for nearly a century, together with the wide administrative apparatus which supported it. And it was there that he took into his service Abul Fazl, the man who would record the details for posterity.

Abul Fazl's two works, the *Akbar-nama* or 'History of Akbar' (2,506 pages in the printed English text) and the *Ain-i-Akbari* or 'Regulations of Akbar' (another 1,482 pages) surely add up to the most complete account that any one man has ever compiled of the affairs of one particular court. In spite of, or perhaps because of, his so-called illiteracy, Akbar had a passionate interest in books. Where others have collected magnificent libraries of manuscripts, he created one—said in about 1630 to have numbered twenty-four thousand volumes.[2] He had copies written out, and splendidly illustrated, of existing works. He set up a translation department, with a special room at Fatehpur Sikri reserved for the translators, producing Persian texts from the Turki of Timurid chronicles, from the Sanskrit of Hindu classics, and even from the Latin of the Christian Gospels, brought to court by Portuguese Jesuits.[3] And for his own biography he not only took the perfectly normal step of commissioning from Abul Fazl a full chronicle, but even organized the writing of primary sources.

At the same time as Abul Fazl received the order to 'write with the pen of sincerity the account of the glorious events and of our dominion-increasing victories',[4] an instruction went out to the older members of the community, who had had first-hand experience of great events, to record their memoirs. Humayun's sister Gulbadan began her volume with the words 'There was an order issued— write down whatever you know of the doings of Babur and Humayun.'[5] Hers is one of the three surviving memoirs of this type, the other two being by Humayun's personal servants Jauhar and Bayazid; the latter had suffered a stroke and dictated

[1] 97, 92–3 [2] 44, 108
[3] 13, II, 356; 125, 236–7
[4] 10, I, 27–8 [5] 6, 83

a rather rambling account of affairs to a clerk of Abul Fazl's at Lahore. Similar orders went out to the provinces for anyone with important local information to come to court and recite it to scribes, and Abul Fazl himself, in his own words, 'planted his foot in the dread wilds of research'[1] and went round interviewing old men and collecting copies of documents and reports.[2] To help him with current events Akbar set up a records department, which always had two clerks on duty recording every minute detail of court life—not only the business done, but such extra daily information as what Akbar ate and drank, how long he spent in the harem, his precise moments of sleeping and waking, his remarks, animals killed in the hunt, bets placed, who came, who went, marriages, births, books read, exercise taken, the dying of horses, the results of chess and card games, not to mention any 'extraordinary phenomena'.[3]

An Englishman at the Moghul court early in the following reign noted that the emperor 'hath writers who by turnes set downe everything in writing which he doth, so that there is nothing passeth in his lifetime which is not noted, no, not so much as his going to the necessary, and how often he lieth with his women, and with whom; and all this is done unto this end, that when he dieth these writings of all his actions and speeches which are worthy to be set downe might be recorded in the chronicles'.[4] Abul Fazl provided himself also with a committee to help interpret all this evidence but unfortunately he found most of the members 'of a retrograde tendency, spinning like a silk-worm a tissue round themselves, immeshed in their own conclusions, and conceding attainment of the truth to no other while, fox-like, artfully insinuating their own views'.[5]

The *Akbar-nama* was a continuing chronicle and Abul Fazl himself, who died three years before Akbar, was not able quite to complete it; but after only seven years (and five drafts)[6] he had produced his *Ain-i-Akbari*, an astounding combination of gazetteer, almanac, dictionary of science, book of rules and procedures, and statistical digest. Obviously much of the research is not directly Abul Fazl's own—he must have accepted wholesale the facts and figures provided for him by the various more specialized departments of state—but he has achieved a masterly feat of coordination. To give only a brief idea of the range of subject matter, the book includes Rules for Estimating the Loss in Wood Chips, and Regulations for Oiling Camels and Injecting Oil into their Nostrils, as well as details of how sixteen matchlocks can be cleaned at one time with the help of a cow[7]: more weighty academic sections explain such matters as different alphabets and comparative etymology, the origin of the many various systems of chronology in the world, and mathematical methods for calculating the nature and size of the earth[8]: of the emperor's table and kitchen, to take only one of the many court departments, we learn that he liked only one meal a day; that on the way from pot to plate his food was tasted for poison at three different stages, after which each dish was sealed with the seal of the master of the kitchen or *mir bahawal*, whose seal likewise had to be on every bag containing bread, curds, pickles, fresh gingers or limes in the long procession, accompanied by guards, to the royal table; that caravans with melons and grapes arrived almost all the year round from whatever district was now in its fruit season; that a boatload of ice called daily at the capital in an unending convoy from the mountains between the Punjab and Kashmir; and that Akbar never drank anything but Ganges water, wherever he might be, but authorized the use of rain water for cooking.[9] The list could be continued almost

100

A living-room within the harem at Fatehpur Sikri, in so-called Palace of Jodh Bai

[1] 11, III, 3 [2] 10, I, 29–32 [3] 11, I, 258–9 [4] 35, 116 [5] 11, III, 379 [6] 11, III, 402–17 [7] 11, I, 226, 146, 115 [8] 11, I, 97–106, and II, 1–36, and III, 25–112 [9] 11, I, 55–65

The central pillar in Akbar's diwan-i-khas at Fatehpur Sikri; and BELOW *Akbar's seat on top of the pillar*

indefinitely since nearly fifteen hundred pages are devoted to recording facts about the emperor himself, his dominions and the various departments of his administration.

One of the most interesting of Akbar's departments at Fatehpur Sikri was that of the painters. Akbar had inherited from his father the two Persian painters Mir Sayyid Ali and Abdus Samad, but the large number of painters under their control in the court studio were nearly all Hindus, trained in the Gujarati school of painting; the resulting Moghul style is therefore a combination of Persian and Indian traditions, and is in most ways an improvement on both. The department of painters was closely attached to the library, since nearly all their work at this period was the illustration of manuscripts, and they operated very much on a manufacturing basis. Each artist developed his own special skill—it might be doing the first outline sketch, or filling this in with colour, or adding details of landscape or facial expression—with the result that three or four artists would often work on one painting. The superintendent would then write at the bottom the names of the artists involved. At the end of each week any newly completed work would be taken to Akbar for his approval or comments, and he would give out rewards or adjust the artists' salaries accordingly.[1] It is a fortunate fact in the history of art that neither the Persians nor the Moghuls paid any attention to the passage in the Koran which forbids figurative art. Mohammed proclaimed that any man who parodies God's power of creation by making an image of a living thing will be required on the Day of Judgment to give that image life and, if he fails so to do, to surrender to it his own—a prohibition which forced artists in the stricter Islamic cultures to concentrate exclusively on calligraphy and abstract decoration.[2]

As with architecture, the Moghul style of painting does not reach its peak until after Akbar's reign. The paintings of his period are full of exquisite detail, but they usually lack the overall sense of design which was to make the paintings commissioned by his son Jahangir so distinguished. The reason may partly be that such a large proportion of Akbar's paintings were illustrations of narrative, and narrative paintings tend to become cluttered with detail. The accompanying advantage, though, is that we do have a great many pictures of contemporary events, and even if they were only painted in the pleasant seclusion of the studio at Fatehpur Sikri the general feeling and the minor physical details can be assumed to be accurate. Akbar's manuscripts are full of paintings of such familiar events as court celebrations, gardens being laid out, forts being constructed or stormed, allies being welcomed or the vanquished submitting, and a general profusion of battles.

Both Abul Fazl's great books abound in details of Akbar's wide-ranging reforms of the administrative system. Of course, one of the first claims which any royal panegyrist makes for his master is that he set up a new and stable form of government, and in sober fact several of Akbar's 'innovations' had existed in earlier stages of Indian history. So, for example, the Moghul system that employed news writers to send full and regular reports from throughout the empire had been prominent under Balban in the thirteenth century; Akbar's attempts to reduce the revenue demands on the peasants by increasing the area under cultivation had been anticipated by Ghiyas-ud-din Tughluq in the fourteenth; and the building of good roads with regular caravanserais, on which a rapid postal

[1] 11, I, 107; 87, I, xxv–xxvii; 92, 202–4
[2] 89, 23; 92, 181 ff.

system could operate, had been variously claimed for Ghiyas-ud-din, Babur and Sher Shah.[1] Indeed Ghiyas-ud-din's postal system, if it worked as well in practice as in concept, could more than outpace Akbar's two centuries later. The Tughluq ruler settled runners with their families in huts every twelve hundred yards along his main routes of communication; when an imperial message came through, each man would run at full speed the distance to the next stage carrying a baton with bells on it, the ringing of which would warn the next man to be ready to continue the relay. The system was economical in the sense that it only re-quired paths rather than good roads, and even allowing a generous five minutes for each man's twelve hundred yards in daylight and twice as much at night, it was technically possible for the message to travel a hundred and fifty miles in twenty-four hours;[2] by comparison Akbar's imperial post was officially ex-pected to fulfil a daily rate of only seventy-eight miles.[3] Sher Shah, in his brief reign of five years (1540–1545), laid many foundations which Akbar could build on, as in the streamlining of the revenue collection, the strengthening of provincial government, the provision of safe roads (a safe road in those days

Abul Fazl presenting the manuscript of his book to Akbar: c. 1605

meant one free from thieves) and the compensation of peasants for damage done to their crops by his armies.[4] But even if many of Akbar's reforms had been anticipated, the credit is still his for taking advantage of a comparatively untroubled reign of fifty years to establish the changes firmly within a unified system which would long outlast him; and in doing so he effectively changed Hindustan from a military dictatorship to a state administered by an extensive civil service.[5]

Akbar's empire was divided into crown lands—those areas in which the revenue was collected from the peasants by Akbar's own agents, and so went straight into the imperial treasury—and *jagirs*, areas given in non-hereditary fief to nobles who were responsible for the revenue collection in that district. This was not, in principle, a method of rent-farming; the revenue of the *jagir* represented that noble's agreed salary and there were imperial auditors to see that any excess which might be collected was paid into the treasury, or, more reluctantly, that any unavoidable deficit should be made up from central funds.[6] The noble's salary depended on his military rank—the structure of society was still military, and everyone in Akbar's service, even the painters at Fatehpur Sikri, had a military rank—and this rank was expressed and paid for in terms of the number of mounted troops the officer was expected to muster when required. The particular form of inflation in Moghul society was that the nobles tended to produce, as time went on, fewer and fewer men on parade; gradually, since no one was prepared to make a big issue of this except in times of crisis, a steadily lessening proportion of the stated numbers became regarded as normal; and as this proportion fell, the emperor raised the nominal level of each rank, and hence the actual salary, in order to maintain the same number of troops in the army. Akbar rationalized this state of affairs and for a time managed to curb the process. He instituted a double rank; a *zat* rank, which regulated the salary of the holder, and a *sawar* rank which stipulated the number of troopers he had to provide, for whom there was now also a special allowance. Those who were soldiers only on paper, such as the painters, the writers, or the middle range of officials in government departments, had as before only one rank, which merely regulated their salary; but the nobles now had two ranks, for example a thousand *zat* and five hundred *sawar*, which meant that they were paid the salary for the rank of a thousand horse and had to produce five hundred on parade. The lower ranks of officers were paid in cash, whereas the nobles or amirs—roughly anyone with a *zat* rank of five hundred horse or over in Akbar's day—were usually given a *jagir* from the revenue of which to collect their own salary.[7]

The *jagirdar*, or holder of a *jagir*, did not necessarily live on his territory or even hold any official secular authority over it beyond the collection of rent. There was in each province a complete hierarchy of administrative officers, repeating exactly the administrative structure at the centre and responsible only to their counterparts at the centre. The four main departments, both at the centre and in each of the provinces, were those headed by the *diwan*, responsible for finance, the *mir bakhshi*, for military affairs, the *mir saman* for factories, stores, transport and trade, and the *sadr* or *qazi*, separate offices but often interchangeable, for religious matters and the law.[8] The higher provincial officers would themselves be holders of *jagirs*, and although their *jagirs* would sometimes be in the province which they administered, just as often they would be elsewhere in

[1]74, 74–5, 128–9; 4, II, 629
[2]4, 129–30 [3]109, 216 [4]9, 413 ff.
[5]111, 248–72 [6]118, 151
[7]107, 36–8, 145; 111, 128–32
[8]108, 146–288

the kingdom. Moreover it was common practice not only to move provincial administrators to another province every few years, much like diplomats today, but also to change peoples' *jagir* from one part of the empire to another at regular intervals. The advantage of this was that it secured the central power by preventing any likely rebels from acquiring strong local support; the disadvantage was that neither as *jagirdar* nor as provincial administrator did a man have any strong motive to develop his own district, because he would soon be elsewhere. It was in his own selfish interest to extract as much profit as he could from the area in the near certainty of leaving it before his unpopularity reached a dangerous level. As a result the best administered parts of the empire were the crown lands.

Money under the Moghul system kept returning pleasantly fast into the imperial treasury. A man hoping to rise at court would find it necessary to give the emperor a valuable present in return for each stage of advancement, as well

An unusual drawing of Akbar: c. 1605

106

as on numerous annual occasions, and most of the property of any noble who died was usually impounded for a variety of excellent reasons. But the supply of available wealth could only be increased by further conquest and annexation, to which there must ultimately be a practical limit, or by raising agricultural production within the empire. The latter, Akbar reasoned, should not prove too difficult. There was at that time in India far more fertile land than was actually under cultivation.[1] The effect of the usual methods of revenue collection was to discourage the peasants from taking on more land—since if they appeared to be becoming richer, they would almost certainly be tormented by the collectors for even higher payments—so Akbar issued instructions for his officials to take every measure possible, such as the granting of loans, to persuade peasants to take in hand unused lands near their villages.[2] As with many of his reforms, the corruption of the minor officials on the spot prevented the new approach from having its full effect,[3] but an indication of the opposite standard, against which Akbar's efforts should be measured, comes from the kingdom of Golconda, to the south of Akbar's empire. The system at this time in Golconda was for collectors to bid at auction for the right to farm the taxes in certain districts; in order to surpass the already inflated level of his bid and so make a profit, the winning collector mercilessly flogged the peasantry; if he failed to honour his bid he was himself flogged, or was sometimes lent money by the central revenue authorities at five per cent monthly (or sixty per cent *per annum*) to tide him over until such time as he could bring pressure to bear more effectively on the peasants.[4] Under Akbar the peasants of Hindustan did achieve a standard of living which, though pitifully low, was nevertheless a peak from which they gradually declined during the next two centuries.[5]

A few examples from the wide range of Akbar's reforms will show the general trend of his efforts to achieve a rational administration. In the field of revenue collection Akbar inherited a system by which the peasants paid in kind, but under the expert guidance of Akbar's *diwan*, Raja Todar Mal, this was now gradually changed for one whereby they paid in cash, the amount being at first a proportion of the value of their crop that year and then, for further streamlining, a proportion of a rolling average over ten years with a built-in system of relief in bad years. Abul Fazl reproduces forty-four printed pages of lists of the annual yield of some fifty crops in seven provinces over a period of nineteen years.[6] Akbar also changed the revenue year from lunar to solar, arguing that it was unjust for the peasants to be taxed every lunar year (354 days) when they only had their crops every solar year.[7] Steps were taken to improve both the manufacture and the marketing of fabrics, and the remission of certain taxes on merchants was expressly designed to stimulate trade, which was also given as one of the reasons for Akbar's extensive road-building programmes; when the emperor wanted to travel to Kashmir 'three thousand stone-cutters, mountain miners and splitters of rocks, and two thousand diggers were sent off that they might level the ups and downs of the road', and on another occasion the Khyber pass was for the first time made accessible to wheeled vehicles, with a bridge over the Indus leading to it, to the considerable alarm of Akbar's neighbours to the north of Kabul.[8] To make the mustering of troops more realistic Akbar reintroduced the branding of horses, a measure used previously by Sher Shah and designed to prevent some Rosinante of the bazaar from reappearing day after day as a different trooper's

[1]118, 129 [2]111, 83–4
[3]13, II, 192–4 [4]117, 241–2
[5]84, 535–7
[6]10, III, 561–6; 11, II, 70–114
[7]10, II, 23, n.1
[8]11, I, 87–90; 10, III, 437–8,
1223, 817, 735, 1052

borrowed mount, and for the same purpose Akbar added a roll-call for the troopers themselves with brief descriptions of each.[1] We have several such descriptions from about a century later, and a typical one reads: 'Qamr Ali, son of Mir Ali, son of Kabir Ali, wheat complexion, broad forehead, separated eyebrows, sheep's eyes, prominent nose, beard and moustache black, right ear lost from a sword cut.'[2] In social matters Akbar busied himself with efforts to ban child marriages, to abolish *sati* (the burning of Hindu widows with their husbands), to regulate gambling, to control prostitution by restricting it to a specified quarter of the town, to introduce standardization into the chaos of Indian weights and measures and to bring in a more efficient and liberal system of education.[3]

The machinery for all this meant a much increased civil service, and the usual tragi-comic antics of bureaucracy were as frustrating at the Moghul court as anywhere else. Before a newly appointed officer could draw his allowance, the following procedure had to be completed. After the emperor had made the appointment and it had been entered in the daily records of his court, an extract was made from these records and was signed by three officials before being handed over to the copying officer for an abridgment to be prepared, which was signed by four officials and sealed by a Minister of State. This abridgment went to the military office, which now demanded a descriptive roll of the officer's troops. When this was provided, a salary statement was made out and was entered in the records of all the departments concerned before being sent on to the financial department, where an account was prepared and submitted to the emperor for his approval. Once formally sanctioned, a pay-certificate was drafted and was passed in turn to the Finance Minister, the Commander-in-Chief, and the Military Accountant. The latter prepared the final firman which, after six people had signed it in three departments, could be accepted by the Treasury as authority for payment of the salary.[4] But at least it was a civil service through which talent could rise. Shah Mansur, who as Akbar's *diwan* later helped to carry through many of Todar Mal's reforms in the revenue system, had first distinguished himself as one of the officers of the Perfumery Department.[5]

At the age of twenty-three Abul Fazl arrived at Fatehpur Sikr to enter Akbar's service—in the very same year, 1574, as another equally brilliant young man, Badauni.[6] From early in his childhood Abul Fazl had known Badauni, eleven years his senior, because Badauni had studied at Agra under Abul Fazl's father, Shaikh Mubarak.[7] Each now immediately caught Akbar's eye; each seemed destined for a most promising career; and they were to become, between them, the two most important historians of the period. But their paths rapidly diverged and the vast difference between their two careers and their two books symbolizes neatly the gulf which opened in the second half of Akbar's reign and which made these seem years of calamity to the more orthodox Muslims among Akbar's subjects, many of whom came to believe that the emperor had become a Hindu. Badauni was a strict Sunni, whereas Abul Fazl was a freethinker, as were his elder brother, Faizi, and his father, Shaikh Mubarak. The appointment of the three members of this talented family to positions at court was an ominous reversal for the rigidly orthodox and until now very powerful members of the *ulama*, or religious hierarchy.

Shaikh Mubarak and his two sons rapidly became the most influential group at Akbar's court, largely because their eclecticism chimed so well with his. The shaikh himself took the leading place among the palace divines. His elder son, Faizi, became the poet laureate. And Abul Fazl launched with a will into the many tasks which would bring him ever closer into the emperor's trust. The more affairs at Fatehpur Sikri went the elegant and carefree way of Abul Fazl and Faizi, the more Badauni and his like felt excluded. Badauni claims to have upbraided Abul Fazl one day for his notorious heresies and to have been enraged by the cool reply 'I wish to wander for a few days in the vale of infidelity for sport',[8] though the story does less than justice to the political seriousness underlying Abul Fazl's wish to broaden the regime's religious basis. With poignant irony the two rival intellectuals were each as young men given the rank of twenty horse and were made to share the same task—supervising the branding of horses for muster. Abul Fazl knuckled down to it, and in Badauni's words, 'by his intelligence and time-serving qualities' managed to raise himself from here to the highest positions in the realm, 'while I from my inexperience and simplicity could not manage to continue in the service'.[9] Badauni soon sank to the official level of a mere translator. Akbar, with characteristic lack of concern for Badauni's bigotry, gave him the four-year task of translating into Persian the Hindu classic the *Mahabharata*, which he predictably found nothing but 'puerile absurdities of which the eighteen thousand creations may well be amazed . . . but such is my fate, to be employed on such works'.[10] Badauni hardly appears in Abul Fazl's book, but the latter looms large in Badauni's as the 'man that set the world in flames' and as being 'officious and time-serving, openly faithless, continually studying the emperor's whims, a flatterer beyond all bounds'.[11] The two men's books make together a perfect pair of commentaries on the reign. Badauni's, crotchety, bigoted, ruthlessly honest with himself as well as with others, is much the more readable and in modern terms is far better written. It was compiled in secret and only discovered in 1615 after both Akbar and Badauni were dead. Abul Fazl's, in which a mere list of Akbar's good qualities can run to several pages,[12] was commissioned by the emperor and was read aloud to him as each stage was completed—and no doubt again and again subsequently. Yet it carries one along by the sheer confident profusion of its flowery Persian metaphors and can also be surprisingly vivid, as when a holy man has 'for thirty years in an unnoticed corner been gathering happiness on an old mat'.[13] The difference between the two histories is that between a brilliant diary and the most magnificent of ornamental scrolls.

Akbar's own bent for religious speculation was encouraged not only by Shaikh Mubarak's family but also by wider currents of opinion in India at the time. Within Islam there had long been a tradition of free-thinking mysticism, known as Sufism, which was opposed to the rigid distinctions of orthodoxy, and in the past century this had been joined in India by similar stirrings within Hinduism, in particular the Bhakti movement and the beginnings of the Sikh religion, both of which included a rejection of the caste system and a belief in a personal God.[14] By 1575 Akbar's interest in comparative religion had become so strong that he built a special *ibadat-khana* or 'house of worship' in which to hold religious discussions. The building, which no longer exists, was an extension of a deserted hermit's cell. It was situated behind the mosque at Fatehpur Sikri and Akbar would go there after prayers in the mosque on Thursday evenings—the Muslim day is calculated as beginning at dusk, rather than midnight, so Thursday

[1] 11, I, 265; 107, 189   [2] 109, 48
[3] 11, I, 277–8; 110, 169–70;
116, 52–3   [4] 116, 78
[5] 10, III, 273; 62, 188–9
[6] 13, II, 175–6; 10, III, 116–18
[7] 134, I, 586   [8] 13, II, 270
[9] 13, II, 209–10   [10] 13, II, 330
[11] 13, II, 201–2   [12] 10, I, 16–23
[13] 10, III, 832–4   [14] 126, 16–19

evening was for Akbar and his mullahs the evening of the holy day, Friday.

His intention, as in his *diwan-i-khas*, was to sit in the middle and digest the arguments from all sides. He was deeply shocked—and sufficiently inexperienced in academic matters to be surprised—when the learned divines whom he invited to participate immediately fell out over who should sit where, but this was finally settled by separating the rival groups to the four sides of the building. The discussions went on long into the night; much perfume was wafted on the air; and Akbar had a pile of money in front of him, as he always did on any comparable occasion, with which he hoped to reward the most persuasive and elegant contributions. But here too he was disappointed. Badauni records that in no time the learned doctors were calling each other 'fools and heretics', and the arguments soon went beyond subtle sectarian differences and threatened to undermine the very foundations of belief, until the participants 'became very Jews and Egyptians for hatred of each other'.[1] The foundations of Akbar's belief, perhaps already shaky, were certainly further disturbed by these performances; such furious differences of opinion within the Muslim community, to whom the discussions were at this stage restricted, seemed to him to cast doubts on Islam itself and his next step was to throw the debate open to learned men from other religions. Eventually he included Hindus, Jains, Zoroastrians, Jews and even a small group who came to play a prominent and most interesting part in the court life at Fatehpur Sikri, three Jesuit fathers from the Portuguese colony at Goa.

The Portuguese had been established on the west coast of India even before the arrival of Babur in 1526 but their dealings with Indian potentates had been mainly confined to their neighbours in Gujarat. In 1579 Akbar sent an envoy to the Portuguese authorities in Goa, expressing his interest in the Christian religion and asking them to send some learned fathers to his court 'with the chief books of the Law and the Gospel'. To the Jesuits this seemed a chance of another Constantine for Christianity, a heaven-sent opportunity to convert a whole empire of heathens from the top downwards. And Akbar was hoping, in addition to his genuine interest in comparative religion, that diplomatic contact with the Portuguese might help to 'civilize this savage race'.[2] All seemed set for a friendly relationship, and so it turned out.

A mission of three fathers reached Fatehpur Sikri in February 1580. They were Rudolf Aquaviva, an Italian aristocrat whose uncle became General of the Society of Jesus; Antony Monserrate, a Spaniard who later left a very full account of his experiences in the land of the Moghul; and Francis Henriquez, a Persian convert from Islam who was expected to act as interpreter. The trio were immediately plunged into the religious debates and with the courage of men whose sights were officially set on martyrdom—a state which Aquaviva later achieved, though not at Moghul hands, becoming beatified in 1893—they proceeded to lay into Islam with such vehemence that Akbar finally had to take them aside and advise caution. But they were anyway interested less in convincing Akbar's bigoted mullahs than in winning for their God the emperor himself, and here they appeared to make the most satisfactory progress.[3]

Akbar always treated the 'Nazarene sages', as Abul Fazl called them,[4] with the greatest courtesy; he liked them to sit near him, and would often draw them aside for private conversation; he sent them food from the royal table; when Monserrate was ill he visited him, and he had even gone to the trouble to learn a special

Shaikhs waiting to greet Jahangir at Ajmer, which remained an important place of Moghul pilgrimage: by Manohar, c. 1615

OVERLEAF *A detail from one Akbar's tiger hunts: c. 1590*

[1] 13, II, 205, 243, 262
[2] 10, III, 37–8 [3] 122, 25–30, 206
[4] 10, III, 368

*Akbar's son, Jahangir,
sharing a window with
Christ — Moghul albums
were often composed like
exquisite scrap-books:
c. 1620*

Portuguese greeting for the occasion; and he could sometimes be seen walking in public places with his arm round Father Aquaviva. On religious matters he was just as cooperative; he was prepared to kiss their sacred books and holy images; he came to see the crib which they had built for their first Christmas at Fatehpur Sikri, and when he entered their little chapel he took off his turban; he appointed Abul Fazl to teach them Persian and allowed Monserrate to become tutor to his son Murad, then about eleven, even tolerating 'In the name of God and of Jesus Christ, the true Prophet and Son of God' at the head of each of the prince's exercises; he allowed the fathers to preach, to make conversions and to hold a large public funeral for a Portuguese who died at court, processing through the streets with crucifix and candles; he even took in good part the Jesuits' chiding him for his surplus of wives.[1]

It is not surprising that the missionaries felt encouraged, but they were soon to be disappointed. They had mistaken Akbar's fascination with all religions for an inclination to join theirs. It seems that Christianity appealed to him at least as much as any other religion—though he was distressed, among other things, that Christ should have allowed himself the indignity of being crucified and felt that once up there he should have used his special powers to get down—and it has sometimes been suggested that Akbar was consciously hoping to find in Christianity a religion with which he could solve his empire's communal hostilities by imposing it from the top on Muslims and Hindus alike, precisely, in fact, as the Jesuits themselves intended. But he was too shrewd a politician to imagine that he could solemnly decree a new religion for India, and it is likely that his interest in Christianity derived almost entirely from his personal love of speculation. It is typical that when he did finally decide on his own religion it should turn out to be so generalized, its main distinguishing feature being a vague nimbus of divinity around his own person, and that he should have made so little effort to spread it beyond his own circle of friends. The announcement in 1582 of this new religion, known as the *din-i-Ilahi* or 'religion of God', finally showed the fathers that their efforts had failed. They returned to Goa but at Akbar's request other missions followed them, and on several more occasions Christian hopes were raised high only to be dashed again. During the next reign, in 1610, three of Akbar's grandsons were even publicly baptized as Christians amid great festivities and were handed over to the Jesuits to be educated, but the fathers' joy was tempered by the subsequent rumour that they had only entered the fold in the hope of acquiring some Christian ladies for the various royal harems, and three or four years later, as a Jesuit writer put it, the princes 'rejected the light and returned to their vomit'.[2] To the very end of Akbar's life—so inconclusive had the *din-i-Ilahi* proved—each religious group still had hopes of the emperor and there was eager competition round his deathbed in 1605 to discover whose God would have the honour of being last on his lips. Even this was uncertain, most of the Christians believing him to have died a Muslim, and many of the Muslims a Hindu.[3]

If the Jesuits were wrong in believing that Akbar was moving towards Christianity, the Muslims were certainly right in their conviction that he was drifting away from orthodox Islam. That he was doing so was as much as anything a matter of policy. The principle of a medieval Islamic state gave very great powers to the mullahs, since it was believed that the correct way of doing everything could

[1]122, 28–35
[2]122, 72–4; 40, 276–8
[3]122, 64–5

be found in the Koran or in one or two long established commentaries on it. The ruler must therefore abide by the book and the book was best interpreted by those who had devoted their lives to religion. A measure of how ill-equipped the orthodox mullahs were to give Akbar helpful advice on running the mixed communities of India can be seen in the attitudes of the highly intelligent and talented Badauni. The man whom Badauni most admired was Husain Khan, in whose service he had spent his early years, and the action of Husain Khan's which had most impressed Badauni is highly significant. As Akbar's governor in Lahore, Husain was sitting one day dealing with public affairs when a stranger entered. Assuming him to be a Muslim the governor 'with his usual gentle humility' rose to greet him. But the man turned out to be a Hindu. Husain was so ashamed of his small misdirected gesture of courtesy that he ordered all Hindus to wear in future a visible patch on their sleeves so that such a mistake could never occur again.[1] And, by the strictest standards of orthodox Islam, Badauni and Husain were right. There was a long tradition stipulating that *dhimmis* should wear distinguishing articles of dress.[2]

Akbar used the undignified squabbles between the Muslim divines in the *ibadat-khana* as an opportunity to limit the power of the priesthood. In 1579 appeared the famous *mahzar* or so-called decree of infallibility, in which it was stated that if there was disagreement among the learned about the meaning of any part of the Koran, it would in future be Akbar who had the deciding say on which of the contending interpretations should be accepted; and further that if he chose to take any step for the good of the state, it should be accepted by all unless it

LEFT *Two Jesuits, Rudolf Aquaviva and Francis Henriquez, taking part in the debate in the* ibadat-khana: *c. 1605*

RIGHT *Christian etchings brought by the Jesuits and lat* *pasted into a Moghul album*

116

could be shown to be against the Koran. The decree was sound Islamic theory in so far as it placed the book above all, but it did represent a fairly startling upheaval, at least in concept, in the relationship between the *ulama* or body of learned men and the temporal power—even if in practice it did not amount to much since both Akbar and the highly orthodox Aurangzeb showed themselves willing and able to dismiss their *qazi*, or religious and legal adviser, when he refused to sanction a course of action.[3] The decree of infallibility was signed by several divines but only one of them, Abul Fazl's father Shaikh Mubarak, put his name to it with enthusiasm, as a note below his signature testified.[4] Having probably been largely Mubarak's idea, the decree marked a definite advance in the power at court of the shaikh and his two sons, and was a serious blow to the orthodox— particularly when coupled with other indications about this time of the direction which Akbar's thoughts were taking. In 1579 he put an end to the custom of sending vast sums of money each year to Mecca and Medina for distribution to the poor; in 1580 he gave up his annual pilgrimage to Ajmer; in 1584 he rejected the Muslim system of dating events from the Hegira, or flight of the prophet from Mecca to Medina, and replaced it with a new chronology beginning with his own accession (Abul Fazl explains that Akbar found it 'of ominous significance' to date things from the Hegira, presumably because of the mention of flight); finally he had had the effrontery to begin preaching and reciting the *khutba* himself in the mosque, although on the very first occasion he had to stop halfway, when he began trembling in what appears to have been another of his quasi-mystical seizures.[5] Together with the decree of infallibility, this personal performance in the mosque was perhaps the most offensive of all to the orthodox. It implied that Akbar was conferring on himself the status of a learned divine. Their next shock was when he seemed to take the process one stage further and present himself simply as divine.

The *din-i-Ilahi*, Akbar's new religion based on a vague and mystical liberalism, was at the very best unspecific about how far Akbar straddled the dividing line between mortal and divine. The new chronology dating from his accession was known as the Divine Era. And considerable outrage was caused when he decided to stamp on his coins the potentially ambiguous phrase *Allahu akbar*; the ambiguity derives from the fact that *akbar* means great as well as being the emperor's name so that the words could mean either 'God is great' or 'Akbar is God'. This has seemed to various modern historians the most blatant assumption of divinity, but it need not have been so. When a shaikh accused Akbar of having intended the second meaning he replied indignantly that it had not even occurred to him. His claim sounds far-fetched; and the fact that he had taken the unusual step of removing his own name and titles from his coins, in order to substitute this phrase, suggests that he was not unaware that it included his name as well as God's.[6] But *Allahu akbar* is a basic Islamic incantation—to give two extreme examples, it was the battle cry of Timur's troops and was wailed by the women during the fire in the Al Aqsa mosque in Jerusalem on August 21, 1969[7]—and it seems likely that Akbar was amused by the ambiguity rather than taking it as a serious statement of his own identity.

In all these steps Akbar was energetically supported if not actually led by Shaikh Mubarak and his sons. Abul Fazl's biography of Akbar is liberally sprinkled with epithets suggesting his divinity, and he attributes to the emperor

[1]13, II, 227 [2]134, II, 228
[3]13, II, 211–13; 49, I, 381
[4]13, II, 278–80
[5]10, III, 405–6, 462–4;
11, II, 30; 13, II, 276–7
[6]13, II, 213; 78, lxv–lxxi
[7]4; *The Times*, Aug. 22, 1969, 4

several miracles, including even the making of rain. The emphasis throughout Abul Fazl's writing is on religious toleration—he was a man who practised what he preached, having a Hindu, a Kashmiri and a Persian wife—and within the space of one paragraph he calls the Muslims of Kashmir 'narrow-minded conservatives of blind tradition' but praises the Hindu priests of the same province for not loosening 'the tongue of calumny against those not of their faith'. His stated aim in studying and describing the culture and philosophy of the Hindus was so that 'hostility towards them might abate, and the temporal sword be stayed awhile from the shedding of blood'.[1]

Akbar's progression away from orthodox Islam towards his own vague religion was no doubt part of a conscious effort to seem to represent all his people—the Rajputs, for example, saw their rajas much like Abul Fazl's image of Akbar, both human and divine—and it fitted in with a general policy which included his adoption of Hindu and Parsee festivals and his increasing abstinence from meat in the manner of Hindus.[2] But it also fulfilled a personal need. He was drawn to mysticism, fond of lonely contemplation, eager for any clue to the truth, and if that truth should touch him with divinity there were always precedents within the family; Humayun had indulged in a mystical identification of himself with light, and through light with God; Timur, more conventionally, used to refer to himself as the 'shadow of Allah on earth'.[3] Akbar's religious attitudes seem to have been a happy blend of personal inclination and state policy.

Needless to say the resentment of the orthodox Muslims grew apace. They saw Akbar's measures as a direct assault on Islam. Rumours flew around of mosques being forcibly closed, even destroyed. It was believed that within the harem people now actually repeated the words 'there is no god but Allah and Akbar is his prophet'. When Akbar in an attempt to curb alcoholism opened a wine shop near the gate of the fort for the use only of those with doctor's prescriptions, it was whispered that the wine, offensive enough in itself, had had pig's flesh mixed in with it on the emperor's orders. The age-old literary game of inventing chronograms, which in their normal use were congratulatory phrases about a particular event elaborately devised so that the values of the letters should add up exactly to the year of the event, now reappeared in underground form with such efforts as 'Publication of Heresy' and 'Decline of Learning' to date the emperor's measures. Even quite unimportant opinions of Akbar's were seen as deliberately anti-Koranic. Badauni was outraged to discover that Akbar considered it more sensible to have a bath before rather than after sexual intercourse. Mohammed had said precisely the opposite.[4]

For the moment, then, the orthodox were in retreat, but even during Akbar's reign there were signs of a backlash which by the end of the century would leave the relationship between the communities worse than Akbar had found it. Muslim criticism of Akbar was led by an orthodox Sunni, Shaikh Ahmad Sarhindi, who was notably fond of Mohammed's maxim that 'anything new which is introduced in my religion is condemnable'; the shaikh had little effect on Akbar and was imprisoned by Jahangir, but his son and grandson continued his cause and were able to move gradually nearer to the side of the throne.[5] Badauni describes Husain Khan, the man he most admired, as never missing a prayer, having nothing to do with any woman apart from his three legally married wives, and living in the trappings of great poverty although extremely rich, and he adds that

Husain 'looked on nuts as a sort of intoxicating food'.[6] His description reads as if almost tailor-made for Aurangzeb, the last of the Great Moghuls whose reign of nearly fifty years, from 1658 to 1707, was one of increasing religious bigotry and heralded the collapse of Akbar's empire. In the long term it was Badauni rather than Abul Fazl who won.

I have dwelt at some length on Akbar's religious policy and its results because it is this attempt at synthesis, both in his own personality and within his society, which has given his reign such a special fascination today in the light of the modern troubles between the two communities of India. Historians have been much exercised as to whether or not Akbar's new religion, the *din-i-Ilahi*, meant that he had renounced Islam or had merely rejected its rigidities while retaining its essential spirit. The question seems both unimportant and insoluble—in the sense that Akbar himself probably neither knew nor cared where he stood in relation to any one religion. To the orthodox, to reject any part is to reject the whole; once that position is itself rejected the whole remains unthreatened until there are no parts left, and Akbar certainly retained a belief in God at least as great as—if not identical with—his belief in himself. In the late sixteenth century, as now, Akbar's spiritual odyssey was important for its effect on his relationship not with God but with the passionate and volatile communities of India.

The simultaneous rebellion in 1580 of the Afghans in Bengal and of Akbar's half-brother Hakim in Kabul was the last serious threat to the security of the empire. During the remaining twenty-five years of the reign Akbar and his generals busied themselves in keeping down unrest in the existing territories—Bengal in particular required almost continual attention—and in adding a few important new ones. The capture of his birthplace, Umarkot, in 1592 was a particularly sweet victory and was part of the incorporation of the whole of Sind into the empire; Baluchistan, further west, and Kandahar followed soon after; but undoubtedly the most important conquest was Kashmir in 1586. The Moghul emperors fell in love with Kashmir. Akbar, in spite of the arduous journey, paid three separate visits to the valley and liked to refer to it as his private garden. He would leave most of the harem in Sher Shah's fort at Rohtas, because the journey was so difficult, and would strike north on roads specially prepared for him. It was a measure of the security of the empire that the emperor was now able to go on long expeditions to a place from which it would be impossible to return very rapidly; and once in the valley he would relax almost into the life of a tourist, going boating and water-fowling, seeing how many men could pack into a hollow *chenar* or plane-tree (thirty-four was the answer) or watching the saffron fields being harvested together with his eldest son, Salim, who as the future emperor Jahangir would develop a love of Kashmir even more obsessive than Akbar's.[7]

Less successful was the attempt to push southwards into the Deccan, a campaign which Akbar waged inconclusively during the last twelve years of his reign and which, as continued by his successors, became an increasing and finally crippling burden on the Moghul state. Hindustan, the name given to the plains of northern India, has natural boundaries for an empire; from the mouths of the Indus to those of the Ganges one vast territory stretches with no internal geographical barriers sufficient to prevent a large army from moving about with speed and ease, but with its own secure and natural boundaries of the sea to the west and east, the curving arc of the Hindu Kush and the Himalayas to the north,

[1]10, III, 876–8; 11, II, 352–3, and III, 2, 449
[2]11, I, 61–2, 276; 10, III, 332–3
[3]92, 185–6; 56, 78
[4]13, II, 281–2, 376, 311, 375–7, 315
[5]120, 145–71 [6]13, II, 228
[7]10, III, 955–8, 1095; 16, I, 93; 13, II, 381

and the rugged territory of the Deccan to the south. By 1595 this entire area was under Akbar's control. To a modern economist, with his eyes on internal development, the empire would now have looked complete. But Akbar was of his own time in seeing conquest as the business of an emperor, and given the nature of the Moghul economy the need to expand was a real one. No less real were the difficulties of doing so into the Deccan.

From 1593 the Moghul army was in operation in the Deccan under the command of prince Murad. By this time Akbar's three sons were all of age (Salim was twenty-four, Murad twenty-three, Daniyal twenty-one) and they had for some years been accustomed to positions of responsibility, both military and administrative. But the almost complete ineffectiveness of the army in the Deccan was due in large part to Murad's drunkenness, a family failing which Akbar managed to control in himself but which affected his three sons to the point of dipsomania— partly an escape, perhaps, from the demands of a highly alarming father. By 1599 Murad's condition was such that Akbar sent Abul Fazl to relieve him of his command. Abul Fazl joined the prince's camp early in May and on May 12 Murad died in a state of advanced *delirium tremens*. Abul Fazl restored some discipline in the demoralized army and marched to attack Ahmednagar.[1]

The sudden emergence of Abul Fazl as a high-powered general requires some explanation. At several points during the *Akbar-nama* Abul Fazl records his disappointment when he volunteers for military service on a dangerous mission and is not accepted;[2] and when he nearly dies of an illness he claims that his willingness to leave this hypocritical world was tempered only by a regret at doing so without having been given the chance to prove himself in battle.[3] To a modern eye such protestations may look hollow, but Abul Fazl probably meant what he said because he knew that in Moghul society promotion led inevitably towards the battlefield and the highest positions at court were virtually reserved for successful soldiers. Like Humayun's ewer-bearer Jauhar, he progressed first from his intimate position at the emperor's side to various minor tasks of administration. He was entrusted in 1581 with finding out the opinions of army officers on a proposed expedition into Kabulistan, was raised to the rank of a thousand *zat* in 1585, was speaking forcefully in the councils of war in 1586, was in charge of the cooks on the journey into Kashmir in 1589, was promoted again in 1592 to the rank of two thousand, and in 1598 was even presented by Akbar with a war elephant when he set off with a force of three thousand men to tell Murad that he must return to Agra and that his brother Daniyal was on his way to take over his command.[4] Murad's death within days of Abul Fazl's arrival left the army temporarily without a general, a hiatus which Abul Fazl eagerly filled. He took to high command with his usual zeal, making excellent arrangements for the safe return of Murad's harem to Agra, summoning people far his social superiors to attend on him in camp and being surprised when they failed to do so,[5] and marching with such speed towards the siege of Ahmednagar that Daniyal found it necessary to write to him: 'Your energy is impressed upon everyone. Your desire is to take Ahmednagar before we arrive, but you must restrain yourself from such an intention.'[6] But only a year later Abul Fazl was indeed taking another fort, Maligarh, with his own detachment of troops, even scaling a ladder himself, and ambassadors were beginning to arrive to offer him, as Akbar's representative, the submission of neighbouring princes. In 1601 he at last found himself in command

[1] 10, III, 1125–9
[2] e.g. 10, III, 719–20 [3] 10, III, 890
[4] 10, III, 552–7, 687, 752, 822, 932, 1119–20 [5] 10, III, 1128–42
[6] 10, III, 1162–6

in a pitched battle, when his force of three thousand managed to defeat an enemy of five thousand almost entirely, he implies, through his own personal intervention: 'The victorious warriors were nearly being defeated. But the writer came up, and the enemy was dispersed.'[1] It was all most intoxicating, particularly to a writer, but it was also highly dangerous. The second most powerful man in the empire, Akbar's eldest son Salim, looked on Abul Fazl's successes with an especially jaundiced eye.

Akbar seems to have been intensely irritated by his eldest son, often it must be admitted with good reason—as when Salim executed three offenders with particularly whimsical and sadistic devices,[2] or when he continually declined the command of expeditions to distant parts of the empire, seeming determined to remain near enough the centre to be strongly placed when his father died. But there was also something exaggerated and obsessive about Akbar's hostility. Abul Fazl tells a very revealing story about a quarrel between the two on the journey to Kashmir in 1589. Salim had been told to bring the harem forward to join Akbar, but he decided that the road was too dangerous and so came on alone. Akbar's response was on the verge of hysterical. He refused to see the prince and laid hectic plans to ride all through the night, almost unaccompanied, over the admittedly perilous path to fetch the ladies himself. Even Abul Fazl for once finds no way of explaining his master's behaviour and expresses surprise that he should have been so angry.[3]

The result of this antipathy was that Akbar openly preferred his other sons, and Salim spent the last five years of the reign in spasmodic rebellion against his father. Compared to the rebellions by Moghul princes later in the seventeenth century this was a very low-keyed affair, and can be more accurately described as Salim mooning about the country with a large army and vaguely referring to himself as emperor while disobeying Akbar's orders to put his troops to any more effective use. Both father and son were careful to avoid any irretrievable step, and even when Salim marched in 1602 from Allahabad towards Agra with a force of thirty thousand men Akbar was able to talk him back into obedience without any open clash. At this point, however, the situation did look serious enough for Akbar to summon his beloved Abul Fazl back from the Deccan for the benefit of his advice. Abul Fazl was known to be hostile to Salim, whom he regarded as debauched and unreliable, and Salim was apprehensive as to how his father's actions might be affected by this man whose already vast personal influence would now be increased by his military successes and by a new official rank of five thousand.[4] Salim therefore laid plans to have Abul Fazl assassinated on his road north to Delhi, and he coolly admits as much in his autobiography; he tells how he sent word to Bir Singh Deo, the Raja of Orchha, near whose territory Abul Fazl would pass, that 'if he would stop that sedition-monger and kill him he would receive every kindness from me'.[5] The shaikh's small band, unarmed, were overwhelmed on August 12, 1602, by five hundred horsemen clad in mail. Abul Fazl had been warned of the ambush and even at the last moment had an opportunity to gallop away from the scene, but he was playing his new role to the hilt and with reckless courage he refused to alter his course and scorned any sober suggestion of flight. His head was sent to Salim in Allahabad, and tradition adds to an already unsavoury story the detail of how the prince defiled it by throwing it into the privy.[6]

The pool in the Moghul garden at Vernag in Kashmir, containing fish descended from those caught and ringed by Jahangir and Nur Jahan

[1] 10, III, 1193 [2] 10, III, 1242
[3] 10, III, 824–5 [4] 10, III, 1209–10
[5] 16, I, 25
[6] 10, III, 1216–21; 12, 154–60

*The south gateway to Akbar's
tomb at Sikandra*

The likelihood of strong retaliation by Akbar against Salim for this callous murder was modified by the unmistakable signs that Daniyal, his youngest and favourite son, was rapidly going the way of Murad. His alcoholism would clearly soon leave Akbar with only one son, so a reconciliation with Salim was effected through the senior ladies of the family, in keeping with a well-established Moghul tradition. During the battles between Humayun and Kamran over Kabul their aunt Khanzada had hurried diplomatically to and fro trying to bring them to some agreement; so now in the same way Hamida, Akbar's mother, and Gulbadan, his aunt, brought pressure on him to forgive his son. Another highly respected lady, Salima, who was both cousin and wife to Akbar and who had spent seven arduous years on a pilgrimage to Mecca with Gulbadan,[1] volunteered to go to Allahabad and persuade Salim to come to his father in Agra. She succeeded in doing so, and brought him to the house of his grandmother, Hamida. This old lady, Humayun's reluctant child-bride of sixty years ago, was now the very energetic and powerful hub of the royal family life. She invariably gave magnificent entertainments in her house for every family occasion — particularly the marriages of Akbar's sons and the satisfactorily frequent births of his grandchildren — and she now stage-managed a moving reconciliation between her son and grandson, the present and future emperors. Akbar came to her house, whereupon she led Salim by the hand and cast him at his father's feet. The emperor raised him up lovingly, mollified no doubt by Salim's gift of three hundred and fifty elephants which amounted to a partial disarmament, and then placed his own turban on the prince's head, a gesture which was always regarded as a mark of special affection. In these particular circumstances it could also be taken as confirming Salim as the heir.[2]

This reconciliation took place in April 1603. Precisely a year later Daniyal died in the Deccan of drink, in even more melodramatic circumstances than his brother Murad. Akbar had sent guards to prevent alcohol reaching him, but the prince's own servants smuggled wine to his tent, sometimes stoppered in the barrels of guns, sometimes concealed under their clothes in cows' intestines. His last and fatal dose was some double-distilled spirit which an enthusiast produced from a rusty gun-barrel, though the rust can only have hastened an inevitable end.[3] But although this left Salim secure as the only surviving son, his behaviour in Allahabad soon began to verge once again on rebellion. In yet another reconciliation Akbar again greeted his wayward son with warmth in public but this time grew sufficiently angry to strike him in the face in the privacy of the harem, after which he confined him within the palace and forbad him both alcohol and opium. The entreaties of the ladies led to his release after ten days.[4]

Salim's continuing pattern of behaviour was perhaps both cause and effect of a new situation in which many people now openly supported his own eldest son Khusrau, aged seventeen, as successor to the throne. The rivalry between son and grandson dominated court life during Akbar's last year, and came to a head in a violent scene at an elephant fight. Akbar, apparently looking for an omen, arranged a most undiplomatic contest between Salim's strongest elephant and Khusrau's. The emperor watched it from his balcony above, and sitting beside him was his favourite grandson, Khurram, a younger brother of Khusrau; 'the affectionate sovereign loved grandsons more than sons', Abul Fazl had written earlier.[5] Salim's elephant won, but an open fight broke out between his supporters and Khusrau's, whereupon Akbar sent the thirteen-year-old Khurram down to tell the

[1] 10, III, 205–6, 569–70
[2] 10, III, 1222–30; 16, I, 56
[3] 10, III, 1254–5; 16, I, 35
[4] 10, III, 1247–8 [5] 10, III, 1096

two princes that he wished this undignified behaviour to cease. The child delivering this royal rebuke to his own father and elder brother was the future Shah Jahan who, before achieving the crown, would spend several years in violent rebellion against his father and would be suspected of murdering his brother. The scene was pregnant with more omens than those taking part could have realized.[1]

A throne used by Salim when claiming to be emperor at Allahabad, shown in its present position on the terrace in the fort at Agra

Within less than a month of this event Akbar died, on October 15, 1605. During the three weeks of his final illness, of which the symptoms were diarrhoea and internal bleeding, the debate on the succession became more favourable to Salim. Khusrau was supported by the two most powerful nobles in the empire, who were respectively his uncle and father-in-law; they were Man Singh of Amber, whose sister Salim had married, and Akbar's foster-brother Aziz Koka. But in an unprecedented conference of nobles, summoned specially to discuss this matter, these two found the majority opposed to them. And Akbar, though he may well have personally preferred Khusrau, refused to risk civil war by saying so. When Salim visited his father on the day of his death, his succession was formally indicated; the emperor motioned him to wear the royal robes and turban, and to buckle on the sword of Humayun which hung at the foot of the bed.[2]

Disappointments within his family had darkened the last years of Akbar's life. His prayers for a son had been answered three times and he himself had achieved more than he could possibly have hoped, only to find his successes undermined

126

by the irony that none of the sons seemed able or worthy to inherit what he had established. The fault was no doubt partly his; for all one's sons to be alcoholics smacks of more than coincidence. His own personality was overwhelmingly powerful and self-sufficient, difficult characteristics in a father. He seems to have had little personal need for his sons, apart from the needs of the dynasty, which meant that they were comparatively unimportant to him between the two dynastic moments of their birth and his death. Indeed the accounts of his life are singularly lacking in the intense family affections which characterize other Moghul reigns; with Jahangir or Shah Jahan one is always aware of the influence of the favourite wife and of strong preferences for some children over others; in Akbar's reign, although the preferences were there, only his mother seems to stand out warmly in his affection. His closest friendship went to courtiers, such as Abul Fazl or Birbal. These particular aspects of the emperor's personality, when combined with a secure and ever more lavish environment, may well have caused the princes to drift into self-indulgence. And Akbar's very invulnerability, the extreme unlikelihood of being able to topple him from the throne, perhaps turned into dissipation the energies which later generations of princes would direct towards rebellion.

It should be added that Akbar did all that he consciously could to train his sons to be good rulers. He deliberately gave them at an early age experience of command, both military and administrative,[3] and Abul Fazl writes out an excel-

A life-size statue standing near Akbar's tomb at Sikandra and said to be of his favourite horse: early 17th century

[1]**64**, 70–1
[2]**64**, 72–8; **62**, 323; **63**, 488
[3]**10**, III, 598–9

127

lent letter which Akbar sent to Murad when appointing him governor of Malwa at the age of twenty-one, in which he outlines his concept of the responsibilities of a ruler. One passage sums up the very essence of his theory: 'Let not difference of religion interfere with policy, and be not violent in inflicting retribution. Adorn the confidential council with men who know their work. If apologies be made, accept them.'[1] By this theory, by using strength to support appeasement, by preferring to change one-time opponents into strong allies rather than weak enemies, by choosing and trusting officers capable of carrying out his schemes, Akbar had in half a century turned a mere foothold in the north-west into control of the whole of Hindustan. And it was control of a new and stable kind. Abul Fazl, listing his blessings in life, numbers high among them 'the prosperity of the age and the general security of the times'.[2] It was not surprising that both men saw this fabric endangered by the apparently feeble character of Salim. What Akbar could not know, and Abul Fazl would certainly have refused to believe, was that as Jahangir the prince would make a far from disastrous emperor.

Jahangir enthroned—and preferring the company of a mullah to that of the Sultan o Turkey or James I of Englanc by Bichitr, c. 1620

[1] **10**, III, 912 [2] **11**, III, 445

Jahangir

After a week of mourning for his father, Salim mounted the throne in Agra on October 24, 1605, and announced that his name as emperor—to avoid any confusion between himself and a recent sultan of Turkey, Selim II—would be Jahangir, 'seizer of the world'.[1]

Historians of a schoolmasterly disposition have tended to award Jahangir very low marks as being debauched, spineless, and susceptible to women, but he is among the most sympathetic of the Great Moghuls, and was—at least in cultural matters—one of the most talented. Certainly no other member of his family comes alive so vividly to a modern student. There are two specific reasons for this, and both are the direct result of Jahangir's own talents and energies. The first is that he left a diary which is just as fresh and immediate as the autobiography of his great-grandfather, Babur; and the second that under his direct guidance the court painters reached unrivalled heights, particularly in portraiture, with the result that the personality of the emperor himself remains exposed to us in a wide range of subtly realistic character studies.

It is a most unjust accident of history that Babur's memoirs should be so famous and Jahangir's almost unknown. Admittedly Babur, writing in a period when other chronicles were scarce, has an extra value as a unique source for many facts and dates, but on any other score Jahangir is at least his equal. Where Babur's autobiography was compiled from his notes some considerable time after the events described, Jahangir—with a vast gain in immediacy—has left a day by day account of his perceptions of nature, science and art. He combined a strong aesthetic response to life with an obsessive desire to dissect, analyse and record what he saw. The combination is an endearing one in anybody, and in reading Jahangir's journal one follows with great sympathy his hopes and excitements.

An example will perhaps convey the special appeal of his diary, in a continuing story pieced together from scattered paragraphs over several months. A pair of cranes, captured when they were only a month old, had travelled with Jahangir for five years, occupying a small enclosure which was always put up for them near his tent, when one day the eunuch in charge of the birds—named Laila and Majnun by Jahangir—reported that the pair had mated in his presence. Jahangir, convinced that this had never been closely observed and recorded, gave orders that at the slightest signs of love-play he should be summoned, with the result that one dawn he was brought running to the scene and was able to write: 'The female having straightened its legs bent down a little: the male then lifted up one of its feet from the ground and placed it on her back, and afterwards the second foot, and, immediately seating himself on her back, paired with her. He then came down, and, stretching out his neck, put his beak to the ground, and walked once round the female.' The emperor added—and it is a measure of the immediacy of the journal—'It is possible they may have an egg and produce a young one.'[2] A little while later the birds did make a nest and the female laid two eggs. Jahangir recorded how they took regular turns at sitting on the nest, one

Jahangir bestrides the globe and embraces Shah Abbas of Persia—but incidentally pushes him into the Mediterranean: by Abul Hassan, c. 1620

Sources (*see* p. 252) [1]**16**, I, 2
[2]**16**, II, 16–17

131

signalling with a sharp peck on the other's back that it was time for a change, though later the emperor had to modify his statement about regularity after the birds suddenly remained on duty for two much longer spells—but this was in cold and rainy weather, and he decided that the new routine was to minimize the amount of damp air that would reach the eggs. Later there is great excitement when both eggs hatch, one after thirty-four days, the other after thirty-six, each chick being about the size of a young peafowl a month old. The mother fed them with locusts or grasshoppers from her mouth. The birds grew up safely (though only after Jahangir had decided to restrain the male, who began holding the chicks in his beak upside down by the leg) and soon the cries of the new family were attracting wild cranes, one of which was captured and was ringed personally by Jahangir before its release.[1]

These events are unusual in the diary in that they form a continuing sequence, but every page has examples of similar interests and experiments; a meteorite is dug up while still hot and Jahangir has swords made of it; there are dissections of the wind-pipes of birds, of a snake with a hare in its belly, of a lion's intestines to see whether any physical explanation can be found for its great courage;[2] any unusually large object is measured and recorded, such as a huge peach offered to Jahangir or a banyan tree;[3] there are discourses on Siamese twins, on animals with albino varieties, on the origin and meaning of place-names, on the gestation periods of elephants;[4] hearing that bitumen was supposed to help in the mending

The turkey painted by Mansu *on Jahangir's orders: 1612*

A falcon: attributed to
Mansur, c. 1620. 'What can I
write of the beauty and colour
of this falcon? There were
many beautiful black
markings on each wing and
back and sides. As it was
something out of the
ordinary, I ordered Ustad
Mansur to paint and
preserve its likeness', wrote
Jahangir in his memoirs

[1]16, II, 23–5, 32, 39, 42
[2]6, II, 204–5, 292, 275, and I, 351
[3]16, I, 119, 351
[4]16, I, 406, 139–40, 98–9, 265
[5]16, I, 238–9 [6]16, I, 364–5
[7]16, I, 84 [8]16, I, 422

of bones, Jahangir had a chicken's leg broken but found that the healing was in no way improved, though he adds that the substance may have been stale;[5] a long tale about the philosopher's stone leads him to the instinctive conclusion 'My intelligence in no way accepts this story. It appears to me to be all delusion.'[6] But where possible he will back up his opinion with proof, as when he dismisses a common theory of why rams butt each other—because of an irritation set up in the horns by a worm—by showing that 'the same worm appears in the horn of the female sheep, and since the female does not fight the statement is clearly untrue'.[7] It is typical of his rational scepticism that when he visits a tomb where miracles are said to occur, his first question to the attendant is 'What is the real state of the case?'[8]

To help him record his impressions Jahangir used his studio of painters, some of whom accompanied him everywhere. When he himself has given an excellent verbal description of a turkey which has been presented to him (of the jowls beneath its beak 'one might say it had adorned itself with red coral'), he orders artists to paint it, explaining that 'although King Babur has described in his Memoirs the appearance and shape of several animals, he had never ordered the

painters to make pictures of them. As these animals appeared to me to be very strange, I both described them and ordered that painters should draw them in the Jahangir-nama [i.e., his diary] so that the amazement that arose from hearing of them might be increased.'[1] Similarly when an old man, Inayat Khan, looked more ill than anyone he had ever seen, Jahangir had him carried before the painters so that such a death-like image should be recorded. And indeed the invalid died the following day.[2]

Jahangir inherited his curiosity from his father, and there had been several such occasions in the *Akbar-nama* where Akbar set up inquiries into various phenomena or curiosities.[3] But Akbar was attracted by mysteries with a hint of metaphysics in them, and would be more rather than less pleased if the results of an experiment pointed to divine intervention; an attempt, for example, to bring babies up without their hearing a spoken word seemed disappointing, when the infants turned out dumb, largely because had they spoken their words must have been divinely inspired.[4] Jahangir's distinction is his fierce empirical rationalism combined with an almost ecstatic response to simple facts of nature, as when he marvels at a tree in blossom and then, as he looks more closely, marvels equally at a single blossom on that tree.[5] The emperor would have found himself much in sympathy with the scientific gentlemen who, many thousand miles away and some thirty years after his death, gathered together in London to form the Royal Society.

That Jahangir was able to devote so much time to these interests was due to the stable situation which he had inherited from Akbar. Indeed the first seventeen years of his reign were a period of unparalleled calm in the central provinces, apart from one early disturbance. This was the rebellion of his son Khusrau, which

The dying Inayat Khan, drawn for Jahangir in 1618

134

Jahangir put down with unusual decisiveness. After his accession, in October 1605, the new emperor had prudently divided his most powerful pair of opponents by effecting a reconciliation with Khusrau and keeping him by his side at court, while sending the boy's maternal uncle, Man Singh, to be governor in far Bengal. But a life of virtual confinement naturally irked Khusrau and six months later, in April 1607, he rode out of the fort at Agra on the pretext of visiting Akbar's burial place five miles away at Sikandra and then made his way, gathering supporters as he went, north and west past Delhi to Lahore. He was besieging Lahore most ineffectually when the imperial army arrived from Agra and easily defeated him. The prince and his two closest colleagues attempted to flee across the river Chenab but were refused help by the professional boatmen. Then, in trying to ferry themselves across, they accidentally grounded their boat in shallows in the middle of the river and sat there pathetically awaiting capture. They were brought before Jahangir in a garden outside Lahore. As on such family occasions in the time of Humayun, there were tears on both sides; but there was nothing half-hearted about Jahangir's retribution. The prince's two colleagues were sewn into the wet skins of a newly slaughtered ox and ass, complete with head and ears, and in this guise were seated on donkeys, facing the tails, and were paraded round the city all day; the effect of the hot sun was to dry and shrink the skins, and one of the two men died of constriction and suffocation (this gruesome charade was not Jahangir's own invention but was long established in India, being traditionally held to have been used on Mohammed, the first Muslim conqueror of Sind, as long ago as A.D. 714). Khusrau himself was forced to ride an elephant along a street lined with stakes, on each of which one of his supporters was impaled alive.[6]

It was a grisly scenario by Jahangir, and it lends support to the argument that he was decadently and whimsically cruel. An Englishman visiting his court decided that the emperor used to watch 'with too much delight in blood' the spectacle of the elephants below his balcony crushing those under sentence of death, a conventional method of capital punishment in India.[7] Certainly there was a streak of sadism in Jahangir, as in many other potentates with such unlimited powers, but fanciful attempts to find punishments to fit the crime were not peculiar to him alone. Indeed they were so common that they rank almost as an accepted form of royal wit. Timur's forcing a coward to run barefoot through the camp in woman's clothes or Akbar's cutting off the feet of a man who has stolen a pair of shoes are of a kind with Jahangir's sending a servant who has broken a china cup to fetch another one from China, or sentencing a man who had killed his mother to be bitten to death by snakes.[8] And atrocities at the hands of the Moghuls were rare by the standards of their own Muslim contemporaries in southern parts of India or in Turkey, or of Christians in many other parts of the world at this time.

Khusrau's rebellion had been crushed within less than a month and the prince himself now spent a year in chains, being moved around with the royal camp during an expedition by Jahangir to Kandahar, which was being threatened as usual by the Persians, and to Kabul. But hardly had Khusrau been released from his chains when he encouraged a plot to assassinate Jahangir on the hunting field, in August or September 1607.[9] Some four hundred nobles and courtiers were said to be involved but Jahangir wisely avoided detailed inquiries, which might have turned so many into confirmed opponents by exposing their disloyalty. He

[1]16, I, 215–16 [2]16, II, 43–4 [3]e.g. 10, III, 581–2, 829, 883–4, 1060 [4]10, III, 581–2 [5]16, I, 97 [6]16, I, 51–69; 64, 138–55; 74, 7 [7]40, 87 [8]56, 128; 10, II, 242–3; 41, 388, 362–3 [9]16, I, 111, 122–3

135

contented himself with executing the four known ringleaders, and this time he did give orders for the blinding of Khusrau. The deed was done, whether intentionally or not, in such a way that the prince later recovered partial sight, but his life was now a desolate one.[1] He remained a prisoner moving around with the court, and on rare occasions was brought into his father's presence for a reconciliation, usually unsuccessful because the unfortunate prince depressed Jahangir; not surprisingly, but to Jahangir's annoyance, 'his appearance showed no signs of openness and happiness, and he was always mournful and dejected in mind'.[2]

The most important development of the first half of Jahangir's reign was the twin rise to power of Mehrunissa—whose official title first became Nur Mahal, 'Light of the Palace', and later Nur Jahan, 'Light of the World'—and of Jahangir's third son Khurram, soon to be known as Shah Jahan, 'Sovereign of the World'. Mehrunissa was the daughter of a Persian, Ghiyas Beg, who before she was born had come to try his luck in the service of the Moghuls. He had risen in Akbar's court, and on Jahangir's succession had been given high office and the title of Itimad-ud-daulah, 'Pillar of the Government'. His daughter Mehrunissa married another Persian, Sher Afkun, whom Jahangir posted to Bengal, and after her husband's death in 1607—which later tradition attributed on no contemporary evidence to murder by Jahangir—she was brought as a young widow of thirty to court, where a position was found for her as a lady-in-waiting to one of Akbar's widows, Salima.

An annual event at court, introduced by Humayun, was the fancy bazaar in which the ladies, including wives of nobles, set up stalls as in an ordinary bazaar. The emperor then went shopping among them, an unusual situation which allowed both sides the pleasure of playing at haggling fishwives with an undercurrent, equally unusual in a harem society, of flirtation. It was in this stimulating situation that Jahangir first met Mehrunissa in March 1611, some four years after her arrival at court. (Perhaps this interval of time gave rise to the later tradition, equally unfounded, that she resisted his advances for four years.) Two months later, towards the end of May, he married her and called her Nur Mahal. She was a lady of great energy and many talents. She was an accomplished poet; she designed fabrics and dresses, ornaments and even carpets in a style of her own which dominated fashion for many years; she was a keen hunter and would shoot tigers from a closed howdah on top of an elephant, on one occasion using only six bullets to kill four tigers. She was reputed to be a great beauty, and Indian albums of the following century are full of portraits of her, though since no artist would have been allowed to set eyes on the queen such pictures can only be taken as generalized images.[3]

The emperor fell deeply in love with her. When combined with her father's already high rank at court, her new status ensured for her family a uniquely powerful role in the affairs of empire. Her brother too, Asaf Khan, was given a high rank and a position of trust among the emperor's official advisers second only to his father, who now was chief minister. Their family became almost an extension of the royal family itself. Itimad-ud-daulah was given by Jahangir the special honour of being allowed to enter the royal harem without the ladies' having to veil themselves, and the emperor and Nur Jahan would go out to dine in Asaf Khan's house over hundreds of yards of specially laid velvets and brocade.[4] And the family's special position was to continue in succeeding generations. Nur Jahan's niece married Shah Jahan and was his famous queen, Mumtaz Mahal. Asaf Khan became Shah Jahan's chief minister, and was followed in that office by his own son, Shaista Khan, who became also a close associate of Aurangzeb's. To add to the family's achievements, Nur Jahan's mother discovered attar of roses and was rewarded by Jahangir with a string of pearls. [5] And as a symbol of their position in the realm, with two successive first ladies and three successive chief ministers within seventy years of Ghiyas Beg's arriving penniless from

*One of the many paintings
said to be of Nur Jahan:
18th century*

[1]64, 163–6 [2]16, I, 261
[3]64, 173–7, 185; 16, I, 22, 375;
113, 14; 115, 122
[4]16, I, 351, 319–20; 40, 137–8
[5]48, 56, 66; 75, 201–2;
16, I, 270–1

Persia, it is a striking fact that the two most perfect Moghul tombs belong not to Great Moghuls but to the Persian adventurer and his granddaughter. The tomb of Itimad-ud-daulah, a small gem of mosaic, *pietra dura* and lattice, stands on the north bank of the Jumna at Agra; some three miles downstream on the opposite bank is the Taj Mahal, built for Mumtaz Mahal by Shah Jahan. They are monuments too to the fluidity of Moghul society.

During the greater part of Jahangir's reign the quartet of advisers whose voices could so easily sway the emperor consisted of Nur Jahan and her father and brother together with Prince Khurram. Although only Jahangir's third son, Khurram rapidly showed himself—by his own talents and by his father's obsessive admiration for him—to be the prince most likely to succeed. Aged only thirteen at his father's accession in 1605, he was four years younger than Khusrau and two years younger than Parwiz, both of whom were his half-brothers. Khusrau quickly spoilt his own position by his attempts at rebellion and Parwiz appears to have been regarded from the start as a nonentity and was given little chance to prove himself anything else, but young Khurram's career seemed an unending series of spectacular successes. In 1608 he was given the territory of Hissar Firoz and the right to pitch a red tent, both of which traditionally belonged to the heir apparent.[1] In 1612 he married Asaf Khan's daughter, Arjumand Banu, who would later be known as Mumtaz Mahal and to whom the prince remained totally devoted for the next nineteen years, until her death in 1631 after bearing him fourteen children. In 1614 he was first able to demonstrate his brilliance both as general and diplomat when he was sent to conquer the territory of Mewar or Udaipur, a task in which Akbar had failed and in which Jahangir, as a prince, had declined to engage. By a ruthless devastation of the countryside, submitting his own army to considerable shortage in order to inflict even greater on the enemy, Khurram brought the Rana to the point where he was ready to make terms, and then had the wisdom to make his conditions comparatively easy. The Rana need surrender no territory; a mere profession of loyalty to the Great Moghul would be sufficient; and he need not even wait on Jahangir in person, but could send his son. The Rana accepted these proposals and so did Jahangir, waiting at Ajmer, who confided complacently to his diary 'my lofty mind was always desirous, as far as possible, not to destroy the old families'.[2] Khurram brought the Rana's son Karan Singh to court at Ajmer, and Jahangir went out of his way to shower the Rajput prince with presents and to put him at his ease, as he 'was of a wild nature and had never seen assemblies and had lived among the hills'.[3] For the young Moghul prince these were exciting days. His father was busy congratulating himself that the submission of the senior house of Rajasthan should finally have been achieved in his reign,[4] but everyone knew where the credit lay.

In 1616 Khurram was given the command of the forces in the Deccan, replacing his brother Parwiz, and he rapidly persuaded the various Deccani rulers to negotiate terms, thus seeming to have pulled off another brief and brilliant campaign. In fact the terms did little to secure the Moghul frontiers to the south, but they did result in the presentation of vast wealth in jewels and goods to Khurram. When he returned to lay these before his father, the spectacle was one of extraordinary magnificence. Jahangir came down from his *jharoka* or balcony to pour a tray of jewels and another of gold coins over his son's head; he announced

[1] 64, 192; 65, 9 [2] 16, I, 274
[3] 16, I, 277 [4] 16, I, 274

Jahangir's twelve gold coins of the zodiac: c. 1620. 'It now occurred to my mind that, instead of the name of the month, the figure of the sign of the zodiac should be stamped . . . This was my own innovation: it had never been done before', he confided to his memoirs

that the prince would in future be known as Shah Jahan, and that a chair would be placed near the throne to allow him the unprecedented honour of sitting down in the emperor's presence; his rank was raised to the unheard-of level of thirty thousand *zat* and twenty thousand *sawar*; and in the emperor's private quarters Nur Jahan, whose steady policy of advancing Khurram had borne such spectacular fruit, threw a victory party for the prince and all his harem at a cost of three hundred thousand rupees.[1]

A distinguished and highly articulate foreigner was present at the Moghul court to witness both Khurram's departure for the Deccan and his triumphant return a year later. He was Sir Thomas Roe, England's first official ambassador to India and thus of sufficient standing to take a personal part in the daily life of the court, unlike most of the Europeans who visited and wrote about the Great Moghuls in the seventeenth century. His experiences lead one through a wide range of royal events and activities at the high point in the reign of Jahangir and at a time very near the middle of the period of the Moghuls' greatest successes, which ranged roughly from Akbar's building of Fatehpur Sikri in the 1570s to Aurangzeb's desertion of Delhi for the Deccan in 1681. His adventures are worth following therefore in some detail.

Sir Thomas Roe had been sent with letters of credence from James I to try to secure from the Great Moghul a trading agreement for the young East India Company. He had been preceded seven years earlier by another Englishman, William Hawkins, on a similar though less high-level mission. Hawkins pleased Jahangir by speaking Turkish and so being able to tell him about the west without the encumbrance of an interpreter, with the result that he too took an intimate part in court life and left an account which usefully backs up Roe's, although only a small part of it survives. The Portuguese had a long start in the lucrative business of bringing calicoes and indigo from India, and the Dutch also were slightly ahead of the English. But the only consideration which impressed the Moghuls was control of the seas. India felt no great need for trade with Europe, but the Muslims needed the protection of (which also meant from) European ships for those sailing to Arabia on pilgrimage. Until recently the Portuguese had commanded the Arabian Sea and pilgrims had only been able to travel with passports bought from the Portuguese, bearing small prints of Mary and Jesus; for the more orthodox it must have been a most painful necessity to assent to idolatry on the very journey to Mecca.[2] In this respect Roe arrived at a propitious time, because twice recently English ships had soundly beaten the Portuguese in Indian waters and he was able to warn Jahangir with some justification that 'the King my master would be lord of all these seas and ports to the prejudice of his subjects'.[3]

Roe landed at Surat in 1615, at the age of thirty-five, and immediately plunged with a will into the activity which usurped most of his energy during his entire stay in India—the struggle to be shown a deference proper to his royal master. Matters of precedence and protocol played an even greater part in seventeenth-century diplomacy than in today's. A favourite story at the court of Shah Jahan was of how the emperor had tried to trick a haughty Persian ambassador into bowing low as he approached by leaving open only a small wicket gate into the hall of audience, but the ambassador retaliated, with great presence of mind, by turning as he stooped, thus contriving to enter the imperial presence backside first.[4]

[1] 16, I, 395–401; 40, 131–3, 171–2, 385–6; 64, 221–8 [2] 13, II, 206; 6, 71–2 [3] 40, 105, 56 [4] 48, 151

Roe's contortions were of a hardly less childish nature. His first concern, admittedly an understandable one, was to prevent the customs officer from rummaging about in his pockets; he then decreed that hands could be laid on his followers only in such a way 'not as to search but to embrace them'; he refused to approach the welcoming committee until they stood rather than sat on their carpets; and he and the governor of Surat spent several days parleying about whose duty it was to visit the other first.[1] When he finally reached the presence of one of the royal princes, Parwiz, who was then at Burhanpur, Roe with considerable courage marched through a lane of mounted troops and courtiers, refusing their command to bow down to the ground, and then insisted that he must either be allowed to climb the three steps up to the prince and stand beside him before conversing, or alternatively be provided with a chair below. It was explained that either of these was out of the question but it was eventually agreed that Roe could lean nonchalantly against the silver pillar supporting the prince's canopy, a position which he could accept as being within his dignity, and Parwiz moreover promised to bring him to a place that evening where they could talk in even greater intimacy. Unfortunately Roe now presented a case of bottles, and by the evening the prince was too drunk to see him.[2]

At Burhanpur Roe lodged in a public *sarai*, where he was disgusted with his accommodation, 'four chambers like ovens, noe bigger, round at the topp, made of brick in a wall syde'.[3] Here he caught a fever which nearly killed him, and then he made his way, still in a very delapidated state, to Ajmer, where Jahangir was holding court. He was enlivened on the journey by a chance meeting with Tom

Sir Thomas Roe LEFT *and his chaplain, Edward Terry*

*n Coryat, who wrote 'I have
rid upon an elephant since I
ye to this court, determining
one day (by God's leave) to
ave my picture expressed in
y next booke sitting upon an
elephant'*

Coryat, the eccentric Englishman who had spent three years walking here from the Mediterranean and who now had plans to kiss Tamburlaine's tomb in Samarkand and thence, via 'Prester Jhac in Ethiopia', home again.[4] But he died, still in India, in 1617 and is buried at Surat. Only his evident oddity had saved his life this far. Roe's chaplain Edward Terry, though himself imprudent enough to refer to Mohammed as the ringleader of the Muslim religion,[5] reports in some awe a private demonstration by Coryat against Islam. Coryat was sick of hearing 'their devout Mullāhs five times every day ascend unto the tops of those high turrets, whence they proclaim *La alla illa alla, mahomet Resul-alla*, that is, here is no God, but one God, and Mahomet, the messenger of God', so one day he climbed to a high place opposite the mosque and shouted back '*La alla illa alla, Hasaret Eesa Ben-alla*, that is, no God, but one God, and the Lord Christ, the Son of God; and further added, that Mahomet was an impostor', for which, Terry admits, he might well have been killed, 'but he was here taken for a mad-man, and so let alone'.[6] The story is possible in that Coryat had learnt Arabic together with Turkish and Persian on his travels and later addressed a begging speech in Persian to Jahangir, much to the embarrassment of Sir Thomas Roe, who was thinking, as ever, of the dignity of his country's image.[7]

Roe arrived at Ajmer on December 23, 1615. He was ill again, and somewhat to Jahangir's annoyance was unable to pay his respects to the emperor for nearly three weeks, but on January 10 he presented himself at four in the afternoon at the daily durbar. He found the emperor seated high under a canopy, with two attendants standing below on the heads of wooden elephants to fan him; a position

[1] 40, 29–42 [2] 40, 70–2 [3] 40, 69
[4] 40, 83, n.1 [5] 41, 242
[6] 41, 248–53 [7] 39, 249, 264–6

far above the crowd was a standard feature of all royal appearances in public, combining dignity with security. The officials and courtiers stood below at precisely measured distances from the throne, the senior being within inner railings and the next grade within a second row, all on a slightly raised platform round which those of lesser importance stood at ground level on three sides. Roe observed that the arrangement was precisely that of a player king sitting high at the back of the stage at a public theatre in London[1] (Plate 30, opposite).

Roe had prudently acquired permission in advance to use the salutation of his own country, so he 'made a reverence', presumably a bow and a flourish with the right hand in the manner of a subdued Osric, at three different points on his approach to the throne.[2] The normal obeisance at the Moghul court, the *kornish*, was not in fact particularly undignified. The courtier was expected to bow with the palm of his right hand pressed against his forehead, signifying that his head was 'in the hand of humility' and was presented to the emperor. Akbar had introduced full prostration from the disciples of his new religion when in private, but even he had forbidden them to use it in public assembly to avoid giving offence to the orthodox.[3] Hawkins describes, however, a very elaborate and rather humiliating series of salaams expected of noblemen returning to court after a long absence, and at a certain time in Jahangir's reign prostration seems to have been the conventional way of offering thanks for any exceptional royal favour.[4] Roe was no doubt afraid that he might be classed in one of these two categories.

The afternoon durbar was only one of the several appearances which made up the emperor's daily programme, a programme so rigidly fixed that Roe described his life as being 'as regular as a clock that stricks at sett howers'.[5] Even if individual emperors changed the precise hours at which their clock would strike, the ingredients of the royal day remained the same from Akbar to Shah Jahan. Before sunrise musicians played to wake the court and at the moment of sunrise the emperor presented himself in his *jharoka-i-darshan*, or 'balcony of appearance'. This balcony was high in the outside wall of each fort or palace, and the common people could gather below for a glimpse of their emperor. The custom by which the ruler showed himself to the public each day to reassure them that he was alive and well and all calm in the kingdom was an old one, but it was one of Akbar's more typical innovations to chime his appearance with the rising sun (but both Akbar and Jahangir went back to bed for two more hours of sleep after this early chore).[6] In concept this public appearance was an occasion for common people to make personal requests direct to their ruler, and successive emperors devised various methods, more symbolic than practical, by which their subjects could attract their attention; Humayun set up a drum which those seeking justice could beat; Jahangir lowered a golden chain from his private quarters in the fort at Agra to the ground outside, designed so that when it was shaken small bells on it would ring; and Shah Jahan sometimes let down from the *jharoka* a string to which petitions could be attached, and so reach him without the intervention of officials.[7] But this aspect of the *jharoka* was probably only effective in the case of a mass demonstration, as when a vast number of starving people presented themselves before Shah Jahan in Lahore in 1641 and moved him to fairly extensive relief measures. As an indication of how difficult it was for ordinary people to bring their case before the emperor, one group of plaintiffs went so far as to pass themselves off as jugglers in order to be brought into Jahangir's presence.[8]

Shah Jahan in durbar, in the raised balcony-type throne which reminded Roe of a player king in a London theatre: by Bichitr, c. 1650

[1] 40, 91 [2] 40, 87 [3] 11, I, 158–9 [4] 35, 119; 24, 170 [5] 40, 270 [6] 108, 68–9; 11, I, 156; 35, 115 [7] 10, I, 651; 16, I, 7, 17, 113; 105, 39 [8] 111, 292, 205

144

Detail of mosaic on the south gateway to Akbar's tomb at Sikandra, built in the reign of Jahangir

At noon Jahangir returned to the *jharoka* to watch elephant fights or a parade, and at four in the afternoon, after the beating of a great drum, he appeared before the assembled court in the *diwan-i-am* or 'hall of public audience', where Roe first saw him. Here was carried out the more public part of state business, such as appointments and presentations, while wrestlers and tumblers were always on hand to fill in gaps if required. The emperor then withdrew to a more private gathering of the highest officials, at which the real decisions of state were argued out and made. This private council was known as the *ghusl-khana*—literally 'bathroom', and thought to derive from Sher Shah's habit of holding council there while his hair dried after his bath.[1]

Under Jahangir the *ghusl-khana* tended to merge, as the evening progressed, into a private party. Those attending had their breath sniffed by a guard at the entrance for signs of alcohol, but business was often 'prevented by a drowziness which possesseth His Majestie from the fumes of Backus'.[2] Sometimes, while the assembly was still in progress, the emperor suddenly lay down and went to sleep for the night (less surprising than it might sound, in a warm climate where people sat among comfortable cushions on a carpet), after which the candles were immediately snuffed and the guests were expected to grope their way out.[3] On more sober evenings serious business was carried out at these assemblies in a mood of lively and indeed often heated debate. Roe gives fascinating accounts of occasions on which, expressing himself with some difficulty through a Spanish interpreter, he indulged in angry three-cornered arguments with Asaf Khan and Prince Khurram in front of the emperor, and found Jahangir surprisingly willing to reprimand his favourite son in public when he felt he had wronged the ambassador.[4]

A main bone of contention between Roe and the prince was that on more than one occasion Khurram's officers had impounded Roe's crates of baggage, which consisted largely of presents for the emperor (possibly why he had such a sympathetic hearing from Jahangir). Presents played an immoderately large part in the routine of Moghul administration, though novelty could impress the emperor as much as lavishness; an unusual box with a glass side, a white china cup, and even a fish of a type which Jahangir happened not to have tasted for eleven months, were all at different times most favourably received.[5] Roe reports that even in the daily public durbar those wishing to speak with Jahangir held up in the air whatever gift they had brought and he then asked them their business; and many of them must already have given presents to several court officials in order to arrive in a position to give one to the emperor.[6] Roe's influence increased to a marked extent when news came of an English ship recently arrived at Surat which might be expected to contain some pleasant 'toyes' for the court, and Jahangir himself asked shamelessly how much was coming for him.[7] What he most wanted was an English horse, and he argued that if six were shipped one might survive the journey and 'though it came leane, he would fatt yt'.[8] In general Jahangir was astounded that his brother on the English throne should send him such pawky offerings as Roe could produce, and Roe sent an angry letter back to the East India Company complaining of the shoddy quality of the goods they had provided him with: velvet that had faded, leather cases that had gone mouldy, and mirrors from which the silvering had peeled and the glue of the frames had come unstuck. He added later that he was having to give away his own personal

[1] 64, 95–7; 11, I, 157
[2] 40, 265, 325; 41, 371–2
[3] 40, 190, 201; 35, 115–16
[4] 40, 128–33, 420–1
[5] 16, I, 165, 379, 414
[6] 40, 94; 35, 119; 42, 57–8
[7] 40, 251–2; 35, 94 [8] 40, 129

possessions to keep up appearances.[1] He scored a modest success with an English coach which had been conveyed here in pieces, though Jahangir immediately had the original upholstery replaced with a much richer brocade and the brass nails changed for silver ones.[2]

For a while Roe seemed greatly to have pleased the emperor with the latest edition of Mercator's maps. When Jahangir went riding it was the custom for anyone whose house he passed to stand outside it and make him an offering. Roe, surprised on one occasion to discover that the emperor was coming his way, had nothing ready but chose from among his belongings this volume of maps, 'which I presented with an excuse that I had nothing worthy, but to a great king I offered the world, in which he had so great and rich a part'.[3] Not long afterwards it was returned, and Terry believed that for a man who claimed in his imperial title to have seized the world it was too much of a shock to discover how much remained —though he does add that Mercator certainly cramps the Moghul unduly in his map.[4]

The only objects with which Roe was really able to impress Jahangir were his English paintings, since European art had for some years been very much admired at the Moghul court. Abul Fazl stated that the artists of Europe were much more accomplished than those of India, and in 1602 the whole of Agra was so impressed by a large painting of the Madonna, which the Jesuit fathers kept on their altar, that Akbar asked them to bring it to the palace and then carried it himself, not allowing anyone to help him, to show it to his mother and wives and daughters. Jahangir made his painters study western prints and copy their Christian subjects on to murals in his palaces and even in his father's tomb at Sikandra; and European etchings can be found pasted into elaborately painted pages in several seventeenth-century albums.[5] When Jahangir appeared in the new year festivities of 1616 the alcove behind his throne was decorated with portraits of the English royal family, though a lack of proper discrimination about such distant

A motley assortment of European paintings, some secular, some religious, above Jahangir on his throne: detail from a painting by Payag, c. 1650

[1] 40, 99, 352–3, 76–7, 117
[2] 40, 98–9; 41, 367–8
[3] 40, 284, 380   [4] 41, 350–2
[5] 11, I, 96, 107; 122, 229–40

people had led to their hanging in company with a 'cittizens wife of London' and the Countess of Somerset, who was at that very moment awaiting trial for the murder of Sir Thomas Overbury; and a similar lack of discrimination from the other side caused Roe even more embarrassment when a painting arrived from the East India Company showing Venus and a satyr, to which Jahangir kept returning and demanding that the allegory be explained, until Roe became convinced that he 'understood the morall to be a scorne of Asiatiques, whom the naked satyre represented, and was of the same complexion, and not unlike; who, being held by Venus, a white woman, by the nose, it seemed that she led him captive'.[1]

OPPOSITE *The principle of the European miniature adapted for a Moghul portrait of a child: late 17th century*

Jahangir was particularly interested in the portrait miniatures which Roe had among his personal possessions, because the emperor had himself introduced into court life the western concept of a miniature—a realistic likeness richly set, which could be worn both as a memento and a jewel. He was so taken with a miniature of Roe's wife (which Roe most diplomatically resisted giving him) that he ordered five copies to be made of it and announced that his principal wives would wear them. He gave Roe a small portrait of himself set in gold with a pendant pearl, a flattering gift in that even the great nobles at court usually received nothing better than a gold medallion with the emperor's head, which was to be worn in the turban and had to be set at their own expense.[2]

It was a new departure of Jahangir's to strike coins and medals bearing his own

LEFT *A miniature of a European lady copied by a Moghul artist: early 17th century*

[1] 40, 125–6, 350
[2] 40, 222–4, 214–15; 16, II, 36, 90

150

portrait, and an added offence, since coins are more public than pictures, against the Koranic ban on images. Akbar had taken his mint very seriously, placing the artist Abdus Samad in charge of it and producing coins which are among the finest in the world for that period, but with one or two very minor exceptions he had limited the design on his coins to calligraphy.[1] Jahangir first used images in substituting the sign of the zodiac for the name of the month,[2] and later progressed not only to portraits of himself but even, on occasion, to portraits of himself holding a wine glass (Plates 28 and 29, pp. 139–40).

The extremely high quality of both paintings and coins during Jahangir's reign was a direct result of the emperor's personal interest. Having grown up at Fatehpur Sikri in the busy days of Akbar's studio, he was a keen student of technique and claimed to be able to tell which master had painted the eye and eyebrow in a face and which the rest of the portrait—though this skill related more to the paintings of his father's reign, since under Jahangir the factory system of several artists working on one picture began to fade out, resulting in a lower rate of production but a higher level of artistic quality.[3] It was Jahangir's special demands which led to the new realism in painting. Where Akbar had required crowded scenes to illustrate events many of which had happened long ago and far away, Jahangir often wanted in effect a photographic record of the wonders of plant and animal life, and this simpler and more precise subject matter led in turn to an improved sense of design. In the same way his interest in portraiture forced his painters to grapple with the deeper problems of character—he sent a painter all the way to Isfahan to bring back a likeness of Shah Abbas, and would frequently show it to people who had seen his great rival to check on its accuracy.[4] In addition, he himself seems to have invented and commissioned from his artists a new style of political allegory in art which, however self-congratulatory and vain, provided some of the most magnificent paintings of the period. One such picture claims to celebrate a new spirit of peace with his Persian neighbour, Shah Abbas, but in fact redresses Mercator's depressing projection of the size of the Moghul empire by allowing Jahangir's lion to sprawl right across Persia and Turkey, pushing the poor Persian lamb into the Mediterranean (Plate 27, p. 130); another professes to show how the humble emperor prefers the company of simple holy men to that of great potentates, but enables the Sultan of Turkey to be placed a pleasing distance away from and below the throne, and James I of England even further—a place no doubt in keeping with the feebleness of his gifts, but Roe could console himself with the fact that the King of Portugal, or Spain, does not even appear (Plate 26, p. 129); and a third is an elegant wish-fulfilment of the death of Malik Ambar, the Abyssinian whose guerilla forces so regularly harried Jahangir's armies in the Deccan. The subject matter can be seen as delightful or silly according to choice, but this blend of realistic painting at the service of a mysterious combination of symbols—such as the globe resting on an ox standing on a fish—was a rich artistic vein hitherto unused in Moghul paintings.

Another innovation of Jahangir's, less important but useful in the dating of pictures, was the use of the nimbus or halo to surround his own head. He had borrowed it from the paintings and prints which the Jesuits had brought, but it had been used long ago in the east as a pagan symbol of holiness, and from there had travelled to Byzantium and so into Europe while dying out in India and

[1] 78, lxvi; 89, 120; 62, 156–7
[2] 16, II, 6–7
[3] 16, II, 20–21; 89, 111
[4] 87, I, xxxii

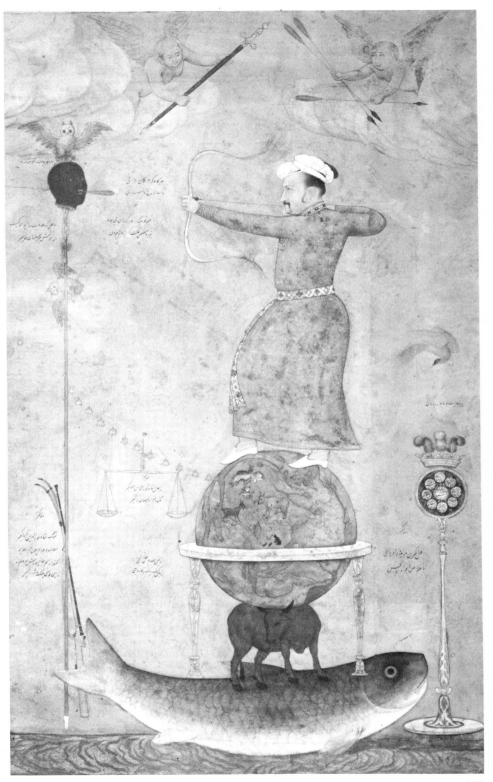

Jahangir (as he imagined)
finishing off Malik Ambar:
by Abul Hassan, c. 1620

Persia. After its reintroduction by Jahangir it was always used in later Moghul paintings to adorn the figure of the emperor.[1]

In November 1616 Jahangir moved south to Mandu in order to be nearer the operations in the Deccan. Roe accompanied him and has left magnificent descriptions of the royal camp and of Jahangir's lavish ceremony of departure. The ambassador, assiduous as ever, 'shuffled' his way through the crowd of courtiers to stand close to Jahangir at the important moment of setting out, and for once even he was impressed:

> The King descended the stayres with such an acclamation of 'health to the King' as would have out cryed cannons. At the stayres foote, wher I mett him, and shuffled to be next, one brought a mighty carp; another a dish of white stuff like starch, into which hee putt his finger, and touched the fish and so rubd it on his forhead, a ceremony used presaging good fortune. Then a nother came and buckled on his swoord and buckler, sett all over with great diamonds and rubyes, the belts of gould suteable. A nother hung his quiver with 30 arrowes and his bow in a case, the same that was presented by the Persian ambassador. On his head he wore a rich turbant with a plume of herne tops, not many but long; on one syde hung a ruby unsett, as bigg as a walnutt; on the other syde a diamond as great; in the middle an emralld like a hart, much bigger. His shash was wreathed about with a chayne of great pearle, rubyes, and diamonds drild. About his neck hee carried a chaine of most excellent pearle, three double (so great I never saw); at his elbowes, armletts sett with diamonds; and on his wrists three rowes of several sorts. His hands bare, but almost on every finger a ring; his gloves, which were English, stuck under his girdle; his coate of cloth of gould without sleeves upon a fine *semian* as thin as lawne; on his feete a payre of embrodered buskings with pearle, the toes sharp and turning up.[2]

To add to the ambassador's delight at the use of the English gloves, the emperor drove away attended by an English servant in a replica which had already been made of the English coach, and was followed soon after by Nur Jahan in the original coach with its rich new upholstery and silver nails.[3]

The emperor gave orders for the camp at Ajmer to be burnt, so that the traders and camp-followers who had been living there for three years would be forced to move with him. At one point in his diary Jahangir calculates that to supply a large army on the move, in unfertile districts, grain-sellers with at least a hundred thousand laden bullocks must be persuaded to accompany the camp.[4] Jahangir's attendance was not on this occasion as large as usual—the main fighting force was with Shah Jahan—but Terry, who described the royal camp as '*ambulans respublica*, a walking republic', said that when on the move it took twelve hours for the whole procession to pass any one place, and Roe calculated that when halted for the night it covered an area twenty miles in circumference and might 'equall almost any towne in Europe for greatness'.[5] It was indeed organized like a town, with regular streets where each noble or tradesman had his own allotted area in which to pitch his tent, so that the camp was identical in each place and people could instantly find their way around—a system deriving from Timur, if not earlier. The king himself and the nobles had duplicated tents, so that one set could always be sent ahead to the next stage to be ready for them on their arrival, as if an entire town were playing leapfrog.[6] British viceroys in India would later move about in precisely the same manner.

In the centre of the camp was the emperor's own enclosure, which was in effect

[1]89, 172–4 [2]40, 283–4 [3]40, 284–5
[4]40, 297; 16, II, 233–4
[5]41, 398–401; 40, 324–5
[6]40, 325, 239–40; 28, 140–4;
11, I, 47
[7]11, I, 45, 54; 40, 286; 28, 162

a small fort of painted wood and canvas. In the time of Akbar it was 'never less than one hundred yards square' and Roe found Jahangir's to be nearly three hundred yards in diameter. The outer wall consisted of wooden screens, painted or sometimes covered in scarlet sackcloth, and held together with leather straps; there was a handsome gate-house and gates which could be securely bolted. Inside there were all the normal buildings which would be found in a royal palace, a hall of public audience, a hall of private audience, and a travelling mosque (Timur carried about with him a beautifully painted wooden one) and in an adjoining enclosure a great deal of private space for the harem. There was even a *jharoka* window in the outer wall in which the emperor could make his usual public appearance; and all the normal activities of court life, such as scholars or artists bringing their work for presentation and approval, continued just as at home in Agra.[7]

Considerable comfort was taken for granted. Jauhar once indicated the dire straits into which Humayun's little party had fallen, after making a hurried escape from a battle with a handful of followers, by saying that there was not even a separate tent available for the emperor's privy; Akbar introduced a large cart, drawn by an elephant, which contained several bathrooms; and in the streets of Timur's camp there were even public bath-houses, complete with boilers for heating the water.[8] The interiors of pavilions belonging to the emperor or his nobles must have seemed profoundly luxurious and attractive, with a profusion of rich carpets under the bright canvas, and indeed the court artists manage to suggest a great deal of the magnificence in their miniatures. Abul Fazl records that to transport the royal tents alone required a hundred elephants, five hundred camels, four hundred carts and a hundred bearers, and Roe described the camp as 'one of the wonders of my little experience'.[9]

There were various conveyances in which the emperor or his nobles, when not on horseback, could travel in comfort between stages. The palanquin was a covered litter, carried on long poles on the shoulders of four or six men, in which there was room for the occupant to recline at full length. Because of the skill of the bearers over rough ground it was regarded as the least painful method of transport for an invalid. In a type of carriage drawn by oxen there was very plush upholstery, and room for four to sit or two to lie down and sleep. And, according to Jahangir himself, lying down to sleep in the howdah of an elephant was so comfortable that one could travel on through day and night without inconvenience. All three types of vehicle were used also to transport the harem, though without doubt the ladies were at their most splendidly remote, a precious and exclusive cargo, when riding on elephants in golden howdahs with the windows covered in gold mesh so that they could see but not be seen. The mahout driving the elephant had a cloth thrown over his head, and they were preceded far ahead by mounted eunuchs and lackeys with large canes clearing the road of male observers. These advance guards took great pleasure in their work, and it was known to be extremely dangerous to let them reach you; later in the century the French physician Bernier once allowed them to do so and had to draw his sword to make his escape.[10]

After a leisurely journey of four months the camp reached the huge hill fortress of Mandu, on March 6, 1617. Roe was still in attendance—his most unsavoury experience on the journey had been to pass 'a cammell laden with 300 mens heads,

A lady travelling in a closed palanquin, with her female attendants riding veiled beside her: c. 1590

10, III, 862; 16, II, 20–21, 257
[8]7, 95–8; 11, I, 275; 28, 140–4
[9]11, I, 47; 40, 324
[10]41, 143–6, 404; 16, I, 226–7;
40, 283; 49, II, 334; 48, 373–4;
45, II, 190–3; 50, 76; 52, 160

sent from Candahar by the Governor in present to the King'—and he now installed himself in a small deserted mosque to save the rent on better accommodation.[1] He and Terry were far from comfortable. There was an appalling shortage of water in the fort and the lions prowled round their mosque and carried off their animals.[2] But Jahangir was much enjoying himself sightseeing in this pleasant spot; he visited the beautiful Friday Mosque, a superbly simple and dignified building from the early fifteenth century (Plate 9, p. 46); he was delighted by the wild plantain trees all around and by the wagtails, a pair of which hatched a couple of young ones in the building which he occupied; he took great pleasure in kicking the tomb of a Mandu ruler, Nasir-ud-din, who had been so brutal as to kill his own father, and then as his indignation increased at such a thought the emperor decided to go further and he had the wretch's body dug up and thrown into the river; and he had a delightful picnic with his ladies in the Nilkanth summer-house which had been built forty years before by one of Akbar's generals on a slope in the south-west corner of the fort.[3]

At Mandu Roe saw the emperor being weighed on his birthday against a variety of precious metals and stones, a ceremony which he had missed the previous year at Ajmer, greatly to Jahangir's anger, because a messenger misled him about the time of it.[4] The emperor sat on one side of a pair of golden scales while bags of gold were placed to balance him on the other, followed by the same weight in silver, jewels, precious cloth and foodstuffs. Roe was unimpressed because the precious metals were not visible ('it being in bagges might bee pibles'), and he argues that since the sacks were carried inside again afterwards it was not likely that the goods would be distributed in charity, as they were intended to be; but it seems improbable that the Great Moghul would have connived at such an easily discovered fraud suggesting poverty.[5] The ceremony of the weighing derived from a Hindu custom known as *tuladana* and is usually said to have been introduced into the Moghul calendar by Akbar, but certainly Humayun was weighed against gold as early as 1533.[6] From Akbar onwards there were two weighings each year, one for the solar birthday in public and one for the lunar birthday, usually in the privacy of the harem; the monarch's solar and lunar birthdays coincided only on the day of his birth, after which they separated by a further eleven days each year. Being fat cost the emperor money but could on occasion benefit a private citizen, as when Jahangir weighed Ustad Mohammed Nayi against rupees to reward him for his flute-playing, or gave the astrologer Jotik Ray his own weight for a correct prediction. The comfortable astrologer turned out to weigh two hundred rupees more than the musician.[7]

After the weighing which Roe attended, Jahangir scattered imitation fruits made of silver among his courtiers. Roe was astounded both by the undignified scrabbling on the floor which ensued and by the extraordinary thinness, and therefore cheapness, of the silver[8]—a detail which will be familiar to anyone who has eaten pure silver leaf on ordinary sweets and ice-creams in India today. Moghul magnificence was by now such that even in the public streets Jahangir frequently scattered rupees right and left from horseback or howdah as he passed.

The other great annual festival at the Moghul court, also witnessed by Roe, was the new year festival of *nauruz*, introduced by Akbar from Persia in 1582.[9] It became the main occasion for granting new ranks and honours and was a particularly pleasant festivity in that it always fell in the spring, thanks to the workings

The Nilkanth summer-house Mandu, where in 1617 Jahangir had a picnic with his ladies

[1] 40, 322, 353–4 [2] 41, 184
[3] 16, I, 365–7, 382–4 [4] 40, 221
[5] 40, 379; 11, I, 266–7; 35, 118–
[6] 11, III, 282; 59, I, 59
[7] 16, I, 376, and II, 203
[8] 40, 379 [9] 10, III, 557–8

of the Persian calendar. It could last anywhere from six to nineteen days,[1] and every evening a different noble gave a party in his house or tent, which Jahangir attended and at which there was much present-giving—a system greatly to the benefit of the emperor, since the custom was for his host to spread out a rich array of gifts and for Jahangir to accept them all, after which he would courteously present whichever he did not want to their original owner. On some occasions the procedure was a little different but almost equally advantageous: Jahangir would take all the goods but would insist on buying them, after which the officials from his treasury would fix the price at only half their worth.[2] Singers and dancing girls provided almost constant entertainment during the days of festivity—'I sawe what was to be seene', said Roe, 'presents, elephants, horses, and many whoores.'[3] The wives of the nobles moved into the imperial harem so that they could celebrate with the emperor's ladies and could all watch together, through lattice grilles, the great central durbar at which the emperor appeared in his most magnificent array. Roe found the throne and its surroundings on this occasion impressive but vulgar, in that it tried to show too many precious objects all together, 'like a ladie that with her plate sett on a cupboord her imbrodered slippers'[4]—a somewhat ungracious response since it was here that the portraits of the English royal family could be seen and they, more than any other item, must surely have qualified as the embroidered slippers.

Roe finally sailed homewards from Surat on February 17, 1619. In his own eyes his stay had been largely a failure—he had long given up his original target of a formal treaty with Jahangir, and had settled for various concessions relating solely to the port of Surat in a grant or firman from Shah Jahan—but the richest harvest of his trip was a diary which gives a superbly vivid glimpse of everyday life at the Great Moghul's court. For Roe himself, who was thirty-five when he reached India and thirty-eight when he left, this was only the first of a series of diplomatic missions which took him successively to Turkey and Sweden and to peace negotiations on England's behalf at Hamburg, Regensburg and Vienna.[5]

It had taken Roe very little time to discover the real power of Nur Jahan. He had written home to Prince Charles, the future Charles I, that the king's favourite wife 'governs him, and wynds him up at her pleasure', and he had informed the Governor of the East India Company that 'all justice or care of any thing or publique affayrs either sleepes or depends on her, who is more unaccesable than any goddesse or mystery of heathen impietye'.[6] The image of some heathen goddess too precious for men's sight was an apt one, since all that Roe had seen of this powerful lady was the occasional closed carriage passing at a distance. But in addition to her great personal influence over Jahangir behind the scenes, her voice was at this stage directly heard in open council through her brother, Asaf Khan, who appears almost more frequently than anyone else in Roe's pages, and through her father, Itimad-ud-daulah, the chief minister. In January 1622, however, Itimad-ud-daulah died, and his death came at a time when relations had been cooling between Nur Jahan and the other two members of what had been her junta, Shah Jahan and Asaf Khan. Seeing her special protégé Shah Jahan become steadily and spectacularly more successful in his own right, she seems to have come to realize that if such a powerful character inherited the throne there would be no effective role for herself after her husband's death. The situation became more urgent when Jahangir fell ill and nearly died in 1620, and from then on his poor health, already weakened by alcohol, opium and asthma, came increasingly to dominate affairs at court.[7] Nur Jahan therefore shifted her support to a younger prince, Shahriyar, whose own natural feebleness was further enhanced, from her point of view, by his comparative lack of status in being merely the son of a slave-girl or concubine. In April 1621 the prince was married to Nur Jahan's daughter by her first marriage, Ladili Begam, amid the most lavish pomp and ceremony at Agra. This event, only nine months before Itimad-ud-daulah's death, created—or rather made evident—a clear political split within the old man's powerful family. One prince, Shahriyar, was now son-in-law to Nur Jahan. Another, Shah Jahan, was already son-in-law to her brother, Asaf Khan. It seemed clear that a granddaughter of Itimad-ud-daulah's would become queen. But as to who should be king, his children had from now on opposing views.

After Itimad-ud-daulah's death, Nur Jahan put in hand the construction in white marble of his exquisite tomb at Agra which was finished as little as six years later, in 1628. Unlike the much larger Taj Mahal, with which it can rank in quality, the appeal of this tomb depends not so much in its outline as in its decoration. It is like a brilliant casket, bejewelled with various styles of inlay, each an advance on previous techniques and a herald of even greater things to come. Its two major innovations—the extensive use of white marble as a material and of inlay as a decorative motif—were to become the distinguishing features of the greatest period of Moghul architecture. Even a plain sandstone wall, as on the riverside gateway to the tomb, is now inlaid with elegant shapes and designs in white marble which enliven the surface much more successfully than the elaborately carved reliefs of the palace buildings at Fatehpur Sikri, or the simple geometrical inlay of white marble in red sandstone which can be seen round the doorways in the Fatehpur Sikri mosque. Geometrical patterns in stones more variously coloured than plain red and white had also been known for some decades in India: such work had been seen, for example, in Sher Shah's mosque in the Purana Qila in Delhi, built in the 1540s, and more recently on the south gate of Akbar's tomb at Sikandra. But the tomb of Itimad-ud-daulah develops this technique into something infinitely more subtle.

One of the elaborately inlaid corner towers of the tomb of Itimad-ud-daulah, Agra

The surface of the gateway at Sikandra, although extraordinarily beautiful (Plate 31, p. 146), is comparatively rough work, being composed on the mosaic principle with shaped pieces of stone laid side by side on a flat ground. The exterior of Itimad-ud-daulah's tomb (Plate 32, p. 163) starts instead with a smooth surface of marble into which geometrical cavities have been cut; within these cavities are laid precise shapes of very varied stones, selected for the maximum textural pleasure in the grain. The lower part of the same wall adapts this inlay technique to a considerably harder task, that of laying unsymmetrical and curved pieces of stone into a marble surface to make free figures of scrolls and flowers. In the alcoves of Itimad-ud-daulah's tomb, and on the small towers round the upper storey, the process becomes even more delicate with the laying in of semi-precious stones such as lapis, onyx, jasper, topaz and cornelian in intricate designs, a craft nearer to the jeweller's than to the mason's because of the hardness of the materials involved.[8] This is the technique which in its European use, developed in Florence in the sixteenth century, is known as *pietra dura*. It has often been argued that the concept and the skill must have travelled from Florence to India.[9] But the Florentine *pietra dura* is more purely figurative,

[1]115, 100; 64, 98 [2]35, 118 [3]40, 132 [4]40, 127 [5]40, li–liv, lxvii–lxviii [6]40, 270, 337 [7]64, 319–22 [8]97, 104 [9]92, 174–5

159

tending to imitate conventional pictures in other media (the only unmistakably Italianate panels of *pietra dura* in India are in the alcove behind the throne in the *diwan-i-am* in Delhi, and they are of a considerably later date and may even have been brought ready-made from Florence[1]), whereas the Indian version, even when including flowers or other recognizable objects, remains essentially decorative and can be seen as a direct refinement of the previous use of patterned mosaic. Refined even further, and used in combination with relief work in plain white marble, it was to become one of the glories of Moghul architecture in the reign of Shah Jahan (Plates 40 and 41, pp. 196–7).

The other comparably important building of Jahangir's reign, the tomb of Akbar at Sikandra, is less successful. Indeed the tomb itself is something of a monstrosity, possibly due to the personal intervention of Jahangir, who visited it for the first time after the work had already been in progress for three years and who then ordered his architects to pull down much of what was built and start again, since it 'did not come up to my idea of what it ought to be'.[2] The first three storeys are of red sandstone, roughly in the style of Fatehpur Sikri, but on top of them sits a white marble courtyard containing the delicately carved sepulchre. The courtyard is in itself extremely beautiful and it points the way to the more extensive use of white marble in the tomb of Itimad-ud-daulah and in later Moghul architecture, but in its present position it is decidedly incongruous. However, the south gateway to the tomb is a complete success architecturally (Plate 25, p. 124), quite apart from the pleasures of its surface decoration. It fulfils the best in Akbar's architecture and leads on towards Shah Jahan's. The gateway itself is in the style of Akbar's more massive and famous victory gate known as the Buland Darwaza, on the south side of the mosque at Fatehpur Sikri, but it has rather better proportions than its predecessor; and the charming white minarets which surround it were an innovation which would reappear, almost unchanged, round the Taj Mahal.

With Itimad-ud-daulah dead, and the interests of Asaf Khan and Shah Jahan becoming increasingly opposed to her own, Nur Jahan's junta had ceased to exist. For the remaining five years of the ailing Jahangir's reign she ruled, therefore, much more directly from inside the harem. To rule directly from within the harem sounds like a contradiction in terms, and this, combined with other details of Nur Jahan's life such as her love of hunting, has often led to the statement that she broke purdah and took a normal part in public affairs.[3] But there seems to be no evidence of this. She shot tigers from a closed howdah on top of an elephant with only the barrel of her musket exposed to public gaze.[4] In 1626 she even rode into battle, but she was in an elephant-litter, which was a closed conveyance slung between two elephants, and she continued to distribute her orders in the normal way through her eunuchs.[5] And on one occasion, when Roe was in a garden awaiting the arrival of Jahangir, elaborate precautions were taken to prevent anyone from seeing Nur Jahan, whom he had brought with him in an open carriage; 'suddenly newes came to put out all lights, the King was come, who entred on an open waggon, with his Normahall, drawne by bullocks, himselfe carter, and no man neare'[6]; with such care taken it seems extremely unlikely that Nur Jahan was not also veiled, and the emperor drove her straight to her quarters before reappearing himself.

The error seems to be in thinking of the harem as nothing more than a gilded

[1] 99, 46, 50–51 [2] 16, I, 152
[3] 64, 186; 113, 108–12 [4] 16, I, 3
[5] 16A, 425–6; 45, II, 190–2
[6] 40, 426

cage full of pretty but idle women, in which only the cock of the roost was seen or heard. No doubt much of the time was spent in self-adornment, or in eying one's own pretty face in the mirror, about an inch in diameter, which each lady wore on her right thumb,[1] but the harem was also a hive of business activity and intrigue, much of it relating to the world outside, and men of sufficient rank were able from a distance to present their compliments to the ladies and to solicit their help.

Admittedly when a man's business involved a visit deep into the private quarters, as when a doctor had to see a sick patient, the precautions taken were elaborate. Two European doctors who attended the royal family later in the century have described their experiences. When François Bernier had to visit a lady 'so extremely ill that she could not be moved to the outward gate', he says that 'a *Kachemire* shawl covered my head, hanging like a large scarf down to my feet, and an eunuch led me by the hand, as if I had been a blind man'.[2] And Niccolo Manucci, a self-taught quack whose vague memories of European medicine enabled him to pass himself off by Moghul standards as an expert, tells of the arrangement when the doctor reached the patient and the shawl over his head was removed. She would be lying out of sight behind a curtain. If she needed to be bled or to have a minor wound dressed, the appropriate arm or leg would appear through the curtain. If some further inspection was required, the doctor was allowed to put his hand through the curtain, and Manucci describes the stimulating dangers, and the need to keep a straight face, when the patient was only pretending illness for the sake of being visited: 'There are some who from time to time affect the invalid, simply that they may have the chance of some conversation with, and have their pulse felt by, the physician who comes to see them. The latter stretches out his hand inside the curtain; they lay hold of it, kiss it, and softly bite it. Some, out of curiosity, apply it to their breast, which has happened to me several times; but I pretended not to notice, in order to conceal what was passing from the matrons and eunuchs then present, and not arouse their suspicions.'[3]

Naturally a great deal of uninformed rumour and gossip circulated about the supposed hotbed of life in the harem, and Manucci may well here be stretching the facts to contribute to it. He repeats, for example, the detail that the eunuchs refuse to allow into the harem 'radishes, cucumbers, or similar vegetables that I cannot name', a pleasantly salacious titbit which has every appearance of a popular bazaar rumour and which had been enlarged on fifty years before by Tom Coryat, who had written home that 'whatsoever is brought in of virill shape, as instances in reddishes, so great is the jealousie, and so frequent the wickednesse of this people, that they are cut and jagged for fear of converting the same to some unnaturall abuse'.[4]

The way for a man to rise, wrote Bernier, was by 'making valuable presents, every year, to a *visir*, a *Eunuch*, a lady of the *Seraglio*, and to any other person whose influence at court he considers indispensablè'.[5] The more important nobles were allowed to the gate of the harem, where they could tell a eunuch to convey their respects to a certain princess or to carry a message of farewell if they were being posted far away. The princess would then, if she felt well disposed, send a jewel or an ornament as a token of her esteem, and if the present was a valuable one the amir could feel reassured that she would speak warmly on his behalf to the emperor. Equally, if a princess were outside the harem, safely behind the gold

Inlay in white marble at the tomb of Itimad-ud-daulah, Agra

[1] 50, 53; 49, II, 340 [2] 48, 267
[3] 49, II, 353 [4] 49, II, 351; 39, 278
[5] 48, 231

*he Jag Mandir—the island in
the lake at Udaipur where
Shah Jahan stayed, in 1623,
during his rebellion*

mesh of her palanquin or howdah, a noble who wished to pay his respects would dismount at a distance and wait for the procession to approach. Again she would send him a present in the hands of a eunuch, or occasionally, if he had misjudged his standing, order him to be driven off with blows.[1]

The princesses were well acquainted with the character and appearance of the various nobles because there were many court functions which they could watch through their protective grilles, as usual seeing but unseen. From their hidden position they even sometimes exerted direct political pressure during a debate in council. On one occasion Jahangir and his advisers were discussing what should be done about Aziz Koka, the father-in-law of Khusrau. He had worked against Jahangir's succession and more recently had behaved with open insolence in the emperor's presence. Some of the nobles now advised Jahangir that he should be executed, others recommended mercy. Then the voice of Salima, one of Akbar's senior widows, was heard from behind the screen. The women, she said, wanted mercy. Jahangir must come into the harem to hear their case; if not, they would come out to him. He went inside, their voice prevailed and Aziz Koka was pardoned.[2]

Roe gives a delightful account of the feeling of the eyes of unseen women surrounding all important events. When he went to observe the king's departure from Ajmer, Jahangir was sitting in his *jharoka* and two of his wives were in a window to one side, hidden behind a temporary screen of reeds to watch the proceedings. But their curiosity was such that they kept separating the reeds to get a better view. 'I saw first their fingers, and after laying their faces close nowe one eye, now a nother; sometyme I could discerne the full proportion. They were indifferently white, black hayre smoothed up; but if I had had no other light, ther diamonds and pearles had sufficed to show them. When I looked up they retyred, and were so merry that I supposed they laughed at mee.'[3]

The ladies in the harem were also extremely rich, and not only in jewels. Each had a monthly allowance and a mere ex-concubine of Jahangir's, now serving as an attendant on Nur Jahan, was said to be worth a hundred and sixty thousand rupees at the time of a scandal in which she was discovered in sexual play with a eunuch, after which 'another capon that loved her killed him'.[4] The senior ladies received income not only from their allowances and the emperor's lavish presents, but also from *jagirs* assigned to them and even sometimes from such perks as customs dues, and with the help of a staff of financial advisers, mirroring in miniature the emperor's own finance ministry, they engaged in business and commerce. Jahangir's mother owned a large ship which traded on her behalf between Surat and the Red Sea and there was a political crisis in 1614 when it was seized by the Portuguese. Nur Jahan carried on a similar business, specializing in the indigo and cloth trades. And later in the century Shah Jahan's daughter Jahanara continued the tradition and was reported to have made enormous profits.[5] For Nur Jahan to rule from purdah was nothing more than an extension of normal activities within the harem.

Shah Jahan had been still in high favour in 1620 when his forces captured the precipitous fort at Kangra, a task specially allotted to him after others had failed and a victory which particularly pleased Jahangir because his own father had been unable to take it.[6] And in 1618 Jahangir had done his favourite son a very great personal honour; he had decided that his journal for the first twelve years

[1]49, II, 353–4, 220 [2]108, 298–9
[3]40, 282–3
40, 190–1; 41, 387; 11, I, 44–5;
16, I, 10 [5]115, 61–70
[6]16, II, 184–6

of his reign should be written out by scribes as one complete volume, and he solemnly presented to the twenty-six-year-old Shah Jahan the first copy of this manuscript which contained so many glowing eulogies of him. When recording the event in the second volume of his diary Jahangir wrote that he considered Shah Jahan to be 'in all respects the first of my sons' and hoped that the presentation would be a 'cause of good fortune'.[1] It was not. Before the second volume was ended the favourite son had shown his hand in a prolonged rebellion; the hero who had risen in the first volume from Khurram to Shah Jahan sank back in the second to Khurram and finally to Bi-daulat, 'the Wretch'. But it was typical of the immediacy of Jahangir's diary that not a single comment on his son seems to have been altered in retrospect. It would have been hard for the father to eliminate the praise in the first volume, since the first copy was in the hands of his enemy and others had been given to Itimad-ud-daulah and Asaf Khan and even, possibly, sent to distant cities.[2] But the glowing terms continue well into the second volume and were left undisturbed in the later days of disillusion. Jahangir seems indeed to have been unusually willing to let historical records stand uncensored. Both the major histories of Akbar's reign have come down to us full of criticism of his own character and behaviour as crown prince. It would again, admittedly, have been difficult for Jahangir to make alterations in a book already so widely known as Abul Fazl's *Akbar-nama*. But the manuscript of Badauni's history, which abounds in such choice pieces of abuse as that the prince 'boasted of being a ripe grape when he was not even an unripe grape',[3] was not discovered until well into Jahangir's reign, in 1615, and the official censorship appears to have been limited to half-hearted efforts to prevent booksellers from distributing it.[4]

Shah Jahan's drift into rebellion was a gradual one and seems to have been the direct result of Nur Jahan's new policy of pushing him aside. In 1620, when the court was at Lahore, trouble broke out again in the Deccan. The Abyssinian Malik Ambar, commanding the army of the Nizam Shahi kings of Ahmednagar, was giving a brilliant demonstration of the guerilla tactics, both in politics and warfare, which would plague the Moghuls in the Deccan throughout the seventeenth century; like Shivaji after him, he manipulated the powerful rulers of the Deccan in a series of shifting alliances both against each other and against the empire, and then used his nimble Maratha horsemen to pester mercilessly in these mountainous districts the much more powerful but therefore also more unwieldy Moghul armies. Jahangir ordered Shah Jahan to march south and to subdue the district once again, but the prince was noticeably reluctant to set out. There were many reasons. He knew the near impossibility of the task, and having already three years ago received the highest honours for apparently solving the problem it was hardly attractive to undertake it all over again. Jahangir's health was now much worse than before, and on the earlier expedition he had moved the court down to Mandu; to campaign in the Deccan while the ailing emperor was nearly a thousand miles away at Lahore, with a known inclination to move whenever possible even further north to Kashmir, must have seemed almost suicidal absenteeism from the centre of affairs. And it may already have been noticeable that Nur Jahan, far from furthering the prince's cause at court, was now actively beginning to work against him.

Shah Jahan's device for protecting himself was to insist on being allowed to take with him his elder brother Khusrau, whom he undoubtedly saw as his chief rival. This pitiful figure, who had now been a prisoner, half blind, at his father's court for some thirteen years, did nevertheless have a considerable following and popularity—partly because of his obvious misfortune, partly because he seems to have had a genuine charm and intelligence, but also because the many nobles who were irked by the dominance of Nur Jahan saw in him their natural candidate for the succession. Nur Jahan's own allegiance was changing, but not—although there had been rumours to that effect—towards Khusrau. With her new plans for Shahriyar she may well have welcomed the prospect of one of his rivals falling into the clutches of another, and Jahangir gave his permission for the transfer of Khusrau to Shah Jahan's care, though some later said only in a fit of drunkenness. It was the last the emperor was to see of either of his sons.[5]

Shah Jahan once again achieved a rapid success in the Deccan, though only in the sense that he was quickly able to frighten his enemies into a treaty which temporarily subdued but far from suppressed them. His achievement brought him the usual honours and presents, but was followed in August 1621 by the news that Jahangir was once again seriously ill. Shah Jahan's response seems to have been to kill his captive brother. Jahangir merely noted in his diary the curt information 'At this time a report came from Khurram that Khusrau, on the 8th. of this month, had died of the disease of colic pains, and gone to the mercy of God', but the evidence suggests conclusively that the colic was at the very least induced by Shah Jahan.[6] The future emperor would murder another brother before finding himself securely on the throne, so establishing a family tradition which would stain Moghul history throughout the dynasty's decline but which, though common enough among their contemporaries, had been conspicuously lacking in the first century of their rule.

The immediate sequence of events which led to open rebellion by Shah Jahan began with the ominous news from the west that Shah Abbas was marching to take Kandahar, the rich trading post on the caravan route to and from India which was a permanent bone of contention between Persia and the Moghuls. Jahangir planned to mobilize a huge army to meet this threat, and in March 1622 Shah Jahan was ordered to come with his troops from the Deccan to join it. He replied that he preferred to wait out the rainy season at Mandu, and then would only come on receiving confirmation that he would be in sole command of the army, with the province of the Punjab also under his control in his rear. Having in the last eighteen months built up a reasonable power base in the south, he was unwilling to relinquish it and to be sent equally far away to the west, unless he could be sure of sufficient strength to march for the throne if Jahangir died and Nur Jahan placed Shahriyar upon it. His worst suspicions seemed to be confirmed at this period by the gradual transfer of his *jagirs* to Shahriyar, culminating even in Hissar Firoz, the traditional *jagir* of the heir apparent which had so significantly been conferred on the young Shah Jahan fourteen years before.[7] Nur Jahan was easily able to persuade Jahangir that the reply about Kandahar was evidence of incipient rebellion, and a strong reprimand was sent to the prince, forbidding him personally to come into his father's presence but ordering him to dispatch his troops immediately for Kandahar. Shah Jahan, alarmed, sent an ambassador with his apologies but Jahangir refused to listen to him. The next news to reach court was that the prince, clearly convinced by now that compliance would harm his cause as much as rebellion, was marching north from Mandu towards Agra in

[1] 16, II, 27 [2] 16, II, 37, 27
[3] 13, II, 391–2 [4] 125, 274
[5] 64, 331–3; 65, 26–7
16, II, 228; 64, 336–9; 65, 35
[7] 64, 354

the hope of seizing the imperial treasure, which was about to be moved to Lahore for the war effort against Kandahar.[1] Jahangir himself now marched south, being forced to divert his attention from Kandahar, which had meanwhile fallen to the Persians, and complaining to his diary: 'What shall I say of my own sufferings? In pain and weakness, in a warm atmosphere that is extremely unsuited to my health, I must still ride and be active, and in this state must proceed against such an undutiful son.'[2] From now on he felt too ill to write his own diary, but entrusted the factual parts to an assistant and added his own personal comments by dictation.

The nominal command of the army against his rebel brother was given to Parwiz. But the real leader of the imperial forces was Mahabat Khan, a talented general who was to play a most surprising role in the later years of Jahangir's reign. He had been a close friend of Jahangir's since the emperor's boyhood, but in recent years his outspoken opposition to the influence of Nur Jahan had led to a series of commands in the most distant outposts. Now the crisis in the empire required his skills, and he was recalled. For nearly three years he and Parwiz pursued Shah Jahan in a great loop of several thousand miles, down through Rajasthan and into the Deccan, eastwards and up again through Orissa to Bengal, back along the Ganges towards Agra and then once more down to the Deccan. Whenever there was a battle or skirmish Shah Jahan had the worse of it, but he was too nimble for the pursuing army and it proved impossible to pin him down. He was accompanied throughout by his wife and children, and their quest for allies brought them into strange new alliances with old enemies. Sharing now a common antagonism to the imperial power of the Moghuls, Shah Jahan briefly joined forces with his old rival in the Deccan, Malik Ambar. And he was also entertained for four months at Udaipur in 1623 by Karan Singh, the prince of Mewar whom he had brought so triumphantly to do homage at his father's court nine years before. Karan Singh, who was now the Rana of Mewar, lodged his fugitive guest in the Gul Mahal, a domed pavilion which had only recently been completed on the beautiful island of Jag Mandir in the lake at Udaipur[3] (Plate 33, p. 164).

Late in 1625 Shah Jahan's flight had come more than full circle and he was for the second time taking refuge in the Deccan. It was clear that stalemate had been reached, and he sued for peace. In spite of the weakness of his position, he was offered surprisingly lenient terms. He was to surrender two fortresses which he had captured, and was to send his two young sons Dara Shukoh and Aurangzeb as hostages to court. He himself would be made governor of the Balaghat, a remote district in modern Madhya Pradesh. The leniency of the terms perhaps reflected Nur Jahan's worry that this long pursuit was beginning to defeat her purpose by concentrating too much power in the hands of Parwiz and Mahabat Khan. Shah Jahan accepted the terms gratefully, and when in early March 1626 the imperial messenger delivered the firman, which was sent by Nur Jahan on behalf of Jahangir, he prostrated himself before it and placed it on his head as a mark of respect. The two princes Dara Shukoh, aged ten, and Aurangzeb, aged eight, bitter enemies of the future, travelled together to the court with lavish gifts for the emperor. They were placed in the care of Nur Jahan—an alarming prospect considering the political situation, but Shah Jahan, like Humayun with the infant Akbar, seems to have been able to rely on a family tradition that no harm would come to them. He himself was too cautious to set foot within the frontiers of the empire, so instead of taking up his governorship in the Balaghat he withdrew to Nasik.[4]

To undermine the power of Mahabat Khan, Nur Jahan had already arranged for him to be replaced as adviser to Parwiz and to be sent as governor to far away Bengal, and at the same time she laid serious accusations against him of dishonesty in his handling of state funds. But the general's reaction to pressure of this sort was, like Shah Jahan's, an aggressive one, and for a brief while he proved a very much more successful rebel than the prince. Ostensibly to give an account of himself, he set out for Lahore and came up with the court in March 1626 when it was encamped on the east bank of the River Jhelum on its way towards Kabul, but rather to the alarm of the royal entourage he arrived with a force of five thousand Rajputs. In spite of this show of force, peaceful so far, he was sent a scornful message forbidding him to attend the court until summoned; and Asaf Khan was so imprudent as to take the main body of the imperial army over the river, leaving the royal tents only lightly guarded on the east bank. At this point Mahabat Khan struck, reasoning that if Nur Jahan and Asaf Khan had been able to rule through the person of the emperor, there was no reason why he should not do the same. He placed two thousand Rajputs at the end of the bridge of boats to prevent anyone crossing back from the west bank, and then rode into the royal encampment.[5]

Mutamid Khan, the scribe who had continued Jahangir's diary when the emperor had found himself too weak to do so, was with the household that day and has left an eye-witness account. Surrounded by a cloud of dust in the dry midsummer plain Mahabat Khan rode into the camp with about two hundred Rajputs on foot, carrying spears and shields. They were trying to get into the bathroom where they expected to find the emperor, and were tearing down the boards which surrounded it, when Jahangir came out of another door. Mahabat Khan persuaded him to mount the royal stallion and to accompany him back to his own tents. Later—so that the crowd could more easily see that the emperor appeared to be going of his own free will—he asked him to transfer to the howdah of an elephant, with all of which Jahangir complied. They arrived safely at Mahabat Khan's tents, and the abduction seemed a total success, until it occurred to Mahabat Khan that it had been most unwise of him to overlook Nur Jahan and Shahriyar. So he persuaded the emperor to accompany him back again in solemn procession to the camp to collect his family. But both wife and son had vanished. The Rajputs at the bridge had not been asked to prevent anyone crossing from east to west, and Nur Jahan had slipped over in disguise, accompanied by one of her eunuchs, to join her brother on the other side. Horrified at the loss of Jahangir, the brother and sister launched the following morning a most ill-considered attack across the river and were soundly beaten and dispersed. Nur Jahan then gave herself up to rejoin her husband, but Asaf Khan escaped with undignified haste to the safety of the great fort built by Akbar at Attock—where he was soon persuaded to surrender when Mahabat Khan reached the fort with Jahangir and Nur Jahan peacefully in his camp. And in this form, with the emperor and his all-powerful wife and brother-in-law under the control of one of their generals, the royal camp continued—like some hollow parody of its former self—its interrupted journey to Kabul.[6]

[1]6, II, 234–9, 246–7; **64**, 351–4
[2]**16**, II, 248 [3]**81**, 127–8
[4]**64**, 394; **65**, 52 [5]**64**, 396–414
[6]**16A**, 420–28

It is hard to see where Mahabat Khan thought this success could lead him or how long it could last, particularly since he allowed his royal guests considerable freedom, but he contrived to remain in command of the situation for a few months and when it came to an end it did so, amazingly, with very little upheaval. Nur Jahan had quietly been building up her support in the camp, but had encouraged Jahangir to comply with everything which Mahabat Khan ordered so that he might believe that his unorthodox position was becoming accepted. On the way back from Kabul, when the camp was near Rohtas, Nur Jahan was ready. Jahangir announced that he wished to review her forces, and he asked Mahabat Khan to march on a few miles so that the two parts of the army should not fall to quarrelling on the occasion of this big parade. That he and Nur Jahan could arrange such a parade and make such a request demonstrates that the situation was one which Mahabat Khan could never have controlled for long; and that he not only accepted the suggestion, but marched the few miles and then carried straight on at a speed that could only be interpreted as flight, shows that he knew his hour had come. Troops were sent in pursuit, but failed to catch him. The very oddity of each part of this saga in the closing months of the sick emperor's life suggests that Mahabat Khan had no clear object which he was trying to attain, no prearranged plan that he was following; finding Jahangir unprotected he had improvised his bold act of kidnapping, finding himself in control he had improvised the rather lax system by which he had imposed his will, and finding himself at a disadvantage again he had improvised his hurried departure. It had been the strangest of interludes, but it is a tribute to the good sense of those caught up in it that it began, continued and ended with comparatively little melodrama or bloodshed.[1]

Mahabat Khan headed south and was soon entering an alliance with Shah Jahan (there was hardly a pair of opponents in this reign of shifting allegiances who did not sooner or later find themselves shoulder to shoulder), but the emperor turned north to the only place where he now could find any real comfort from his illnesses. For several years he had made an almost annual journey to Kashmir, which from his earliest visits with his father had been his favourite province. He had found it a natural paradise but he and his court had done much to make it an artificial one too: the Moghul gardens which are one of the main glories of Srinagar are the direct result of his enthusiasm.

The distinguishing feature of a Moghul garden is the water which falls from terrace to terrace, slithering down marble inclines gouged with scallops to make it splutter and spurt, curving over a ledge like a sheet of clear ice, plunging into the ground to gush and sprinkle from fountains below, or resting in a deeper pool on its way round some elegant pavilion reached only by the low stone bridges which seem to float on its surface. Ideally a spring was used to provide the water supply, but if there was none the Moghuls were prepared to make other arrangements; in one garden near Agra thirty-two pairs of bullocks were permanently at work raising water from wells to keep the fountains playing.[2] Kashmir provided sloping hillsides and a plentiful supply of water after the winter snows, all in the most majestic natural setting.

The two great gardens at Srinigar, the Shalimar Bagh and the Nishat Bagh, have the expanse of the lake in front of them and craggy hills, still snow-capped in spring, immediately behind. The Shalimar Bagh, built by Jahangir, is distin-

In Shah Jahan's Shalimar Bagh at Lahore, a garden complex of marble pavilions waterfalls, fountains, bridg and thrones

[1] 16A, 429–31 [2] 16, II, 75–6

guished by a series of summer pavilions standing on elegantly carved black pillars (Plate 34, opposite), surrounded by pools with seats in them which can only be reached by stepping stones. The nearby Nishat Bagh relies more on the natural beauty of its site, tumbling down from hillside to lake in a series of terraces adorned with the huge *chenar* or plane trees of Kashmir; it was built by Asaf Khan, and Jahangir expressed slightly pained surprise that a mere subject should create anything so splendid. Some forty miles further south, at Vernag, is the most dramatic example of a spring tamed for the use of a Moghul garden. The River Bihat has its source here, welling up in a broad clear pool some forty-two feet deep (according to Jahangir's careful measurement) and of a lovely turquoise blue. Jahangir built an octagonal series of small domed pavilions around the pool, and when they were completed he gave a party there, offering his guests alcohol and some fine peaches which had been brought by runners from Kabul for the occasion. The pool is full of large fish, and Jahangir and Nur Jahan put gold rings in the noses of some of them. When François Bernier visited Vernag forty years later he found that the largest still wore their gold rings. Their descendants, unadorned, can be seen there today[1] (Plate 24, p. 123).

But this year, 1627, even Kashmir could do little to help the emperor. His asthma grew ever more oppressive; he lost his appetite; and, though he lasted out the summer, the autumn journey south towards Lahore proved too much for him. He still did his best to amuse himself with sport, and he had arranged a day's sedentary hunting in which beaters were to drive deer towards where he sat with his musket resting on a wall. Unfortunately one of the hunt servants fell from a precipice and was killed, and Jahangir, in whose presence violent death had at other times been a fairly common occurrence, was profoundly disturbed by this accident. He took it as a glimpse of the angel of death arriving for himself. He had no more rest and was even unable to swallow a glass of wine he had called for, a fact which deeply impressed those around him with the seriousness of his condition. Three days after the hunting accident, on October 28, 1627, he died.[2]

It was undoubtedly a weakness in Jahangir that he was so easily influenced by others—indeed the strange months when he continued to rule the empire while himself the captive of Mahabat Khan can be seen merely as the logical extension, the *reductio ad absurdum*, of his many years on the throne with Nur Jahan pulling the strings from behind the scenes. But it should be added that the disorders in the empire towards the end of his reign were not directly the result of his abrogating of power, but were inherent in the problem of succession under the Moghul system, or, as a European put it, arose 'from the want of good laws, concerning the Title of Birthright'.[3] It had been one of the greatest strokes of good fortune for the Moghul dynasty that two successive emperors, Akbar and Jahangir, came to the throne with no strong rivals among their relations and that their two reigns spanned the seventy years during which the empire was established. The death of every subsequent Great Moghul would be accompanied by upheavals even more disruptive than the rebellion of Jahangir's favourite son.

Disturbances darkened the last five years of his reign, but during the previous twelve Nur Jahan and her faction had been equally powerful, in a period when the empire was on the whole well governed and was in a state of unusual calm. In all respects Akbar's policies were continued, and if there were an error due perhaps to the diffusing of power at the top, it was that good policies were carried

One of the black pillars in Jahangir's Shalimar Bagh at Srinagar

OVERLEAF *A detail of the extensive mid-17th-century tile-work along the outer wall of the fort at Lahore*

[1] 16, II, 141–2, 170, 173–4; 48, 414; 35, 119–131
[2] 16A, 435; 17, 5; 64, 432–3
[3] 52, 233–4

The hunting lodge and tank built by Jahangir at Sheikhupura in memory of a favourite deer

out with too little energy. Jahangir's diary is full of his ideas for promoting social justice and administrative efficiency, and in most of them he tries to follow or outdo the liberal ideas of his father,[1] but he was less successful in putting them into effect. Akbar had made at least a dent in the great bulk of official corruption, and under his officers reserves of cash were steadily built up to give an underlying strength to the empire; under Jahangir corruption increased again and the reserves declined.[2]

The memory of his father dominated Jahangir the emperor as much as Akbar himself had dominated Salim the crown prince. He never tasted a new fruit without wishing his father were alive to share his pleasure; his greatest joy in subduing Udaipur or taking the fort of Kangra was that his father had been unable to do so; he deliberately received with favour the disciples of Akbar's religion, recounted with approval in his diary the principles of the *din-i-Ilahi* and the need to 'follow the rule of universal peace with regard to religions', and continued Akbar's Thursday evening discussions.[3] He encouraged the Jesuits at least as much as Akbar, and his favourite holy man was a Hindu ascetic named Jadrup whom he loved to visit whenever possible for long discussions in the 'narrow and dark hole' cut into a hillside where the hermit lived without mat or fire and naked except for his loincloth.[4] But Jahangir's religious attitudes were largely matters of impulse where Akbar's had been of policy. His tolerance of other religions derived from the receptive quality of his mind, but a shock of aesthetic disgust could well make him behave quite inconsistently—as when at the lake of Pushkar, a holy place to the Hindus, he was deeply offended by the sight of an idol, a 'form cut out of black stone, which from the neck above was in the shape of a pig's head, and the rest of the body was like that of a man'. So he ordered his followers to 'break that hideous form' and throw it into the water, and for good measure disposed too of the local belief that there was no bottom to the lake by establishing it to be 'nowhere deeper than 12 cubits'.[5]

As a measure of the extent to which Jahangir's religious position appeared to his contemporaries to be a direct continuation of his father's, it is interesting that Roe describes him in words which read as if written about Akbar: 'His religione is of his owne invention; for hee envyes Mahomett, and wisely sees noe reason why hee should not bee as great a prophett as hee, and therfore proffesseth him selfe soe . . . hee hath found many disciples that flatter or follow him.' And Roe adds that 'all sorts of religions are wellcome and free, for the King is of none'.[6]

Jahangir's abiding vice was his addiction to alcohol and opium, a family failing of which he was far from being the most extreme case—his brothers Murad and Daniyal had both died of drink before Jahangir inherited, and in 1626 his son Parwiz went the same way, leaving Shah Jahan and Shahriyar the only two princes alive to contend the succession. But Jahangir was undoubtedly the most addicted of the reigning emperors. In his diary he describes with characteristic frankness his own case history as an alcoholic; from the first sweet cup of yellow wine at the age of seventeen he progressed until wine ceased to affect him, he then changed to arrack and, when that too lost its power, to double-distilled spirits of which in his late twenties he was consuming twenty cups a day. But he had the strength of character to pay heed to a doctor's advice that this course would lead to death within six months, and he gradually reduced his daily ration to six cups of a mixture two parts wine and one part arrack, a level to which he claims to

g. **16**, I, 1, 7, 47, 82, 150–1, 157, 168, 417, and II, 50–2, 170
[2]118, 126 [3]16, I, 350, 37–8, 61, 20–1
, I, 355–6, and II, 49, 52, 104–5
[5]16, I, 254–5 [6]40, 270–1

have kept for the rest of his life. It was backed up by a daily allowance of opium of the weight of fourteen berries.[1]

Jahangir could be monstrously unpredictable and cruel—particularly under the influence of alcohol, as when he gave instructions one evening for his companions to drink with him, forgot the next morning that he had done so and punished the less powerful among them most brutally for having indulged them-selves[2]—but for the most part he was unusually mild and he is described in European accounts as 'gentle, soft and good of disposition' or 'gentle and debonaire'.[3] Roe was highly impressed by the courtesy which he always received from Jahangir; and the emperor's considerable charm can be seen again and again in the ambassador's pages, as for example when Jahangir ends a diplomatic discussion about whether he should present a portrait of himself to Roe or through Roe to James I with the observation 'Your King doth not desier one, but you doe: therefore yow shall have it.'[4] And he is certainly the warmest, the most emotional of the Great Moghuls; his responses to the death of one grandchild and to the miraculous escape from a high fall of another would rank as touching passages in any diary;[5] and if his feelings at times spilled over into the rankest sentimentality, as in the vast drinking tank for animals built at Sheikhupura in memory of a favourite deer, we can at least enjoy the resulting architecture (Plate 36, p. 176). Perhaps Edward Terry left the most convincing and concise statement of his character: 'Now for the disposition of that King, it ever seemed unto me to be compared of extremes; for sometimes he was barbarously cruel, and at other times he would seem to be exceeding fair and gentle.'[6]

Events moved fast in the royal camp after the emperor's death. Asaf Khan now showed his hand with unexpected forcefulness and diplomatic skill, and for once his sister Nur Jahan was outwitted. Since neither Shah Jahan nor Shahriyar was with the royal camp, he persuaded a majority of the nobles to join him in pro-

Jahangir with a portrait of his father, c. 1605; and with a picture of the Virgin Mary, 17th century

claiming as emperor Dawar Bakhsh, the young son of Khusrau who was brought from confinement to receive this honour. This purely tactical move meant that Shahriyar who was at Lahore, some thousand miles nearer than Shah Jahan in the Deccan, would now have to fight as a usurper against the imperial forces instead of being able to mobilize them around himself against Shah Jahan. The luckless Shahriyar had been with the camp in Kashmir until recently, and Shah Jahan's succession would have been more problematical if his rival had been at Nur Jahan's side when the emperor died. But Shahriyar had developed a form of leprosy which caused all his hair to fall out, including even his whiskers, eyebrows and eyelashes; embarrassed at his appearance, and advised that he ought to seek the warmer air of the Punjab just as his father was seeking the cooler air of Kashmir, he had left the royal party during the summer and had moved back to Lahore. Here he now received a hasty message sent from Nur Jahan to mobilize — virtually her last political action, as Asaf Khan immediately confined her to her quarters and removed from her care the two sons of Shah Jahan, Dara Shukoh and Aurangzeb. Shahriyar seized the imperial treasure at Lahore and used it to gather together a large but inexperienced army with which to meet the imperial forces, proceeding south under Asaf Khan and Dawar Bakhsh. Shahriyar's impromptu mercenaries stood little chance against the professional soldiers under Asaf Khan when they faced them within three miles of Lahore, and a few days later the poor bald Shahriyar was himself winkled out of his hiding-place in the fort. Asaf Khan imprisoned him, and soon gave orders for him to be blinded.[7]

Immediately after Jahangir's death Asaf Khan had sent word to Shah Jahan, and a message was now received from the prince, on his way north with Mahabat Khan towards Agra, 'to the effect that it would be well if Dawar Bakhsh, the son, and [Shahriyar] the useless brother of Khusrau, and the two sons of Daniyal, were all sent out of the world'. Asaf Khan duly arranged for the murder of the brother, two nephews and two male cousins of the new emperor. Shah Jahan's blood-stained footsteps to the throne were a precedent which would be quoted to him by his own son, Aurangzeb, to justify a similar policy, and which would prove a pattern for events in the royal family throughout the eighteenth century.[8]

On the last day of 1627 Shah Jahan was in his absence proclaimed emperor in Lahore and on January 24, 1628, he completed his journey from the Deccan to Agra and mounted the throne. Of the figures who had dominated court life during the years of Jahangir's illness, Asaf Khan was rewarded with the position of chief minister and Mahabat Khan was appointed governor of Ajmer. Nur Jahan, too positive a character to quibble when her defeat was plain, accepted retirement and a pension of two hundred thousand rupees a year, and occupied herself with building a tomb for her husband at Lahore. It derives in style from the tomb she had built for her father in Agra, and is larger but less distinguished than its predecessor, particularly nowadays since a marble pavilion on its roof was dismantled in the last century.[9] But it does contain some magnificent *pietra dura* work around the sarcophagus. Nur Jahan survived her husband by eighteen years and designed a similar but smaller tomb for herself nearby. Between her tomb and Jahangir's rose that of Asaf Khan. Today a railway line separates her on one side of the tracks from her brother and husband on the other, accurately reflecting the losing and winning alignments in the first of the Moghul wars of succession.

[1]16, I, 8, 307–10 [2]40, 264–6
[3]40, 273, 259 [4]40, 201
[5]16, I, 326–8, and II, 151–3
[6]41, 386 [7]16A, 435–7; 65, 58
[8]16A, 437–8; 19, 356, 367;
71, III, 155

Shah Jahan

The first of the two family tragedies which darkened Shah Jahan's life happened early in his reign. There had been a joyful reunion in February 1628, only a month after he reached Agra, when the two princes Dara Shukoh and Aurangzeb arrived safely from Lahore with Asaf Khan. Neither he nor his queen, Arjumand Banu, who from the time of the coronation was to be known as Mumtaz Mahal, 'Chosen One of the Palace', had seen the two boys since they were sent as hostages to Nur Jahan two years before. For the next eighteen months, apart from one brief expedition to Gwalior, Shah Jahan lived in style at Agra, enjoying with his family an ease and security which had not been theirs for more than six years. But towards the end of 1629 there were the usual troubles in the Deccan, by now the routine gathering place for dissidents from the empire, and in December Shah Jahan once again set out southwards. Mumtaz Mahal accompanied him, just as she always had on his campaigns as a prince. He scored a series of successes against the rebel Khan Jahan, and against the kingdoms of Ahmednagar and Bijapur. But near Burhanpur, on June 7, 1631, Mumtaz Mahal suddenly died in giving birth to her fourteenth child. Of the previous thirteen, four sons and three daughters had survived. The eldest son, Dara Shukoh, had been born in 1615, and the third son, Aurangzeb, on October 23, 1618.[1]

Mumtaz Mahal had been as influential a companion to Shah Jahan as her aunt Nur Jahan to his father, but whereas Nur Jahan's role had been one of dominance hers was essentially a matter of support and advice. He was known to have discussed all state affairs with her, and when state documents had been finally drafted he would send them into the harem for her to affix the royal seal.[2] Her death left a profound gap in his existence; it was said that for two years he lived the life of one in mourning, rejecting all indulgence or ostentation, and going without gorgeous clothes or rich food or music.[3] On the larger stage of public affairs too, there seemed a change. Having been very much a man of action, he from now on preferred to leave the command of expeditions to his sons while he remained at the centre, in Agra or Delhi or Lahore, occupying himself with his other great love, architecture. This may have been pure coincidence, since Mumtaz Mahal's death came at a time when her sons were approaching the age where they would be appointed nominal leaders in military campaigns. Nevertheless the first great building to which the emperor now devoted himself was his monument to his wife, the very name of which is a colloquial abbreviation of hers —the Taj Mahal (Plate 37, p. 185).

Even as a boy of fifteen Shah Jahan had been interested in architecture, and had much impressed his father by immediately remodelling in excellent taste the quarters assigned to him at Kabul.[4] He was to take an active part in the many impressive architectural projects of his reign. For the Taj various designs were submitted to him and modified according to his own suggestions, and the resulting ideas were tried out in the form of wooden models.[5] There has been argument for many decades over which architect should be credited with the final design.

The Taj Mahal from the surrounding fields

Sources (*see* p. 252)
[1]71, I, 2–4; 65, 309–10; 75, 186
[2]115, 41 [3]99, 37 [4]65, 10–11
[5]99, 39

181

For a while it was fashionable to accept the statement of an Augustinian friar, Sebastien Manrique, that it was designed by Geronimo Veroneo, a Venetian goldsmith and jeweller.[1] Manrique was told this by the executor of Veroneo's will, but it is a highly improbable story; it seems likely that Veroneo may well have been called in to advise on minor details of decoration, and in later gossip among his own circle this was sufficient to credit an old friend with the whole design. A slightly stronger contender is a certain Ustad Isa Afandi, about whom nothing is known except that he seems to have come from either Turkey or Shiraz, but who is referred to in later Persian sources as the architect. Yet another candidate is Ustad Ahmad from Lahore. It would seem probable, however, that there was no one architect, but that master masons and other craftsmen translated directly into working models and drawings the ideas of the emperor himself, who had used the various designs submitted to clarify his own thoughts.

The Taj was the logical conclusion and synthesis of several strands which already existed in Moghul architecture. The garden setting, square and divided by stone water-courses, had been brought by Babur from Kabul. The slender flanking minarets had been prefigured in the gateway to Akbar's tomb, as had the pleasures of inlay in white marble in the tomb of Itimad-ud-daulah. And the exterior shape, with its swelling dome above an arched alcove, is a concept which derived originally from Persia but which developed a very individual character in India and achieved its perfection in the Taj. Its growth and decay as a form span roughly a century. In Humayun's tomb, impressive but gawky and commenced in 1564, it is still in the bud; in the graceful lines of the Taj (1632–48) it is in perfect bloom; and in the tomb which Aurangzeb completed for his wife in 1678 at Aurangabad, spindly and almost Gothick but with far more charm than it is usually allowed, it has gone to seed. In a very real sense the only architects of the Taj Mahal are Shah Jahan and the Moghul tradition.

Work began early in 1632 and later in the same year an English traveller, Peter

The Moghul tomb in the bud, in full bloom, and gone to seed—the tomb of Humayun, the Taj Mahal, and the tomb of Dilras Banu at Aurangabad

OPPOSITE *The outer wall of Shah Jahan's new fort at Delhi, with his private quarters above*

[1]46, II, 173

Mundy, found already that 'the buildinge is begun and goes on with excessive labour and cost, prosecuted with extraordinary dilligence, Gold and silver esteemed common metall, and Marble but as ordinary stone';[1] by 1643 the structure was sufficiently complete for the annual memorial service for Mumtaz Mahal to be held there for the first time; and by 1648 the Taj itself was quite finished, though work continued on the subsidiary buildings until 1653.[2]

Meanwhile the emperor was already engaged on other even more extensive projects. The central axis of his empire was the road running from Lahore through Delhi to Agra—a continuous and beautiful avenue of trees for four hundred miles, which Tom Coryat praised most highly after walking its length in twenty days in 1615 and which continued to be admired by European visitors[3]—and during his reign Shah Jahan provided himself with a magnificent marble palace in each of these important cities. To do so he pulled down many of the existing buildings in Akbar's forts at Agra and Lahore. In Delhi, to which he officially transferred his capital from Agra in 1648, he founded yet another entirely new city called Shah-jahanabad (the area known today as Old Delhi, to Sir Edwin Lutyens's New Delhi) and between this new city and the river he built himself a fort, surrounded by a massive red sandstone wall copied from his grandfather's at Agra.

Shah Jahan's buildings have themselves been much altered or demolished at Lahore, but the more important components survive in excellent condition at Delhi; and at Agra the entire complex can still be seen, providing a perfect setting in which to reconstruct the daily routine of the Great Moghul. With the increase of the pomp of empire, and with a marked change from a life spent often in camp to one of almost permanent residence in one of the three main cities, Shah Jahan's day seems to have become even more full of fixed public obligations than Jahangir's or Akbar's.

Shah Jahan woke an hour or so before dawn in his marble apartments on the east side of the Agra fort, overlooking the Jumna towards the spot where, a mile away across the sand banks of the gently curving river, the Taj Mahal was rising. After his ablutions he walked along the series of white terraces and pavilions with gilded Bengali roofs, where various of his women lived (Plate 45, p. 225), and on past the octagonal tower or Saman Burj, private quarters intended for the queen, before turning left up the narrow staircase which leads to perhaps the tiniest mosque in the world—the Mina Masjid, only a few yards square but of the finest white marble, where the emperor said his morning prayers alone. He continued to count his beads until sunrise, when he had to walk only a few paces back to the outer wall of the palace to show himself to the people in the *jharoka-i-darshan*. While the public gazed up at him, he amused himself by looking down at newly captured elephants being paraded in the open space between the fort and the river, or at elephant fights in the same area—the low skirting wall which now partly blocks this space was added by Aurangzeb. From here he went back again, beyond the little mosque, to the first important business of the day in the *diwan-i-am* or hall of public audience.[4]

All the officers of state and everyone else who had business with the court were by now standing in strict order of rank among the pillars of the *diwan-i-am*, and no doubt had been for some time already, awaiting the moment a little before eight when the emperor, to the accompaniment of hidden drums and trumpets, would appear in his throne alcove at the back of the hall. It was to grace this

The Taj Mahal, seen from within its own garden

[1]45, II, 213 [2]92, 160–1; 99, 52 [3]39, 244; 48, 284; 47, I, 78 [4]27, 164–6; 65, 238–40; 85, 17

Shah Jahan holding a turban jewel: by Abul Hassan, 1617. The painting is inscribed in the margin in Shah Jahan's hand 'a good portrait of me in my twenty-fifth year'.

alcove, and to add even greater splendour to this most formal of public appearances, that Shah Jahan commissioned his famous peacock throne, which he moved from here to the similar alcove in the *diwan-i-am* at Delhi after transferring his capital there in 1648. Stone grilles in the wall to either side meant that the ladies could watch any important occasion without being seen. A flight of steps led from the floor of the hall up to the throne, but only one or two very senior officials were allowed to ascend them; when an assassin tried in 1654 to rush up these steps in Delhi he was cut down by attendants before he had set foot beyond the first.[1]

In this public audience appointments were made, reports were received from various departments, dispatches from provincial governors were presented and replied to, horses and special elephants were paraded for inspection. Newsletters surviving from the following reign reveal that even quite minor and intimate details in the lives of the emperor or his chief nobles, such as bleedings that had been administered, purgatives taken, or dreams dreamt, were considered worth reporting and recording in this open court.[2] On Wednesdays the business of the court was devoted to matters of justice (in Jahangir's reign the day had been Tuesday, in Akbar's Thursday).[3] Sentences were rapidly passed on those who had committed serious criminal offences, but there always seemed to be fewer plaintiffs appearing with their problems or to seek redress than Shah Jahan himself hoped.[4] His officials explained that the reason was the excellence of the judicial system throughout the empire, by which the citizen could demand justice in any of four different types of court; at the local level there remained the ancient Hindu arrangement of caste and village *panchayats*, and at each subsequent level there were three separate courts, one for financial and revenue affairs headed in the provinces by the provincial *diwan* or finance minister and in the centre by the chief *diwan*, one for religious affairs headed respectively by the provincial *qazi* and the chief *qazi*, and one for general matters headed by the governor of the province and at the centre by the emperor himself. In practical terms, however, it was hard to decide which case should go to which court since all Muslim law, on secular as well as religious topics, was held to derive from the Koran and from a few long established Koranic commentaries on which the *qazi* and his *ulama* were the acknowledged experts. The explanation given by Shah Jahan's officials for the lack of plaintiffs appearing before him was that anyone dissatisfied with the verdict of a small local court could take his case to the *diwan* or *qazi* or governor of the province, and if still dissatisfied to the chief *diwan* or *qazi* in the capital, and 'with all this care, what cases, except those relating to blood and religion, could become subjects of reference to His Majesty?'[5] The more likely reason was that most plaintiffs who might have benefited from a direct interview with the emperor were laying a complaint against an official, so officialdom blocked their path. And the emperor's court was too alarming a place to venture lightly. Hawkins had described the bevy of officials at the foot of Jahangir's throne: 'Right before the King standeth one of his sheriffes, together with his master hangman, who is accompanied with forty hangmen wearing on their heades a certaine quilted cap, different from all others, with an hatchet on their shoulders; and others with all sorts of whips being there, readie to do what the King commandeth.'[6] And if the emperor ordered punishment it was frequently carried out on the spot.

[1] 47, I, 80; 27, 166–70; 5, 240–4, 317–19 [2] 130, 12–13 [3] 110, 11 [4] 24, 172–3 [5] 24, 173 [6] 35, 115

187

After about two hours in the *diwan-i-am* Shah Jahan withdrew again towards his private quarters, to be joined by his senior advisers in the *diwan-i-khas*, or hall of private audience, on the south side of an open terrace overlooking the river. Here, in contrast to the formal proclamations of the *diwan-i-am*, important matters of state were fully debated and argued out; here foreign ambassadors and important visitors were received and listened to in detail; if a powerful official had to defend himself against complaints, it was here that he did so. This was the effective hub of the empire, and appropriately the two *diwan-i-khas* at Agra and Delhi are the most exquisite of Shah Jahan's administrative buildings, their marble pillars adorned with lovely floral patterns carved in relief or inlaid with semi-precious stones (Plates 40 and 41, pp. 196–7). Here too, in this appropriate setting, recently completed works of art such as paintings or embroidery would be presented for the emperor's inspection, together with plans of new or proposed buildings. Each day's endless parade of animals also continued, but at a more suitably refined level—only such elegant creatures as cheetahs and falcons were presented in these delicate surroundings.[1]

Where one private council, the *ghusl-khana*, seems to have been enough for

The steps up into Shah Jaha diwan-i-khas at Agra

Akbar and Jahangir, Shah Jahan retired from his magnificent *diwan-i-khas* to an even more select session in the Shah Burj, or royal tower, where he was attended only by the princes and by three or four senior officers, each of whom had to leave as soon as his own business was concluded.[2] By the time this most secret council of state was over it was past noon, and Shah Jahan returned again to his own private quarters in the harem, where he had a meal, for which he sat cross-legged on rich carpets ('all their bravery is upon their floors', said Terry on the furnishing of Moghul houses).[3] To protect the carpet large sheets of stitched leather were laid out and covered with white calico cloths, on which would be spread an almost infinite variety of food in gold and silver dishes. Even Terry, dining with a nobleman, found fifty separate dishes in front of him as his own personal selection and made a point of sampling every one.[4]

When Shah Jahan had washed and was ready to eat, eunuchs handed the dishes in turn to two beautiful girls who knelt on either side of him and by whom he was served. The emperor almost invariably ate within the harem and descriptions of the procedure are naturally rare, but the Augustinian friar Sebastien Manrique claims to have observed a banquet at Lahore in 1641 when Shah Jahan was enter-tained by his father-in-law, Asaf Khan. He says that at considerable risk he was smuggled by a eunuch through subterranean passages to a gallery high above the hall, and was instructed to make absolutely no sound, but to withdraw to another room should he become forced to rid himself of 'unrestrainable and importunate phlegm'. This banquet was a family affair and was probably typical of any special occasion within the royal harem. Apart from Asaf Khan and his three guests—the emperor, his son Dara Shukoh and his daughter Jahanara—there was no one present except the ladies of Asaf Khan's harem and his eunuchs, and of course the impertinent Manrique. He says that he watched for four hours and he has left a fascinating description of the rich furnishings, the gold and silver vessels, the ceremonies of ablution, the protocol and processions, the continual music and songs of praise for the emperor's victories, the dancing girls, and the presentation to the guest of honour of three large golden dishes full of jewels.[5] One needs to treat travellers' tales of the time with some caution, since there was a convention of presenting hearsay under the guise of personal experience; but if Manrique concocted this scene from what he had heard he did so with unusual flair, and many of his details seem convincing. The lesser nobles also ate normally within their harems, but they occasionally entertained guests to a meal, similar in form but served exclusively by men, in the front part of their houses. It was to meals of this sort that Europeans, such as Roe and Terry or the Dutch factor at Agra, Francisco Pelsaert, were sometimes invited.[6]

After his midday meal Shah Jahan had a brief siesta and then dealt with any business or problems brought to his attention by his senior ladies or by the officials of the harem. Exactly as if in any other of his courts, except that he was reclining in perfumed air surrounded only by women and eunuchs, the emperor now sat in judgment on harem matters and dispensed large sums in charity for ladies outside the harem, providing dowries for destitute girls or pensions for widows and orphans, news of whose distress had filtered up this feminine grape-vine to the royal ear. Ladies from the harems of the senior nobles often visited the imperial harem, and sometimes stayed being lavishly entertained by the royal princesses for as long as a month.[7]

[1]65, 241–2; 27, 170–2; 20, 95
[2]65, 242; 27, 172 [3]41, 185–6
[4]41, 195–8 [5]46, II, 213–20
40, 209–13; 41, 195–8; 42, 67–8
[7]115, 79; 65, 242–3; 27, 172–3

he white marble style of Shah Jahan's reign—the tomb of Shaikh Salim Chishti at Fatehpur Sikri

By the time Shah Jahan had satisfied the ladies' demands to the best of his financial ability, it was nearly three o'clock and time to take part in public prayers—in Agra at his beautiful white marble Moti Masjid or Pearl Mosque, and in Delhi at the huge Jami Masjid, which he began in 1644. After prayers there was more administrative work in the *diwan-i-khas*, illuminated when necessary by huge chandeliers, and then at about half past seven a final half hour's session in the Shah Burj. After this exhausting day of nearly twelve hours of administration, Shah Jahan retired for supper in the harem with musical accompaniment by his women. By ten o'clock he was in bed. Behind a screen to one side of his chamber were readers chosen for the pleasing tone of their voices, who would soothe him with books of travel, lives of the saints, or history. Above all he loved to hear passages from the *Babur-nama*, the inspiring memoirs of his great-great-grandfather. And this routine was followed every day except Friday, when no court was held.[1]

Provincial governors, generals on campaign, and princes when away from the capital all followed a routine similar to the emperor's, though less elaborate. The French traveller Jean-Baptiste Tavernier visited one evening in 1652 the tent of Mir Jumla, who later became a leading general in the service of the Moghuls but who at the time was commander-in-chief of the army of the king of Golconda, and Tavernier has left a very vivid account of the great man dealing at the end of the day in a highly jumbled and informal manner with precisely the affairs which occupied the emperor in his capital in such high state. Mir Jumla was sitting on a carpet with two secretaries. In the gaps between all his toes and between the fingers of his left hand he held documents and letters, which he took and replaced one by one while dictating replies to his secretaries as well as writing some himself. The secretaries then read the letters back and he affixed his seal, but during these proceedings four criminals were brought to the door of the tent. Mir Jumla paid no attention to them for half an hour, but then had them brought in and after various questions was able to persuade them to confess their crimes, an important condition of Muslim law. After their confession he paid no more attention to them for another hour, during which he continued with his correspondence while a succession of officers 'came to pay their respects with great humility, to whose salute he replied only by an inclination of the head'. By now a meal was about to be served, so he turned his attention to the four prisoners, sentencing one to have his feet and hands cut off and to be left in a field to bleed to death, another to have his stomach slit open and to be thrown into a drain, and the remaining two to have their heads cut off. The sentences were carried out while Tavernier and various of the officers sat down with him to dinner, after which he granted Tavernier an audience and gave him a passport and an escort to accompany him to Golconda.[2]

The kingdom of Golconda was admittedly a more barbarous state than the Moghul empire, and under the Moghuls every death sentence was supposed to be confirmed by the emperor before it could be carried out; but in practice provincial governors and generals often took the law into their own hands.[3] Mir Jumla's administrative evening would have been in essence no different a few years later when he was in the service of the Moghuls, and Tavernier provides us with a rare glimpse of one of the recipients in the field of all the firmans and decrees and letters which flowed from the dignified proceedings in Shah Jahan's *diwan-i-am* and *diwan-i-khas*.

[1] 65, 243; 27, 173–4
[2] 47, I, 218, 233–4
[3] 105, 16; 111, 222

191

The white marble of the Taj and of the emperor's private quarters at Delhi and Agra stands as the peak of Moghul architecture, but it was far from being the only style used in Shah Jahan's reign. The beautiful figurative *kashi* or tile-work, for example, stretching for several hundred yards and to a considerable height along the outer wall of the fort at Lahore, is a most spectacular achievement in a very different vein (Plate 35, pp. 174–5). These Lahore tiles, which were used also at the same period on the nearby mosque of Wazir Khan, are something of an oddity in the development of Moghul art and are often explained as being due to the comparative nearness of the Punjab to Persia; but with their elephants and birds and flowers they are much closer to the spirit of the tiles on the outer wall of the palace of Gwalior than to the abstract decorations of Persian mosques and colleges. Also at Lahore is Shah Jahan's Shalimar Bagh, the best surviving Moghul garden outside Kashmir; it does admittedly use the pleasures of white marble for a spectacular pavilion and waterfall, but one of its most striking features is the huge red wall surrounding the garden, broken only by a variety of little decorative alcoves in the very distinctively Moghul style introduced by Akbar on the gateways of the fort at Agra. Pavilions and wall combined make the Shalimar the most architectural of Moghul gardens, appropriately enough in this most architectural of Moghul reigns. But in spite of these more varied achievements, and although white marble had been used occasionally for both Hindu and Muslim buildings before the Moghul period, the profuse and consistently elegant use of this material by Shah Jahan made it virtually his own architectural trade-mark. And it symbolized perfectly, as no doubt was intended, the opulence of his empire—particularly when supported also by his own prodigious display of jewels.

Terry had described Jahangir as the 'greatest and richest master of precious stones that inhabits the whole earth',[1] and Shah Jahan had far outdone his father. He was so fascinated by jewels, reported Manrique, that even when there appeared before him after the banquet twelve dancing girls with all the allures of 'lascivious and suggestive dress, immodest behaviour and posturing', he hardly raised his eyes to them but continued inspecting the jewels with which he had been presented by Asaf Khan.[2] On his accession he had commissioned his famous peacock throne, surmounted by a canopy held up by twelve emerald pillars, at the top of which were two peacocks on either side of a tree set with rubies, diamonds, emeralds and pearls.[3] His idea of an appropriate present to send to the holy city of Mecca was a huge gem-studded candlestick for the prophet's tomb. It was reported that it would take an expert fourteen years to go through and value all the emperor's personal jewels. And he was himself generally agreed to be a considerable connoisseur of precious stones, able at times to give a more accurate judgment than professional jewellers on the quality of a particular item.[4]

But already the marble and jewels were little more than an empty show. A historian writing in Aurangzeb's reign announced proudly that the imperial revenue had been trebled between the reigns of Akbar and Shah Jahan, but added on the next page, apparently without realizing the implication, that expenditure had in the same period grown fourfold.[5] Shah Jahan did his best to curb the most noticeable form of inflation—the ever increasing number of nobles being awarded higher and higher ranks while maintaining a lower and lower percentage of their official number of troops. Akbar had temporarily cured this same abuse by

The wall decorated with alcoves in the Shalimar Bagh at Lahore

[1] 41, 373 [2] 46, II, 219–20
[3] 17, 45–6; 47, I, 303–5; 80A, 19
[4] 18, 84; 49, II, 21; 47, II, 100–1
[5] 24, 171–2

recognizing it, and by allowing his nobles a personal salary in addition to the allowance for their troops; but the official and actual number of troops maintained had again drifted apart during Jahangir's reign. Shah Jahan tried to repeat his grandfather's remedy by recognizing that nobles need not provide their full official complement of troops but stipulating that certain levels—a third when serving in the noble's own *jagir*, a quarter when elsewhere—would be insisted on.[1] But this provided only a temporary halt in the process, and meanwhile a far deeper ill remained.

The empire had expanded little since the days of Akbar, and the constant attempts to push south into the Deccan were a drain on the exchequer rather than the opposite even though at certain times, as in the campaigns of 1636 to 1637, a considerable amount of treasure did travel north.[2] It was clear, therefore, that more revenue had to be found from the existing territories. Shah Jahan and his finance ministers achieved this not by increasing agricultural produce or en-

OPPOSITE *Shah Jahan kills a lion: cameo, mid-17th century*

OVERLEAF LEFT *Pillars inlaid with semi-precious stones in the* diwan-i-khas *at Agra*

OVERLEAF RIGHT *Inlay of semi-precious stones in the* diwan-i-khas *at Delhi*

couraging trade, even if they paid lip-service to these ideals, but by condoning ever more oppressive methods of tax-collection by the *jagirdars*. However, the demands of the revenue department, reinforced by the illegal extortions of increasingly unscrupulous provincial governors and officials, had a self-defeating effect.[3] There was, throughout the seventeenth century, a steady flight of peasants from the land. And, apart from the nobles and one or two very rich merchants, anyone who could gather together a little wealth found it safer to hide it rather than to use it or enjoy it at the risk of attracting predators.[4] In an economic sense even Shah Jahan's peacock throne, although ostensibly designed to show rather than to hide his jewels, represented precisely the same form of stagnation as the tradesman's hidden gold. From the financiers of ancient Rome to modern tourists astounded at the gold bangles of even the poorest classes, observers of India have continually expressed amazement at the way precious metals flow into the country and become to all intents and purposes, and in some cases literally, buried there. And never was this lavish stagnation more evident than in the reign of Shah Jahan. When the Moghul empire appeared to be achieving ever greater splendours, it was already past its prime.

The sectarian hostilities too were beginning to reassert themselves, inevitably perhaps in a country where a majority of one religion had been ruled for so long

LEFT *Jewel merchants with their wares: detail from the border of a portrait, mid-17 century*

[1]117, 270; 107, 36–8 [2]71, I, 50
[3]117, 283–305; 114, 319–30
[4]48, 225–6

194

The 17th-century palace of
Bir Singh Deo at Orchha

by a minority of another. Shah Jahan was three-quarters Hindu—both his mother and grandmother had been Rajput princesses, so that of his four grand-parents only the free-thinking Akbar was by birth a Muslim—but unlike his father and grandfather he himself married no Hindu wives. His mother, known as Manmati or Jogat Gosawini, had died in 1619.[1] So, as emperor, there was no personal Hindu influence in his life. And after the death of his Shia wife, Mumtaz Mahal, the orthodox Sunnis of the *ulama*, who had been so outraged by the religious eclecticism of the two previous reigns, at last seemed to have an emperor virtually to themselves. Undoubtedly the pressures of the orthodox Muslim hierarchy at court had built up to such a point that in the short term it was by now politically advantageous for Shah Jahan to side with them, but the natural severity of his own character suggests that it also suited his inclination to do so. Certainly two of his earliest decrees to have been motivated by religious considerations were both of a specifically self-denying nature. He forbad the custom instituted by his father of courtiers' wearing the emperor's portait in minature in their turbans, and he abolished a form of obeisance sometimes used in Akbar's and Jahangir's courts which involved the placing of the forehead on the ground, as during prayers, which therefore smacked of worshipping the emperor as God; his son Aurangzeb would go even further and abolish, for the same reason, the morning appearance to the people in the *jharoka*.[2]

In 1632 Shah Jahan took the more aggressively orthodox step of ordering the demolition of all newly built Hindu temples throughout the empire. A great many were duly destroyed, particularly in Benares, and the emperor followed this with a ban on any further building; a long tradition of Muslim jurists, although not Mohammed himself, had decreed that *dhimmis* or unbelievers should be allowed to retain existing places of worship but not to build new ones.[3] But the later years of the reign proved less rather than more repressive. Shah Jahan himself enjoyed and patronized Hindu music and poetry—indeed his reign became something of a Golden Age for literature in Hindi—and at one point he even reprimanded his eagerly orthodox son Aurangzeb for pursuing an anti-Hindu policy.[4] It may be that the ageing emperor was increasingly affected by the ideas of his eldest and favourite son, Dara Shukoh, an aesthete who followed the religious eclecticism of Akbar and Jahangir and was a keen student of Hindu mystical philosophy, translating himself the Upanishads into Persian and reaching in his own beliefs a form of pantheism which naturally horrified orthodox Muslims; he even presented a stone railing to the important Hindu temple built recently by Bir Singh Deo in Mathura.[5] The order to demolish the temples in 1632 was therefore something of an anomaly in Shah Jahan's reign. But it proved, when taken with the activities for which Prince Aurangzeb had to be rebuked, an ominous foretaste of what was to follow.

The same period as the order to demolish the temples had seen also the first full-scale Moghul assault on the Christians. The Portuguese had long established a trading settlement at Hooghly, a harbour a little to the north-west of modern Calcutta on one of the many waterways which make up the mouths of the Ganges, but they supplemented their trading activities with piracy, with the selling of local people into slavery or their forcible conversion to Christianity, and with levies on passing ships which did considerable commercial harm to the Moghul port of Satgaon further upstream. In addition the Portuguese idolatry was

[1]16, II, 84 [2]24, 170; 26, 284;
65, 244–5, 293
[3]17, 36; 65, 293–4; 45, II, 178;
69, 106–39
[4]126, 94; 65, 259; 130, 21
[5]69, 38–48; 124, 261

offensive in the spirit of the early 1630s. In this respect the Protestantism of the English and Dutch was a considerable advantage—the Portuguese, wrote a Muslim historian, 'had set up figures in wood, paint and wax, with great gaudiness, but in the churches of the English, who are also Christians, there are no figures set up as idols'.[1] To add to their sins the Portuguese of Hooghly had made an eternal enemy of Shah Jahan by refusing to help him when he was in Bengal during his rebellion against his father, and later by foolishly omitting to send him a present on his accession.

Shah Jahan therefore ordered Qasim Khan, his governor in Bengal, to suppress these troublesome foreigners. Qasim Khan built a barricade of boats across the river to prevent the Portuguese, far better seamen than the Moghuls, from escaping by water, after which he set about besieging the town. Three mines were sunk below the fortifications, two of which were discovered by the Portuguese and were neutralized; but the third reached its position under a large building without being detected. The Moghul army then massed opposite the mine, which had the intended effect of drawing the maximum number of Portuguese to this part of the town, whereupon the mine was blown causing enormous loss of life. After directing a Moghul fire-raft against the barricade many of the Portuguese did

Shah Jahan entertaining a party of mullahs: a double-page painting, c. *1650*

200

succeed in escaping by water, but about four thousand—mainly women and children—were taken captive and were marched on an arduous journey of eleven months to Agra, where the survivors were paraded before Shah Jahan, who explained the benefits of becoming converted to Islam. The majority were by now in no mood to disagree. The men were found employment in Agra, and the women and children were distributed among various harems, but a few, including the priests, suffered imprisonment, whippings and parades through the bazaar being pelted with filth, rather than deny their faith. But as with the anti-Hindu policy of the same period, things soon cooled down again. Within a year or two the Jesuits of Agra, who had themselves been persecuted in the early 1630s, were sufficiently back in favour to be able to help their imprisoned brethren from Hooghly; and by the end of the decade, in spite of the demolition of their church, the Christian community at Agra was almost back to normal.[2]

All the other important campaigns in Shah Jahan's reign were entrusted to the royal princes. In 1635 the emperor's third son Aurangzeb, still only sixteen, was appointed to command an army to put down Jhujhar Singh, the rebellious Raja of Orchha. Jhujhar Singh's father had been Bir Singh Deo, the raja who had obliged Jahangir by assassinating Abul Fazl and who had as a result become a special favourite during Jahangir's reign, growing steadily in power and wealth and building himself magnificent palaces at Orchha and Datia in his territory about a hundred miles to the south of Agra. Bir Singh Deo had died a few months before Jahangir, and his son—rich and powerful in his inheritance, and with no special loyalty to the new emperor—began to assume an unwelcome air of independence. By 1635 a punitive campaign against him seemed inevitable, and the Moghul army under Aurangzeb cut its way slowly through the densely wooded country towards Orchha, a beautiful palace on a monkey-infested promontory formed by a great loop in the Betwa river (Plate 42, p. 198). Jhujhar Singh continually harassed the Moghul army but was not strong enough to halt it, and he was pursued far south until he was murdered for reward by wild Gond tribesmen. By the end of 1635 Shah Jahan was able to lodge in his precocious son's first conquest, the palace of Orchha, near which he arranged for the demolition of the massive temple of Bir Singh Deo and for the erection of a mosque on its site.[3]

Shah Jahan joined Aurangzeb a little to the south of Orchha, and together they moved on into the Deccan, of which Aurangzeb was now appointed viceroy. The emperor wanted to bring some order to this long-troubled district before installing his son in such a difficult position, and his presence with a huge army rapidly persuaded Bijapur to sign a treaty and Golconda to offer a token submission. By July 1636 Shah Jahan was marching north again. During the next eight years Aurangzeb remained viceroy of the Deccan, a post which he filled very successfully, being promoted to a rank of twelve thousand *zat* and seven thousand *sawar* in 1637, and then to fifteen and nine thousand respectively in 1639. It is therefore all the more surprising to find him dismissed in disgrace from his position in 1644, and stripped of his rank and allowance.[4]

His dismissal occurred during a visit to Agra in the summer of 1644 to see his elder sister Jahanara, who had acted as first lady since the death of their mother Mumtaz Mahal in 1631 but who had almost died in March of this year when her fine muslin dress caught fire from a candle. Two of her maids who had thrown themselves on her to stifle the blaze had died of their wounds, and Jahanara

[1] 26, 212
[2] 17, 31–5, 42–3; 26, 211–12; 46, II, 323–33, 392–424; 48, 176–7; 122, 99–106; 65, 104–113
[3] 17, 6–7, 47–50; 71, I, 14–31; 65, 79–91 [4] 71, I, 54, 76

herself was on the verge of death for four months, during which Shah Jahan made only the briefest of appearances at his daily durbar in the *diwan-i-am* and spent much of his time praying at her bedside. Her brothers returned from their various posts to be with her, and it was in this charged atmosphere that Aurangzeb was dismissed and humiliated. But by the autumn she was safe. In late November a great palace celebration was held for her recovery, and among the general bestowing of honours and gifts Aurangzeb was reinstated in his former rank.[1]

The reason for Aurangzeb's sudden dismissal seems to have been the bitter hostility between his eldest brother Dara Shukoh and himself, a crucial factor in the remaining years of Shah Jahan's reign which now made itself felt for the first time. Such a clash was probably inevitable between the two most talented and ambitious of the princes, but it was accentuated by the policy of Shah Jahan, who seems to have learnt the wrong historical lesson from his own experiences during Jahangir's reign. Having himself been a favourite prince who rose against his father, his first concern was to prevent his own favourite son, Dara Shukoh, from rising against himself; and since he knew that his own motive for rebellion had been that he felt threatened, far away from court, by those trying to influence his father against him, his solution had been to keep Dara almost permanently at his side, lavishing him with affection and wealth and honours in the civilized and secure setting of the court.[2] But the conclusion that the emperor should have derived from his own youth was that a prince sent out to gain valuable experience in command and warfare, as he himself had been, becomes the one best able to return at the head of an army to seize the crown. It was not Dara Shukoh busy with his books in Agra but the ill-favoured Aurangzeb, campaigning in the Deccan, who was being allowed to conform to the blueprint of Shah Jahan's own success.

Meanwhile everything seemed to favour Dara Shukoh, and it appears to have been Aurangzeb's complaints against his brother's influence which led to his own dismissal in the summer of 1644. After his return to favour on the crest of Jahanara's return to health, Aurangzeb was sent in early 1645 to govern Gujarat and his efficiency in controlling this turbulent province so impressed Shah Jahan that he appointed him, late in 1646, to take over the campaign in distant Transoxiana in which his younger brother, Murad Bakhsh, had recently failed. Shah Jahan, avid reader of the *Babur-nama*, was dazzled like all his house by the distant and elusive prize of Samarkand, and local disturbances in Transoxiana encouraged him to hope that he might be able to step in and succeed where Babur had failed. It was to prove a vain and expensive hope. In the spring of 1646 Murad Bakhsh, aged twenty-two, led an army of fifty thousand into Badakhshan, two hundred miles to the north-east of Kabul, but after a summer of successful campaigning both he and his army wanted to return to the more congenial winter climate of India without reaching their goal of Samarkand—the very problem in reverse which Babur had faced a century before when his followers wanted to withdraw from India's summer back to Kabul. When Shah Jahan ordered his son to remain in Badakhshan, Murad deserted his army and proceeded back to Lahore alone. It was at this point that Shah Jahan, depriving Murad of his rank and forbidding him the court, appointed Aurangzeb to take command of the stranded army. He reached it in the spring of 1647. Another summer of more arduous campaigning followed, in which the Moghul army could make no permanent gains against the guerilla tactics of the Uzbegs, although it was during this summer that Aurangzeb made the most memorable contribution to his future reputation for piety and courage; the hour of evening prayer happened to fall while a battle was raging, and the prince calmly spread out his carpet and knelt, unarmed, in the middle of the fray. In the autumn, almost too late, he led his army back through the snowy passes of the Hindu Kush to Kabul, losing a great number of men and animals on the way. The two-year campaign had cost the Moghul treasury a fortune and had achieved almost nothing. It was the final and most expensive tribute to the magic of Samarkand, and the first of Shah Jahan's serious reverses as emperor.[3]

hah Jahan presenting a jewel to Dara Shukoh: c. 1650

Another series of disasters soon followed, in connection with that perennial problem on the western border, Kandahar. Shah Abbas had captured Kandahar in 1623, while Jahangir's attention was diverted by Shah Jahan's rebellion, but in 1638 the Persian governor had for reasons of his own entered into secret negotiations with the Moghuls and had delivered the fort again into their hands. Now, in February 1649, Shah Abbas II repeated his great-grandfather's triumph of twenty-six years before, by successfully besieging and recapturing Kandahar. Aurangzeb was summoned from Multan, where he was now governor, to lead a large army to recover the fort, but he was sent ill-equipped for a siege and could make no headway against the superior artillery of the Persians, who were invariably more advanced than the Moghuls in the science of gunnery, being regularly subjected to many a useful lesson by their Turkish neighbours to the west. Aurangzeb had to retire at the end of the year with nothing achieved. But Kandahar, by now a traditional bone of contention between the two rival empires, had become a matter of prestige and Shah Jahan immediately set about preparing a more effective force to recover it. The new army was ready in 1652—the long gap had been taken up with casting large cannon, laying in supplies, safe-guarding the lines of communication back to Kabul and other such preparations. Again Aurangzeb was put in command, but this time his power was more nominal. A system of runners carrying messages in four days to and from Kabul, where Shah Jahan was waiting, meant that the emperor himself would be taking all important decisions. Once again the siege was a complete failure. The Moghuls had their large guns now, but failed to put them to much effect; they were not sufficiently well made to stand prolonged use without cracking, and several even exploded after being packed by inexperienced gunners with too powerful a charge.

By the end of the summer Aurangzeb was in disgrace, much to the delight of Dara's followers, and he was now sent all the way back to the Deccan. But he was to get his revenge the following year. Dara had boasted that he could take Kandahar in a week. Making one of his rare appearances in the field, he set off in 1653 with an even larger and better equipped force, with the added benefit of hired European gunners. In spite of these advantages, he failed just as dismally. The Moghuls were never again to occupy Kandahar and their triple failure in an undertaking on which so much had been staked was a severe blow to their military prestige. From now on there was always a fear of an invasion by Persia. It did not come for another eighty years, but it was a constant threat.[4]

Aurangzeb arrived back in the Deccan in early 1653 and in this second vice-royalty he showed more effectively than ever before his great administrative and military talents. But it was also a period, through none of his own doing, of increasing estrangement between himself and his father—or, in more real terms,

[1] 71, I, 72–9 [2] 18A, 128–9
[3] 17, 70–2; 18, 76–83;
71, I, 83–114; 65, 182–209
[4] 17, 64; 18, 87–96, 99–102;
71, I, 126–69; 65, 223–36

between himself and the brother at his father's side. An almost constant stream of reprimands came south from Delhi; the prince's requests for more money to administer areas impoverished by decades of warfare were interpreted as personal greed; his recommendations were repeatedly disregarded, or his appointments countermanded; he was accused of appropriating as presents to himself objects which should have been classed as tribute to the empire, and even of keeping the best mangoes from Shah Jahan's favourite Deccani tree before forwarding the crop to the imperial table; he and his family were conspicuously neglected in the regular presentations of lavish gifts; his supposed incompetence was openly discussed at court, and at one point his brother Shah Shuja was asked if he would take on this viceroyalty in which Aurangzeb was said to have failed. Indicative of the widening rift was the fact that in his previous spell of eight years in the Deccan the prince was four times invited north on visits to his father's court, but in this five years, from 1653 to 1658, not once. Most offensive of all, both of Aurangzeb's major campaigns in the Deccan—against the two immensely rich kingdoms of Golconda and Bijapur—were halted by orders of Shah Jahan, after direct intervention by Dara Shukoh and his faction, in each case just before a fully successful conclusion seemed almost certain.[1]

The pretext for Aurangzeb's invasion of Golconda in 1656 had been the interesting case of Mir Jumla, a Persian adventurer—son of an oil merchant of Isfahan—who like many of his countrymen had come to the Shia kingdoms of the Deccan to seek his fortune. He rapidly amassed considerable wealth as a diamond merchant and his great administrative abilities led to his becoming chief minister for Abdullah Qutb Shah, the king of Golconda, in whose service he conquered the Karnatic, a district made unusually desirable by its famous diamond mines. As merchant turned conqueror Mir Jumla ensured, hardly surprisingly, that his personal wealth and power kept pace with his prestige, and the feeble Abdullah tried too late to curb him. Mir Jumla's response was to offer his services and his possessions, among which he now listed the Karnatic, to the Moghuls. Abdullah retaliated by imprisoning Mir Jumla's son, whereupon Aurangzeb— after Shah Jahan had hurriedly agreed to appoint Mir Jumla and his son to Moghul commands of five thousand and two thousand respectively—marched in January 1656 to rescue one of his own.[2]

Aurangzeb sent ahead his own son Mohammed Sultan with a body of light cavalry, and at his approach Abdullah withdrew from his rich new city of Hyderabad into the old and almost impregnable fort of Golconda, five miles to the west. As a result Mohammed Sultan was able to secure, almost unopposed, the vast amounts of treasure in the city. In February Aurangzeb arrived with his larger army and settled down to besiege Golconda. He was by now intent on nothing less than the complete surrender of this wealthy kingdom, but meanwhile Dara Shukoh had been bribed by Abdullah's agents at Delhi to plead their case with the emperor. The bribe in itself can have done no more than sweeten his own inclination, since a major military achievement by Aurangzeb would have been highly unwelcome, and he now persuaded Shah Jahan to accept Golconda's offer of a heavy indemnity in return for peace. An order was sent to Aurangzeb to withdraw, accompanied by a public reprimand for the admittedly rather cavalier way in which he had delayed or suppressed various earlier orders of Shah Jahan's. By May 17 Aurangzeb and Mohammed Sultan, now married to the

The fort of Golconda   king of Golconda's daughter, were back in Aurangabad, the city which Aurangzeb had founded as his viceregal capital in the Deccan.[3]

Mir Jumla was meanwhile on his way to Delhi, and his prestige was such that
almost immediately after his arrival in July 1656 he was made chief minister of the
Moghul empire. It was said that Shah Jahan wanted this famous general to set off
on his behalf in yet another attempt to recapture Kandahar, which by now had
come to enjoy the almost symbolic status of Samarkand, but that the extraordinary
profusion of Deccani jewels presented by Mir Jumla whetted the emperor's
appetite for further adventures in the south—a policy which Mir Jumla and
Aurangzeb, already firm allies, were united in recommending.[4]

An opportunity occurred in November of that year with the death of Mohammed Adil Shah, the king of Bijapur, with whom Shah Jahan had been on friendly
terms since their treaty of 1636. The crowning of an heir who was still a boy, and
rumoured by some to be not even his father's son, led to the usual troubled waters
in which it was customary for neighbours to fish. Mir Jumla marched south to
join Aurangzeb, and they set out together from Aurangabad on January 18, 1657.
Bijapur was an infinitely stronger kingdom than Golconda, but even so steady
progress was made. In March the strong fort of Bidar was taken after a siege,

[1]71, I, 170–205; 69, 16
[2]71, I, 216–28 [3]71, I, 228–41
[4]49, I, 237–8; 48, 22–3

followed by that of Kaliani at the end of July. But then the story of Golconda repeated itself. Envoys from Bijapur had been in touch with Dara at Delhi, and he again needed little persuasion to press an early peace on Shah Jahan. Soon the order reached Aurangzeb and Mir Jumla to accept another fat indemnity offered by Bijapur and to withdraw. It is hard to know how long Aurangzeb would have continued to tolerate such constant thwarting of his enterprise, but now a new disaster befell the empire which brought matters to a very sudden head.[1]

In September Shah Jahan fell seriously ill with a retention of urine lasting three days and bringing him, it was feared, to the verge of death. Gossip had always credited him with a very active sex life, and it was immediately rumoured that the cause had been an over-stringent aphrodisiac intended to revive his flagging powers.[2] His failure to make his daily appearances in public led, as always on such occasions, to the belief that he was dead, and Dara aggravated the situation by clamping down on any news and even preventing letters from being sent to his three brothers in their various provincial commands. The princes, hearing through their own agents the simple fact of their father's illness but receiving no official information from the centre, naturally assumed that the decisive moment had arrived and that Dara, as one of Aurangzeb's historians later put it, was 'endeavouring with the scissors of greediness to cut the robes of the Imperial dignity into a shape suited to his unworthy person'.[3] In fact Shah Jahan was recovering, but he had indeed handed over the reigns of government to Dara, raising him to the unprecedented rank of sixty thousand. Shah Jahan himself now retired to Agra—either because he still thought he was about to die, or because he was glad of the occasion to install his favourite in power.[4]

Each of Dara's three younger brothers now began feverish preparations to march on Delhi and contest the throne. Shah Shuja, who had been governing Bengal, immediately proclaimed himself emperor. Striking coins and having the *khutba* read in the proud new name he had chosen, Abul Fauz Nasiruddin Mohammed, Timur III, Alexander II, Shah Shuja Bahadur Ghazi, he marched west to prove himself indeed a second Alexander and a third Tamburlaine.[5] Murad Bakhsh, now governor of Gujarat, murdered the finance minister appointed by Shah Jahan to supervise his affairs and plundered the city of Surat to provide himself with funds for a larger army. Then he too proclaimed himself emperor. Aurangzeb, characteristically more canny, showed no outward signs of rebellion but busied himself with gathering the very useful indemnity promised recently by Bijapur. But Dara knew that he was the greatest danger, and his first step to curb him was to order Mir Jumla to return with his army to Delhi, hoping thus to separate the two allies of the Deccan campaigns and to provide himself at the centre with some much needed support and a general of genius. Mir Jumla's position was an awkward one since the presence of his family in Delhi made open disloyalty dangerous, but Aurangzeb solved his dilemma by arresting him, with Mir Jumla's tacit consent, on some trumped up charge and then confining him to the fortress of Daulatabad until such time as they could cooperate more openly. Meanwhile he would be able to use Mir Jumla's army for his own ends, and he was in contact also with Murad, whom he was easily able to persuade that they would do best to combine their efforts. Indeed there is evidence that ever since 1652 there had been a secret pact between all three younger brothers to combine against Dara when an opportunity presented itself.[6]

A lady in a palace painting a portrait of her lover: an illustration to a raga, or musical mode, 18th century

[1] 18A, 128–30; 71, I, 259–80
[2] 49, I, 240; 48, 24–5 [3] 22, 178
[4] 23, 143; 69, 49–51; 71, I, 302–1 [?]
[5] 71, II, 130
[6] 26, 214–18; 49, I, 249–51;
48, 28–30; 19, 292–7;
71, I, 318–32; 69, 12–13

Inside the Pearl Mosque built by Aurangzeb in the fort at Delhi

It was believed later that Aurangzeb assured Murad that his own ambitions were for nothing more than a hermit's cell but that as a devout Muslim he could not tolerate the free-thinking Dara as emperor and therefore would help his brother to the throne before retiring to a life of contemplation; and it was said that in their private conversations they referred to each other as *Hazrat-ji* ('Your Holiness') and *Padishah-ji* ('Your Highness').[1] The story is probably little more than a later tribute to the subtlety and dissimulation with which Aurangzeb conducted his campaign. As a public image at this dangerous time it might well have pleased Aurangzeb, but it was certainly not possible that Murad could have believed such a charade. He and Aurangzeb had between them a written agreement whereby Murad would have Afghanistan, Kashmir, the Punjab and Sind, and Aurangzeb the rest of the empire with presumably, since his share included Delhi and Agra, the title of emperor. And the booty captured after their first victory together was shared out in the proportion of two-thirds to Aurangzeb and one-third to Murad—hardly an appropriate division, in either case, between a holy man and His Highness.[2]

Since Shah Shuja had been the first to march, the main body of the imperial army was sent against him under Dara's son, Suleiman Shukoh, together with the Rajput general Jai Singh of Amber. They met Shuja near Benares at Bahadurpur in February 1658 and routed him, after which he fled back down the Ganges to Monghyr. Meanwhile another army, also headed by a Rajput, Jaswant Singh of Marwar, had marched south to prevent Aurangzeb and Murad from joining their forces but had failed to do so and had been defeated by Aurangzeb in command of the combined army at Dharmat on April 15, 1658. Throughout these adventures all three rebellious princes had been sending letters to their father to assure him that their one concern was to visit him dutifully in his illness, and that they were approaching with their armies only because they feared that Dara was hostile to them. Shah Jahan himself, now completely recovered and haunted perhaps by his own painful memories of three years of family war, wanted to meet with the princes and solve the matter in council. But Dara, after the defeat at Dharmat, was determined to march out himself and to win his crown in the field.[3]

Niccolo Manucci, an Italian gunner and spare-time doctor in Dara's service, has left an eye-witness account of the departure of the crown prince's magnificent army from Agra on May 18, 1658. Ranks of elephants in shining armour covered the plain together with squadrons of cavalry, their neat rows of lance-heads gleaming in the sun, and at the centre Dara himself resplendent on his high elephant. But Manucci himself admits that the majority of soldiers in this vast army 'were not very warlike; they were butchers, barbers, blacksmiths, carpenters, tailors, and such-like'.[4] The problem was that the best of the army was away in the east with Suleiman Shukoh. Dara's plan was to march south from Agra to Dholpur and there hold all the fords over the River Chambal, to prevent Aurangzeb and Murad from crossing until Suleiman Shukoh should arrive with the better trained forces.[5]

But Aurangzeb was not prepared to wait. After a rapid and arduous journey some forty miles downstream, he reached at Bhadaur a little-known ford which was still unguarded and so established himself on Dara's bank of the river. Dara, for reasons partly astrological, partly vainglorious, decided not to send a rapid detachment under one of his commanders to attack Aurangzeb's forces while

[1]48, 26–7, 32–3; 71, II, 88–9
[2]19, 400–5; 71, II, 22–3; 69, 78–80
[3]26, 219–20; 71, II, 129–36; 69, 52–7, 86
[4]49, I, 266–7 [5]71, II, 35

they were exhausted, but withdrew towards Agra to avoid being outflanked by Aurangzeb's continuing march northwards. On May 29 the two armies met on the sandy plain of Samugarh, eight miles to the east of Agra. The sun was so hot that men's skin was blistered by their armour, and the battle was fiercely enough contested for Murad to have been at one point completely surrounded, and to have suffered several arrow wounds; the howdah from which he fought was said to be studded as thick with arrows as a porcupine, and for several generations it was kept as an honourable curiosity in the fort at Delhi. But the inexperience of Dara and his forces perhaps made defeat inevitable, and Dara himself seems to have given way to panic when the tide began to turn against him.[1]

Dara fled back the eight miles to Agra, arriving in a state of extreme exhaustion at about nine in the evening. He felt too ashamed to see his father, in spite of a kindly message asking him to do so, and remained shut away in his own house until about three in the morning, when he was ready to slip out of the city, with his wife, children and grandchildren and a few choice slave girls on elephants, and a small retinue of close followers on horseback. Shah Jahan sent mules laden with gold coins to accompany him, and gave orders for the governor of Delhi to open the treasury to his fugitive son. Before dawn they were well on their way, and as it turned out their haste was not unjustified. Manucci, galloping out of Agra the following day to join up with Dara on the road to Delhi, found his way already blocked by squadrons of Aurangzeb's troops and had to turn back.[2]

The victorious army arrived outside the unwalled city of Agra on June 1, to the terror of the inhabitants. Shah Jahan, from the safety of the fort, sent a friendly delegation to invite Aurangzeb to visit him. He also presented his son with a famous sword called *Alamgir*, which meant 'Seizer of the Universe' (one better than *Jahangir*, 'Seizer of the World'), and which Aurangzeb later adopted as his official title as emperor. Aurangzeb sent his son Mohammed Sultan to reply to Shah Jahan that he would only visit him if he would make over the fort to Aurangzeb's officers. Shah Jahan naturally declined to do so and Aurangzeb, markedly dropping the pretence that he had only come to be by his father's bedside, proceeded to lay siege to the old emperor. From now on Aurangzeb's self-justification was the argument that Dara had effectively deposed Shah Jahan in order to spread Hinduism and suppress the true religion and that Aurangzeb felt it his duty, as a pious Muslim, to safeguard the kingdom and the faith; if Shah Jahan would not cooperate, he must accept the consequences. Aurangzeb mounted one cannon on the terrace of the Friday Mosque, and another in Dara's house, but they made little impression on Akbar's magnificent red sandstone wall. But then one of Aurangzeb's advisers suggested the much simpler device of seizing the gate to the Jumna through which all the water needed for the fort was carried. The wells, disused for years, were bitter and Shah Jahan was able to tolerate what they could produce for only three days before he capitulated. The gates were opened to Aurangzeb's officers, who seized the treasure and armaments accumulated over three prosperous generations.[3]

Shah Jahan was confined to his marble quarters in the harem, with his grandson Mohammed Sultan as his guard and only contact with the outside world. Three days later Aurangzeb expressed a new willingness to visit his father and indeed was on his way to do so, riding an elephant in a triumphal procession towards the fort, when a rumour reached him that Shah Jahan's Tartar slave-girls, who still

[1] 26, 223–5; 49, I, 269–82; 71, II, 35–64; 69, 56–7
[2] 26, 225; 48, 57–8; 49, I, 288–90; 71, II, 65–9
[3] 26, 225–6; 48, 60–2; 71, II, 74–82; 69, 60–6

attended the emperor in the harem, were preparing to murder him as he approached his father. Aurangzeb appeared reluctant to turn tail at such a petticoat threat, but more tangible evidence of his father's attitude arrived at almost the same moment. Aurangzeb was shown a letter from Shah Jahan to Dara which had been intercepted, and in which the emperor promised his eldest son his continued support. Aurangzeb turned his elephant and went back to his lodgings in Dara's house, where he continued with his preparations to pursue his elder brother.[1]

Aurangzeb set out north towards Delhi on June 13. His army was followed, reluctantly it seemed, and at a distance, by that of Murad. With so much already achieved, the inevitable power struggle between the two princes was beginning to make itself felt. Murad's jealousy had certainly increased during the days at Agra, where Aurangzeb had played such a stirring role while he, still suffering from his wounds at Samugarh, had had to sit idly by. On the other hand it was Murad's army, where pay was higher and discipline more lax, which was growing faster than Aurangzeb's. The two princes became more and more wary of each other. It was rumoured that Murad was being urged to invite Aurangzeb to his tent and there overpower him, but in the event it was Murad himself who was first lulled into accepting hospitality from his brother, at Mathura, on June 25.[2] It was a convivial evening in Aurangzeb's tent. Aurangzeb himself was too pious a Muslim to touch alcohol but Murad, as was intended, drank far too much. He felt drowsy and accepted Aurangzeb's suggestion that he should rest. A slave-girl was sent in to 'shampoo' him (the original Hindi word means 'massage') and soothed by her hands he fell asleep, safely guarded by his own eunuch, Shahbaz, who stood fully armed in the tent. But Shahbaz was induced by a trick to step out of the tent and was silently strangled. When Murad woke he found himself stripped of his arms and surrounded. That same night four elephants, each bearing an identical closed howdah, left the camp—one to each of the four points of the compass, to complicate any attempt at pursuit and rescue. The one heading north carried Murad to his confinement in the fort of Salimgarh, on an island in the Jumna at Delhi. That done, Aurangzeb—a wise eight months after his impetuous brothers—proclaimed himself emperor.[3]

The view from the private quarters
in the fort at Agra to the Taj Mahal

[1] **71**, II, 82
[2] **48**, 66; **49**, I, 263; **69**, 83
[3] **26**, 228–9; **48**, 66–9; **49**, I, 302–5; **71**, II, 86–97; **69**, 83–4

Aurangzeb

It was typical of Aurangzeb that even when finally proclaiming himself emperor he wasted no time on those conventional symbols of power, so attractive to most rulers, the striking of coins and the reading of the *khutba* in his name. Instead, after a brief ceremony in a garden outside Delhi on July 21, 1658, at an hour said by the astrologers to be most auspicious, he hurried on in pursuit of his elder brother.[1]

With Shah Shuja gathering fresh forces to the east and Dara Shukoh doing the same to the west, the new emperor was to spend the next few months shuttling back and forth to protect what he had seized. Of the two brothers, Dara presented the more urgent threat. He had collected vast wealth from the imperial treasury at Delhi, but confronted by Aurangzeb's rapid advance from Agra he had withdrawn from the city before being able to translate his wealth into an effective army. The same pattern was to repeat itself at Lahore. Here he found more treasure, together with all the armaments which Shah Jahan had been gathering for another attempt on Kandahar, but within a month or so of his arrival in the city Aurangzeb was again dangerously near and Dara decided on flight. With his wealth and armaments he set off down river towards Sind. Whether he remembered it or not, he was following precisely the route taken by Humayun when, in very similar circumstances, he fled from the newly proclaimed Sher Shah. Dara's journey was to be at least as painful as his great-great-grandfather's, and its outcome far worse. He had by now a large, though not particularly experienced army, and it was widely expected that around Multan he would make a stand against his brother. But Aurangzeb was a master of underhand diplomacy; genuine letters were smuggled into the camp to seduce the disloyal among Dara's generals, while false letters fell neatly into Dara's own hands to cast doubts on the loyal. The resulting mood of uncertainty, combined with Dara's seeming reluctance ever to face his brother's veteran army, led to snowballing desertion; and with an ever dwindling band Dara fled on southwards. Like Sher Shah after chasing Humayun this far into the wilderness, Aurangzeb now turned back to attend to affairs at the centre and sent his generals in pursuit of the prince.[2]

It was now late September 1658 and Shah Shuja was on the march again, up the Ganges from Bengal towards Agra, on the pretext, much more plausible now than when used by Aurangzeb, of coming to rescue his father.[3] Aurangzeb summoned Mir Jumla from his formal imprisonment at Daulatabad, and in early January 1659 the two old allies from the campaigns in the Deccan joined forces again to the west of Benares, a few days before confronting Shah Shuja at Khajwah. Unlike Aurangzeb's earlier battles in this war of succession, the odds were this time greatly in his favour, yet it turned out to be the narrowest of victories. Part of the reason was the slippery allegiance of Jaswant Singh, the Raja of Manwar, whose turncoat talents became an increasingly important factor in the affairs of this period. It was he whom Aurangzeb had defeated at Dharmat, when Jaswant Singh was fighting for Dara, and it was said that his flight from that battlefield was

Aurangzeb at his prayers:
c. 1660

Sources (*see* p. 252) [1]**26**, 229
[2]**26**, 227–32; **71**, II, 101–28
[3]**71**, II, 138

215

considered in Rajasthan to have brought such dishonour on his house that his wife, a princess from Udaipur, refused him her bed until he should redeem his good name.[1] His subsequent actions seem unlikely to have restored her favours. Fighting now for Aurangzeb, and being placed in command of the right wing, he sent a note to Shah Shuja that in the night before the battle he would turn to attack the imperial army in the rear and that Shuja, hearing uproar in the enemy camp, should attack simultaneously from the front. It was Aurangzeb's reputation for deviousness which saved him. Shah Shuja assumed that Jaswant Singh's letter was part of a trap set by Aurangzeb, and—even when he heard the sudden clamour in the camp—did nothing. Even so Jaswant Singh's treachery was a considerable disaster. He and his Rajputs captured a large proportion of the army's baggage and animals and made off with them towards Rajasthan; and in the confusion, among rumours of a sudden defeat, a great many others fled. But Aurangzeb's own exemplary calm—as usual he finished his prayers before responding to the crisis—prevented the panic from spreading, and when day dawned his forces still outnumbered Shah Shuja's by almost two to one. By subtle and unexpected tactics Shah Shuja very nearly reversed the odds, but by the end of the day numbers told; and once again, as at Bahadurpur eleven months before, he fled back down the Ganges. Aurangzeb sent Mir Jumla to pursue him, but after a campaign lasting fifteen months the prince escaped with his family by boat to Arakan, an area to the east of Bengal inhabited by barbarous pirates. And by the pirates, it seems, they were murdered. But nothing certain was ever heard of their fate, in spite of considerable efforts by Aurangzeb to establish that they were dead and so rid himself of recurrent rumours that Shah Shuja was about to return and claim the throne.[2]

Dara Shukoh had turned east from Sind to struggle through the parched salt desert of the Rann of Kutch; then, finding the governor of Ahmedabad sympathetic to his cause, he had built up yet another army in Gujarat. He now received an invitation from the volatile Jaswant Singh to march north again towards Agra, where the raja would join him with his army of twenty thousand Rajputs for a combined march on Agra to rescue Shah Jahan. Dara readily agreed, but Aurangzeb—wisely putting expediency before his indignation at Jaswant Singh's treachery at Khajwah—wrote offering Jaswant a pardon and new honours if he returned to loyalty, but threatening otherwise severe retribution. The raja sized up the armies of the rival brothers, and once again changed sides. So Dara found himself near Ajmer without the promised support from the Rajputs, and with Aurangzeb approaching rapidly from the north. He prepared a strong defensive position in the narrow pass of Deorai, with Ajmer behind him, and waited. His position was extremely well chosen but after three days of hard fighting Aurangzeb's forces overran it. Night had fallen on the third day, March 14, 1659, when Dara fled south, unnoticed, with his son Sipihr Shukoh and only a dozen followers. Fearing this conclusion, Dara had given orders that his women should wait all that day, ready mounted on elephants with his treasure, by the banks of the Ana Sagar—a lake outside Ajmer—where he would join them. But in his haste he missed even this vital rendezvous. Not till they were surrounded by the unmistakable chaos of an army in flight did the eunuchs and the women decide to leave without him. Plundered by their own servants and by local villagers, they somehow straggled their way south and miraculously succeeded in joining Dara

Decorative marble arches by Shah Jahan on the bank of the Ana Sagar, where Dara's women waited, ready for flight

[1] 67, 244
[2] 26, 232–6, 249–51, 253–4; 48, 111–12; 49, I, 369–78; 71, II, 138–61, 237–88

and his party before reaching their refuge at Ahmedabad. Their condition is vividly described by François Bernier, the French physician who met them on the road and who accompanied them for a few days. 'The cords of the *kanates*, or screens, which concealed his wife and women (for he was without even a tent) were fastened to the wheels of the carriage, wherein I reposed. This may appear almost incredible to those who know how extremely jealous the great men of *Hindoustan* are of their wives, and I mention the circumstance as a proof of the low condition to which the fortunes of the Prince were reduced.'[1]

At this point the next blow fell. News came that the authorities in Ahmedabad no longer thought it wise to open their gates to the fugitives. 'The shrieks of the females drew tears from every eye', wrote Bernier, and Dara walked about 'more dead than alive . . . stopping and consulting even the commonest soldier'.[2] There was no option but another journey across the blazing Rann of Kutch. Dara almost persuaded Bernier to accompany him on this dangerous journey, as one of his wives had a bad wound in the leg, but of the three oxen pulling Bernier's cart two were dead or dying and the third too exhausted to move, and the prince seemed unable to provide even an animal to carry the doctor. Niccolo Manucci, the other European in Dara's train who was keeping a journal of events, had joined up with the prince again in Lahore but had been left in Sind, in charge of

LEFT *A mid-17th-century Moghul portrait said to be of François Bernier; and* BELOW *a portrait of Manucci painted for him in India, c. 1700*

the artillery defending the fort of Bhakkar on an island in the Indus on Dara's behalf.[3]

Pursued by a Moghul army under Jai Singh, Dara struggled back again across the desert to Sind. He planned, like Humayun at the same point in his flight, to continue westwards and to seek refuge in Persia, but more disasters intervened. His favourite wife Nadira Banu (to whom he gave the beautiful Dara Shukoh album now in the India Office library, which bears an inscription to her in his own hand) died of dysentery and exhaustion. Dara depleted his own dwindling force in order to send her body under escort north to Lahore, since her last wish was to be buried in Hindustan; and now a local chieftain, Malik Jiwan, dealt the final blow to the defenceless prince. Dara Shukoh had saved Malik Jiwan some years before, when Shah Jahan had sentenced him to be trampled by elephants and Dara had personally interceded for his life, so he not unnaturally expected some assistance in return. But after a few days of hospitality the chieftain seized his valuable guest and sent word to Aurangzeb. Dara, together with his fifteen-year-old son Sipihr Shukoh, was sent in a closed howdah to Delhi. They arrived outside the city on August 23, 1659, and on August 29 Aurangzeb arranged for them to be paraded, clothed in rags, on a meagre female elephant covered in dirt, through the streets and bazaar of Shah Jahan's new city. Behind them sat a slave with drawn sword, ready to slash off their heads at any sign of rescue.[4]

Delhi had known Dara as the magnificent heir apparent, and had last seen him arming himself with all the treasure of the capital against his upstart brother. The aim of this public humiliation was to underline the absolute power of the new emperor, and to deflate in advance any pretenders who might appear and claim

[1]18A, 131; **48**, 85–90; **49**, I, 339–44; **71**, II, 166–92 [2]48, 90 [3]26, 242–3; **48**, 90–1; **49**, I, 309, 318–19, 345–6; **71**, II, 192–3 [4]26, 243–5; **48**, 91–8; **49**, I, 345–55; **71**, II, 193–212

to be Dara Shukoh. But the policy nearly misfired. Dara had been extremely popular. His had been the pleasant role of a rich prince, without direct personal responsibility, whose voice could sometimes modify the stern justice of the emperor, as indeed it had on behalf of Malik Jiwan. Bernier sat on horseback in the most crowded part of the bazaar that day, and he records that on all sides people were weeping and wailing for their favourite, hardly Aurangzeb's intention.[1] No one dared to make a show of force, but the feelings of the crowd were vented on Malik Jiwan, who was pelted with stones and dung. This demonstration in itself made Dara's death a desirable expediency for Aurangzeb, but there is evidence in his letters that from the very start of the war of succession his intention had been to annihilate his elder brother.[2] However, a debate in the *diwan-i-khas* now gave a legalistic gloss to a foregone conclusion. The discussion centred on Dara's religious unorthodoxy, which had been Aurangzeb's justification for his own actions throughout. Aurangzeb had long ago branded his brother 'chief of the atheists' and had claimed that he had 'not even the resemblance of a Musulman',[3] but the value of the debate was that the decision to execute him could be presented as having been forced on the emperor, who encouraged the rumour that he personally had only wanted the prince driven out of India.[4] A party of slaves entered Dara's prison on August 30 and hacked his head from his body. The body was again paraded through the bazaar on an elephant, before being buried in the tomb of Humayun, and the head was sent to Aurangzeb. Bazaar rumour soon provided a gory tale of his having jabbed his brother's face three times with a sword and then sent it to Shah Jahan in Agra, to be placed on the old man's table in a covered dish.[5] But the account rings more true to character which describes Aurangzeb as saying, when being presented with the head, 'As I did not look at this infidel's face during his lifetime, I have no wish to do so now.'[6]

Meanwhile Murad had been transferred in January 1659 from Salimgarh to the state prison in the fort at Gwalior, where Aurangzeb now arranged for his death by means of a private vendetta. Under Muslim law murder is a matter in which not the state but the relatives of the victim demand justice. Murad had killed his finance minister before proclaiming himself emperor. The man's second son—the eldest declined—was now encouraged to demand justice, and after the pious emperor had informed the official *qazi* or judge at Gwalior that such a case must be tried without fear or favour according to holy law, there was regrettably no orthodox alternative but to allow retribution to take its course. The avenging son refused any financial compensation for his father's life, so on December 4, 1661, the prince was executed in the plaintiff's presence. But to emphasize his distaste for such vindictiveness, Aurangzeb then rewarded the eldest son for refusing to enforce the vendetta.[7]

The emperor's slightly more distant relatives were no safer. Dara's son, Suleiman Shukoh, had taken refuge with a raja in the hills of the Punjab, but diplomacy and threats persuaded the raja to release his guest. He followed Murad to Gwalior, where he was given *pousta*—an extract of poppies which the prisoner had to drink each day before being allowed any food, and which had the usefully undramatic effect of very gradually weakening the body and mind until life finally drained away after several months. Suleiman Shukoh's two sons had been murdered for Aurangzeb in the fort of Bhakkar in Sind at the time of Dara's capture.[8]

Sipihr Shukoh, the young son who had been paraded through Delhi with Dara, was a little more fortunate. After the murder of his father he was sent to Gwalior. But, while his uncle Murad Bakhsh and his elder brother Suleiman Shukoh were killed there, he was spared. After fourteen years imprisonment in the fort Aurangzeb suddenly, in 1673, married him to one of his own daughters and fitted up an apartment for the couple in the island prison of Salimgarh at Delhi. Here they joined another of Aurangzeb's daughters, who was already married to a son of Murad Bakhsh. The emperor was mellowing. This marital nest of cousins, secure in their island fort, was his new solution for the youngest generation of his rivals. And there Sipihr Shukoh remained until his death in 1708, outliving Aurangzeb by a year.[9]

Shah Jahan had been determined to prevent his favourite eldest son from rebelling, but he had lived to see far worse. From a state of impotent imprisonment the most magnificent of the Great Moghuls had watched his family annihilated by the son he liked least. But although it was unusual that he should be alive to watch this horrifying process, and although his pampering of Dara had probably made him the least fit to survive the struggle, there was in fact little that Shah Jahan could have done to prevent this chaos from occurring after his reign. It was inherent in a system which accepted the belief that any prince who could seize the throne had as much right to it as any other. Sons are a blessing, but it was Shah Jahan's particular misfortune—not shared by any of his predecessors since Babur—that he was blessed with four, all of whom were able-bodied and intelligent, and none of whom was incapacitated by alcohol. The chaos was inevitable.

Since Dara was in character diametrically opposed to Aurangzeb, it is tempting to speculate how different the subsequent history of the Moghul empire would have been if he, rather than Aurangzeb, had won. Hindus, to whom he was as well disposed as Aurangzeb was hostile, have often felt that India's coming century of disasters might have been avoided. But it seems more probable that under Dara the collapse of the Moghul empire, though different in kind, would have been just as rapid. The Great Moghuls had built their astonishing achievement on a combination of talents and sensibilities which had been present in Babur and had reached practical fruition in Akbar. The problems besetting an empire which had reached its natural limits of expansion required at least another Akbar to solve them, but his full range of characteristics were now neatly and precisely divided between Dara and Aurangzeb. Dara had inherited the interest in culture, the inquiring mind, the intrinsic tolerance and eclecticism; Aurangzeb had the decisiveness, the physical courage, the ability to inspire and to lead. If Dara had reigned, the family achievement might well have crumbled more pleasantly. Under Aurangzeb's stern hands, it was to grind to its end with blood, toil, tears and sweat.

From 1660 to 1666 Aurangzeb was in the unusual position of being an emperor who held prisoner at one and the same time his father in the fort at Agra and his eldest son, Mohammed Sultan, in the fort at Gwalior. Mohammed Sultan had been sent with Mir Jumla against Shah Shuja in Bengal and had been unwise enough to desert the imperial army and to join for a short spell his uncle's forces. In retaliation Aurangzeb kept him imprisoned for the remaining fourteen years of the young prince's life; and if, in his last two years, he was suddenly more leniently treated and offered hope of a return to favour, the reason was only that Moham-

[1]48, 98–9 [2]19, 401–5 [3]19, 358, 392–7 [4]47, I, 282 [5]26, 245–6; 48, 99–103; 49, I, 355–60; 71, II, 212–20 [6]71, II, 219 [7]18A, 131–2; 26, 266–7; 49, I, 381–3; 71, II, 97–100 [8]18A, 131; 49, I, 362, 378–81; 71, II, 221–36 [9], I, 356, and II, 58, and IV, 461

med Muazzam, the emperor's second son, was beginning to seem troublesome.[1] An atmosphere of mistrust and suspicion became the hall-mark of Aurangzeb's style of government. From his own family down to his lowest officials he seems to have positively encouraged a sense of insecurity which kept the reins more securely in his own hands but which was hardly conducive to good administration.

A view of the Taj Mahal from inside the fort at Agra

Shah Jahan survived eight unhappy years after his deposition. In the beautiful white marble buildings which he had constructed in the Red Fort for the comfort of himself and his harem, he struggled hard against the ever more stringent restrictions imposed by his son. At various periods he was forbidden writing materials and was limited even in his use of his own wardrobe. An acrimonious correspondence dragged on, indignant on Shah Jahan's side, stern and hypocritical on Aurangzeb's. The new emperor, with a haste almost indecent in a man of such religious disposition, was determined to prize away all the jewels in Shah Jahan's possession, including even the pearl rosary with which he said his prayers. Shah Jahan was equally determined to retain them, and replied that he would grind the pearls to dust with a pestle and mortar rather than part with them. Usually, though not in the case of the pearls, Aurangzeb won. And gradually Shah Jahan seemed to accept his position.[2]

He was soothed by the gentle care of his eldest daughter, Jahanara, who had acted as his first lady ever since the death of Mumtaz Mahal, and who now devoted herself to him as his nurse. He would sit staring across the curve of the Jumna towards the memorial to his beloved wife, and his own most famous achievement, the Taj Mahal. He spent long hours with mullahs in studying the Koran. Deprived of the spectacular elephant fights outside the fort which he had once watched from these very buildings, he now diverted himself with a domestic parody of those mighty encounters, in which tame antelopes were set against each other in the marble courtyards. Finally, when the bitterness of the annihilation of three-quarters of his descendants had given way to an acceptance that there was no longer a practical alternative to Aurangzeb, he even seemed to soften in his hostility towards his ruthless son.[3] But they never met again and Shah Jahan, after a recurrence of his urinary complaint, died a peaceful death on January 22, 1666, while listening to verses from the Koran. The next morning his body was taken by water to the Taj Mahal, where he was buried beside his wife.[4]

Jean-Baptiste Tavernier, who was in India at the time, recorded that Shah Jahan had intended a replica of the Taj in black marble to be built as his own mausoleum on the opposite bank of the Jumna, connected with his wife's by a bridge, but that the parsimonious Aurangzeb refused to carry out this grand design and placed his father without more ado in the existing Taj.[5] The legend has been current ever since, although there is no other contemporary evidence to support it. The relative position of the two marble coffins is often pointed out in confirmation of Tavernier's theory; Mumtaz Mahal occupies the very centre of the building, immediately below the point of the dome, while the Great Moghul himself, though his plinth is raised a little above hers, is forced into an inferior position slightly to one side. But exactly the same relationship can be seen in the tomb of Itimad-ud-daulah at Agra, which was certainly designed to contain both husband and wife, and on this occasion it does seem that the unfilial image of Aurangzeb is unjustified.

[1] **71**, II, 260, 275, and III, 50
[2] **19**, 378–9; **49**, II, 77; **71**, III, 140–58
[3] **49**, II, 116–17; **48**, 116
[4] **71**, III, 158–64 [5] **47**, II, 191

Almost a year after his hurried proclamation of himself as emperor Aurangzeb staged at Delhi a second and more formal coronation, which must have been the most magnificent of all such Moghul ceremonies. To the splendours of previous coronations were added now the elegant buildings of Shah Jahan and his sumptuous peacock throne. The astrologers chose Sunday June 5, 1659, as the best day, and three hours and fifteen minutes after sunrise as the most perfect moment. Their advice was so carefully followed that Aurangzeb waited behind a screen in the *diwan-i-am*, while the astrologers watched their water and sand clocks to give him the signal when he should step out and seat himself among bolsters on the jewel-encrusted throne.[1]

Part of Shah Jahan's private quarters, where he was imprisoned for the last eight years of his life

Soon after his coronation Aurangzeb issued a number of ordinances designed to bring public life nearer to strict Islamic precepts, and appointed a *muhtasib*, or censor of morals, to regulate abuses. These were the first of a series of such measures during his reign, increasingly puritanical in intent and often anti-Hindu in effect. Argument has long raged, much of it along strictly partisan lines,[2] as to whether Aurangzeb was a fanatic determined to persecute an infidel population into accepting Islam, or a man of normal religious seriousness attempting to rule the country strictly but justly according to the law in which he devoutly believed, that of the Koran. Considerable heat has been engendered in the debate because the hostilities between Muslims and Hindus which undeniably increased during his reign were precisely those which led, two and a half centuries later, to the partition of the subcontinent and the appalling communal massacres of 1947.

The truth about Aurangzeb seems to lie somewhere between the two. He emerges from his letters—dry, stilted, full of conventional religious precepts—as someone much lacking in imagination and unusually obsessed with the letter of the law, though it should be added that such an obsession can itself be seen as a virtue by many orthodox Muslims (one of his own historians wrote, admiringly, that the emperor was 'remarkable for his rigid attachment to religion').[3] He also, in his constant desire to avoid personal indulgence or ostentation, seems a man much concerned with his own salvation—as well he might have been, with the record behind him of his climb to power. His measures reflect his intrinsic puritanism, both personal and public. He discontinued the morning appearance of the emperor in the *jharoka* window, because it smacked of human worship; in 1668 he forbad, presumably for similar reasons of modesty, the writing of any histories of his reign; music was prohibited at court, as were effeminate styles of dress, and one courtier appearing in a coat too long and elegant suffered the indignity of the bottom being snipped off there and then in Aurangzeb's presence; alcohol was of course forbidden, and the cultivation of cannabis (known as *bhang*) made illegal throughout the realm.[4]

The more extreme and laughable side of the emperor's obsession with the letter of the law appears in a firman of 1669 which deals at some length with the rules for the cultivation of dates and almonds, crops which play an important part in the agriculture of Arabia and therefore appear prominently in the Koran but which are almost unheard of in India, and in his insistence on returning to the orthodox lunar year for revenue collection, although, as a contemporary historian admitted, 'mathematicians, astronomers, and men who have studied history, know that the ripening of the corn and the fruit of each season are

[1] 71, II, 289–300
[2] e.g. 71, III, 283–318; 69, 106–; 325, 156–7 [4] 26, 282–3; 20, 60; 49, II, 5–8; 71, III, 92–103; 75, 230

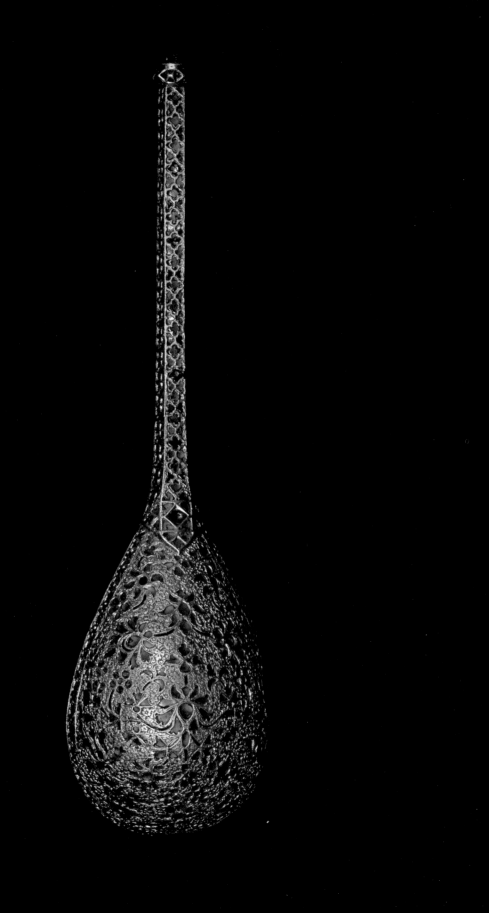

*A rare spoon, gold encrusted
with rubies, emeralds and a
large diamond, dating from
the reign of Akbar. Very little
Moghul jewellery has survived
intact.*

dependent upon the solar reckoning, and cannot be regulated by the lunar'.[1]
But the most harmful side of his orthodoxy was the imposition on Hindus of
restrictions which are sanctioned by Islamic law with regard to *dhimmis* or unbelievers, but which were hardly wise in the context of India. The two foremost
examples were the attempts to enforce the law which says that no new temples
may be constructed and that recently built ones must be pulled down; and the
reimposition in 1679 of the *jizya*, the tax which was ostensibly in return for
military protection by the faithful but which had been abolished by Akbar
exactly a hundred years before.[2]

Aurangzeb's orthodoxy was undoubtedly a matter of genuine religious conviction, but it also brought considerable short-term benefits; it had provided, for
example, both the justification and the support which he had needed for his
campaign in the war of succession. In marching to annihilate the free-thinking
Dara, who was all too reminiscent of Akbar, he had unleashed on his own behalf
all the pent-up frustration and hostility which the orthodox *ulama* had felt since
Akbar had pushed them so inconsiderately to one side. Bigotry of any sort, once
allowed its head, is hard to restrain and it is impossible to say how much Aurangzeb was personally responsible for the many minor discriminations practised
against Hindus during his reign. His apologists argue that he himself disapproved
of discrimination in secular matters (they rely mainly on a saying attributed to
him: 'What connection have earthly affairs with religion? and what right have
administrative works to meddle with bigotry? For you is your religion and for
me is mine'[3]), and they argue that the outburst of desecration of temples by
Muslims and of mosques by Hindus in his reign was an expression of deep existing hostilities within the community rather than the direct result of the emperor's
own pronouncements.[4] The hostilities were certainly there, just as they had been
among Badauni's orthodox circle in the reign of Akbar. But Akbar's policies had
to a certain extent defused them. Only under an emperor prepared to propound
the strictest demands of Islam were they fully released again. Because of the
precisely opposed attitudes of Akbar and Aurangzeb, great-grandfather and
great-grandson each governing India for half a century, they have remained the
two most controversial of the Great Moghuls. To most Hindus Akbar is one of the
greatest of the Muslim emperors of India and Aurangzeb one of the worst; to
many Muslims the opposite is the case. To an outsider there can be little doubt
that Akbar's way was the right one. One needs perhaps to share Aurangzeb's own
strong faith to approve of his policies, and even then it would be hard to admire
his character. Akbar disrupted the Muslim community by recognizing that India
is not an Islamic country: Aurangzeb disrupted India by behaving as though
it were.

From the Moghul point of view the most damaging practical result of Aurangzeb's attitude was the pointless quarrel which he picked with Rajasthan in 1679.
For the past century his ancestors had agreed on the wisdom of maintaining a
friendly alliance with the powerful Hindu kingdoms of Rajasthan, by which the
rajas were allowed complete internal autonomy in return for accepting the Great
Moghul as their emperor; the advantages had included peace in an area which
was vital to Moghul communications, and strong contingents of Rajputs serving
in the Moghul armies. This arrangement was still working satisfactorily when—at
a time when his attentions were already divided between the two usual trouble

[1]**26**, 241–2; **118**, 139–40
[2]**69**, 108–9; **26**, 296 [3]**27**, 99
[4]**69**, 127–9

227

spots, the north-west frontier and the Deccan—Aurangzeb suddenly decided in 1679 to invade Marwar. The immediate cause was the old turncoat Jaswant Singh, though for once his part was beyond reproach; he merely died, commanding an outpost on Aurangzeb's behalf to the south of Kabul, but he left behind him no immediate heir to his throne as Maharaja of Marwar. It would have been normal procedure for Aurangzeb to recognize another member of the family as his successor, and the problem was in any case unexpectedly solved when one of Jaswant's widows gave birth after his death to a son, Ajit Singh. But Aurangzeb brushed aside the unmistakable claim of this infant—offering merely to bring him up in his own harem and to heap him with honours later—and sent into Marwar an army which rapidly overran the province, increasing local hostility by destroying a great many temples on its way. But this rapid conquest of Marwar inevitably involved the neighbouring Rana of Mewar.[1]

The story of Mewar during the past century had been an excellent testimony to Moghul policy. This senior of all Rajput dynasties had successfully resisted Akbar, but had been brought to make terms during the reign of Jahangir. Since then a particular form of tepid allegiance, much to the advantage of both sides, had survived without trouble. The Rana was technically a vassal of the Great Moghul, but the emperors avoiding insisting on this status to the point of injuring his dignity; no Rana had been required to attend the court in person, no princess of Mewar had been requested for the royal harem. The Rana in return respected his part of the bargain by repeating, when required, the formal expression of allegiance and by not acting in opposition to the empire. It was an ideal arrangement between two potentates, the leaders of the two main communities, neither of whom was liable to be defeated by the other; the Great Moghul was too strong, and the Rana too well protected by the deserts and mountains around his territory.

But the Moghul invasion and conquest of neighbouring Marwar upset this *status quo*, by exposing Mewar's flank. The Rana marched against the Moghul army, and the resulting war—covering both Mewar and Marwar—started a chain of events which led to disaster for Aurangzeb. Peace with Mewar was admittedly re-established quite soon, in 1681, though Marwar remained turbulent for another twenty-eight years until Ajit Singh finally established in 1709 his claim to the throne. But the real damage lay in a more domestic conflict which rose directly from these wars—the rebellion of Prince Akbar, in alliance with the Rajputs, against his father.

Akbar, Aurangzeb's fourth and favourite son, had been placed in command of the army against Mewar in 1680, but his failure to make any real headway against the Rana had led to a humiliating dismissal by his father. He was transferred to the command in Marwar, but here also he seemed able to achieve nothing. Messengers from Aurangzeb, who was conducting affairs from Ajmer, brought a string of rebukes; but at the same time secret agents from the Rajput leaders were arriving with much sweeter proposals. The bigoted Aurangzeb, the Rajputs argued, was tearing Hindustan apart. What was needed was an emperor in Delhi who would follow the tradition of the Great Moghuls and be a friend to the Hindus. Believing Akbar to be such a man, the Rajputs would be willing to march with him to overthrow Aurangzeb and to place him on the throne. The plan was particularly enticing because it was so feasible. Aurangzeb had only about ten thousand troops with him at Ajmer. Akbar had an entire Moghul army, which would be supplemented by thirty thousand Rajputs. He agreed, and the combined forces turned towards Ajmer.[2]

It was a most dangerous moment for Aurangzeb. If Akbar had marched rapidly to Ajmer he would certainly have been able to seize his father, but once again Aurangzeb's devious talent for intrigue saved him. While summoning other Moghul armies which were farther afield, he slowed Akbar's advance by suborning astrologers in the prince's camp to advise delay. As a result reinforcements had reached Aurangzeb before Akbar confronted him in January 1681 at Deorai, the very place where Aurangzeb had finally defeated Dara Shukoh twenty-two years before. The size of Akbar's Rajput contingent still made his victory probable, but Aurangzeb produced another of his most effective letters. He wrote to his son congratulating him on having brought the Rajputs into the trap according to their agreed plan, and reminded him that he was to place them in the vanguard during the next day's engagement so that while Aurangzeb assaulted them from the front Akbar could butcher them from behind. The letter fell into Rajput hands while Akbar was asleep in his tent. By the time he awoke the bulk of his army had vanished. He too fled; first into Rajasthan, then by a devious route, hunted all the time by Aurangzeb's armies, down through Gujarat to the Deccan. Ever since Aurangzeb's second viceroyalty in the Deccan, from 1653 to 1658, affairs in the area had remained in their usual turmoil, but Aurangzeb had wisely entrusted the province to his generals. Now, with his son joining forces with his enemies in the Deccan, the problem seemed to demand his own presence. In the autumn of 1681 he moved south to begin a campaign which lasted the twenty-six years until his death. Indeed he was never again to return north to Hindustan. At the end of a chain of events which seems to follow relentlessly from his invasion of Rajasthan, the entire centre of gravity of the empire was altered, with disastrous results, and the emperor himself reverted from the sumptuous stability of court life at Delhi or Agra to the unproductive nomadic existence, on permanent campaign, of one of his Mongol ancestors.[3]

Aurangzeb's move south put an effective end to the tradition of patronage of the arts which had played such a large part in his family's history. Not surprisingly the twenty-three years of his rule in the north, already longer than the entire reign of Jahangir, had produced far less cultural achievement than had become normal under his predecessors. Music had been banished. In literature the emperor had little interest beyond the sacred texts and commentaries, or the repertoire of classical Persian verses with which like any educated man of the time he sprinkled his letters. He allowed painting, in spite of its prohibition in the Koran; he did little to maintain the imperial studio, but the resulting dispersal of many of the court artists was not without its compensations, since they sought patronage elsewhere and the many thriving regional schools of the eighteenth century, producing beautiful work at minor courts during the disintegration of the empire, were all descended from Moghul artists needing a new home.[4] In architecture, however, Aurangzeb's achievements can certainly match his predecessors', though the tendency among modern writers has been to dismiss his buildings as unsubtle. Admittedly the tomb of his wife Dilras Banu at Aurangabad unwisely echoes the shape of the Taj Mahal, and the comparison has often obscured its own very considerable charm. But Aurangzeb's Pearl Mosque in

[1] 71, III, 365–84
[2] 71, III, 384–407
[3] 26, 298–304; 49, II, 243–9; 71, III, 407–25 [4] 89, 103–4

229

the Red Fort at Delhi develops with great delicacy the relief work in white marble pioneered by Shah Jahan's sculptors (Plate 44, p. 208). And similarly his mighty Badshahi Mosque in Lahore, though sometimes dismissed as an inferior copy of Shah Jahan's Friday Mosque at Delhi, is in many ways, with its greater simplicity of line and decoration (Plate 47, opposite), the more assured and successful of the two.

Inside Aurangzeb's Badshahi Mosque at Lahore

In the twenty-three years since Aurangzeb had marched north to seize the throne, the area of the Deccan had been dominated by a small Maratha chieftain, Shivaji, whose guerilla tactics were to prove fatal to the Moghuls and who thereby became a very special hero to Hindus in the political climate of the early twentieth century. With the independence movement under way to eject the British and to restore India to the Indians after nine centuries of domination by rulers whose roots were outside the subcontinent, there was a magnetic appeal about a Hindu who, from comparatively humble beginnings, had risen to shake the very foundations of the Moghul empire. In the words of Sir Jadunath Sarkar, the leading Hindu biographer of Aurangzeb, writing in about 1915, Shivaji 'proved by his example that the Hindu race can build a nation, found a State, defeat enemies; they can conduct their own defence; they can protect and promote literature and art, commerce and industry; they can maintain navies and ocean-trading fleets of their own, and conduct naval battles on equal terms with foreigners. He taught the modern Hindus to rise to the full stature of their growth'.[1] So, when viewed with hindsight through twentieth-century glasses, Aurangzeb on one side and Shivaji on the other come to be seen as key figures in the development of India. What Shivaji began, Gandhiji could complete—the addition of *ji* is in both cases a mark of respect, and Indians today speak in conversation of Gandhiji rather than Gandhi—and what Aurangzeb stood for would lead to the establishment of the separate state of Pakistan.

Like Malik Ambar before him, Shivaji employed guerilla tactics and a shifting pattern of alliances to create a perpetual turmoil among his three powerful neighbours, Bijapur, Golconda and the Moghuls, and in the turmoil he was able steadily to advance his own interests and frontiers. But where Malik Ambar used the armies of the kingdom of Ahmednagar, Shivaji welded the scattered Maratha people into a political and military unit deriving great strength from a new sense of identity. In establishing himself as leader of these tribes he was no doubt helped by the highly colourful incidents of his own life. His exploits were as ruthless as anyone's, but they had an unusual touch of fantasy which made them the perfect raw material for a legendary hero.

[1] **71**, III, 238
[2] **26**, 258–61; **49**, II, 27–8; **71**, IV, 34–40

Shivaji's tiger-claws

The most famous of Shivaji's adventures was undoubtedly the murder of Afzal Khan, a general commanding the army of Bijapur. Shivaji, whose territory was threatened by the Bijapur army, met him at a parley at which each was supposed to be unarmed. But Shivaji had a breastplate beneath his cloak and a set of steel 'tiger claws' attached to the fingers of his left hand. The sources differ as to whether Afzal Khan also intended treachery. Some say that as the two men embraced he thrust at Shivaji's chest a dagger which was stopped by the hidden armour; others claim that he opened his arms in genuine friendship. But whether he was provoked or not, the brief embrace ended with Shivaji ripping out his rival's belly with the hidden tiger claws. In the ensuing confusion Shivaji's army, hidden in the woods around, fell on the Bijapur forces and massacred them.[2]

*A typical page from a later
Moghul album, bringing
together miscellaneous
paintings from the early 17th
century*

Shivaji's next exploit of comparable melodramatic appeal was at the expense of the Moghuls, and was a good example of how a daring guerilla raid can demoralize a much more powerful opponent. Aurangzeb's uncle, Shaista Khan (the brother of Mumtaz Mahal) had been made viceroy in the Deccan and was living in a 'small fortress called Poona'.[1] On April 5, 1663, Shivaji and a small band of his followers made their way by a trick into the Moghul camp and, after picking a hole in a wall, succeeded even in entering Shaista Khan's harem, hoping to assassinate him as he slept. Before escaping again, almost without casualties of their own, they had wounded Shaista Khan and had killed or injured many of his attendants. Needless to say such an adventure greatly added to Shivaji's reputation and appeal among the Marathas.[2]

Aurangzeb, highly displeased at what at the very least was an excellent joke at the Moghuls' expense, replaced Shaista Khan as viceroy with his own son, prince Muazzam. But Shivaji promptly added injury to insult in a much larger scale affront when, between the 6th and 10th of January, 1664, he seized and looted the rich city of Surat. Aurangzeb responded by sending south a far more powerful general, the veteran Jai Singh. By the use of Shivaji's own type of diplomacy, such as playing neighbours off against each other, and by laying energetic siege to Shivaji's key forts, Jai Singh in the short space of three months persuaded the Maratha chieftain to make terms. In return for peace, and the recognition of his right to twelve of his forts, Shivaji would owe allegiance to the imperial throne and would moreover hand over the remaining twenty-three of the forts which over the years he had seized or otherwise acquired. This much already was a great victory for Jai Singh, but Aurangzeb was determined that Shivaji should come to court in person to pay his respects. Shivaji resisted this strongly, pointing to the exception made for the Rana of Mewar and asking for the same dispensation, but finally Jai Singh, on a solemn promise of safe conduct, persuaded him to make the alarming journey to Agra, where Aurangzeb was then holding his court.[3]

Shivaji's reception at Agra was a muddle which, though not intended, probably reflected the deep hostility between himself and Aurangzeb. He happened to arrive, in May 1666, during the celebrations for the emperor's fiftieth lunar birthday, and in the larger ceremony less attention was paid to him than he felt was his due. After approaching the throne, he was directed to stand among a group of nobles whose rank was only five thousand, and as he gradually discovered the identity and status of his immediate neighbours his indignation mounted. Suddenly, as the proceedings dragged on, he burst out in a noisy protest which shattered the reverential calm of the *diwan-i-am*, and then he left the hall without receiving the elephant, the robe and the jewels which Aurangzeb had been intending to present to him at the end of the durbar. The emperor, offended in his turn, gave orders for Shivaji to be confined to his house. For three months Shivaji suffered virtual imprisonment, until—having slowly and painstakingly accustomed his guards to a daily routine, by which each afternoon he sent out large baskets of sweetmeats as gifts to worthy Brahmans in the city—he one day in August hid himself in one of the baskets and so escaped. He made his way back to the Deccan, avoiding recapture by the choice of a long and improbable route and by travelling with his face covered in ashes like a Hindu ascetic. For a while he appeared to respect his treaty with the Moghuls, but in 1670 he

[1] 49, II, 104
[2] 26, 269–71; 49, II, 104–5
[3] 71, IV, 51–83

233

began to take back the forts which he had ceded in 1665. During the next ten years he continued to expand, until a vast area around Bombay was indisputably his and the Maratha nation was firmly established. He died in 1680. Even his enemies allowed him a character nearer to Robin Hood than Dick Turpin. A contemporary Muslim historian wrote that 'he persevered in a course of rebellion, in plundering caravans, and troubling mankind, but he entirely abstained from other disgraceful acts, and was careful to maintain the honour of the women and children of Mohammedans when they fell into his hands'.[1] And a European described him as a 'chief of bandits' but 'both courteous and liberal'.[2]

Shivaji had died a year before the rebellious prince Akbar, in the summer of 1681, made his escape south to the Deccan; so Akbar entered an alliance with his son, Shambhuji, and it was their combined threat which brought Aurangzeb himself south to Aurangabad a few months later. Akbar hoped that Shambhuji would march north with him to gather up reinforcements in Rajasthan for a quick assault on Delhi. Shambhuji agreed in principle, but, with other campaigns to pursue in the rugged security of his own wild countryside, he was in no hurry to risk his armies in the plains of the north. The months dragged on. Akbar had no local support of his own, the daily life of these hill people was very different from the comforts to which a Moghul prince was accustomed, and his father's campaign increasingly threatened his safety. Finally, after the fall of Bijapur in 1686, Akbar despaired of his new allies. He sailed from the west coast and made his way to Persia, where he was given hospitality but no military support for an attack on Hindustan, and where he finally died in 1704.[3]

The flight of his son removed the immediate reason for Aurangzeb's presence in the Deccan, but having moved south he was determined to calm this turbulent area by subduing the three major powers of Bijapur, Golconda and the Marathas. For the first eight years his campaign had every appearance of success. Bijapur was captured in 1686 after a long siege, in which the bribe offered to any soldier willing to risk his skin by throwing a bucket of earth into the moat rose from a quarter rupee to one rupee and finally to a gold coin. Corpses of animals and even of men had been added to the buckets of earth before the moat was finally level and the wall could be stormed. The assault failed, but a week later the garrison capitulated. On September 12, 1686, Aurangzeb entered the city in considerable pomp, scattering coins. He had an inscription carved on the great Bijapur gun, the Malik-i-Maidan, to celebrate his victory, and installed himself in Sikandar Adil Shah's palace after having some offensive murals erased.[4]

Six weeks later he moved towards Golconda and its neighbouring city of Hyderabad, famous throughout India for its wealth and its decadence, with a reputed twenty thousand registered prostitutes, a selection of whom danced before the king in a public square every week on the holy day of Friday.[5] Hyderabad had been seized and sacked by Aurangzeb's son Muazzam in 1685, but the king had once again withdrawn to his virtually impregnable fortress of Golconda five miles to the west. It was this vast and high fortress which Aurangzeb now began to besiege, but it lived up to its reputation and for eight months his army, suffering great discomfort through the rainy season, made no headway. Finally, in September 1687, bribery prized open the gate to the fort and the Moghuls entered. Previous campaigns against Golconda had ended in treaties, in which the Qutb Shahi dynasty accepted allegiance to Delhi. This time Aurangzeb was

The victory inscription carved by Aurangzeb on the muzzle of the great gun at Bijapur

taking no further chances. The kings of both Golconda and Bijapur were imprisoned, their royal lines disinherited, and their two countries annexed as part of the Moghul empire.[6]

The otherthrow of Aurangzeb's third enemy was considerably simpler. Shambhuji, who had inherited little of his father's military genius, was ignominiously captured in February 1689 by a small party of Moghuls while amusing himself with some followers in the town of Sangameshwar. He was paraded on a camel through Aurangzeb's camp, dressed in a fool's costume with cap and bells, but he was true to his father in the courage which he showed in refusing to divulge where his family's treasure was buried, or with which officers in the Moghul camp he had held correspondence. After two weeks of torture, during which he kept up a stream of personal abuse of Aurangzeb, he was hacked limb from limb while each piece, as it was cut off, was fed to the dogs.[7]

So, by 1689, Aurangzeb appeared to have triumphed, and the Moghul empire covered a larger area of land than it ever before had or ever again would. But there was a new spirit of resistance abroad, inspired originally by Shivaji, and it was one that could not be stopped by individual victories or even by the death of particular leaders. It was typical of this new attitude that when Chhatra Sal, a

[1]**26**, 305
[2]**26**, 276–81; **47**, I, 147; **49**, II, 135–40; **71**, IV, 83–98, 174–238
[3]**26**, 312–3; **71**, IV, 280–6, 392–6
[4]**71**, IV, 300–29; **52**, 264–5
[5]**47**, I, 127–8
[6]**71**, IV, 330–86; **52**, 265–6
[7]**26**, 337–42; **71**, IV, 398–404

young prince of Bundelkhand, had deserted in 1670 from the Moghul army and had offered his services to the Maratha cause, Shivaji had advised him to return to his own kingdom and to organize uprisings there which would distract and weaken the Moghuls.[1] In the same way the death of Shambhuji did not break Maratha resistance, but merely splintered it for several years into local groups under separate leaders.

But Aurangzeb was determined, with increasing obstinacy, to hold this vast territory which he had at last succeeded in conquering. The last years of his life were to be spent in a futile series of sieges of comparatively insignificant hill forts. Sooner or later each fell, almost invariably by bribery or stratagem—indeed during Aurangzeb's entire quarter century in the Deccan only one fort was actually taken by storm[2]—but as soon as Aurangzeb marched to besiege the next, the Marathas usually returned to reoccupy the last. The emperor, soldiering on well into his eighties, was like an old bear plagued by bees, and he and his army suffered appalling hardships. The landscape over which they had to drag themselves and their cannon was described by one contemporary author as a 'specimen of hell' in which 'all the hills rise to the sky, and the jungles are full of trees and bushes',[3] and their own effect on the countryside, by their very numbers alone, was devastating. According to the official records the Moghul fighting force in the Deccan numbered a hundred and seventy thousand, without taking into account the far more numerous non-combatants and camp-followers required by any army. The total in Aurangzeb's camp was nearer to half a million, and so many extra mouths made the normal system of trade and supplies virtually impossible.[4] To add to the futility of the whole enterprise some of the subsidiary Moghul armies, undertaking sieges without the presence of the emperor himself, soon discovered that a slightly more pleasant way of life could be achieved by an understanding with the enemy. Shambhuji's younger brother, Raja Ram, had escaped to a magnificent fort south-west of Madras called Jinji. A Moghul army was encamped at the foot of this fort on and off for seven years, making no progress in the siege by mutual agreement with the besieged. And when Aurangzeb finally demanded a result, the Moghul commander arranged for his friend to escape before the fort fell.[5]

In the middle of one of these sieges Aurangzeb was visited by another ambassador from England. Early in 1699 William III sent Sir William Norris on precisely the same mission as Sir Thomas Roe more than eighty years before—to attempt to secure a beneficial trading agreement from the Great Moghul for the East India Company. Norris, after a most troublesome journey ending in a dangerous trek through wild country held by bands of Marathas, finally reached Aurangzeb's camp in April 1701. He found the emperor besieging the fort of Panhala. It had been captured by the Moghuls ten years before, but as soon as they had repaired the fortifications the Marathas had scaled the walls and taken it back. The present siege had already dragged on for six months, and negotiations were now under way as to how large a bribe the commander of the fort would require if he were to surrender it. Norris found the camp deep in mud, conditions extremely insanitary, and the pay of the army more than a year in arrears. The courtiers were as corrupt as they had been in less puritanical reigns, and just as enthusiastic 'Lovers of English spiritts' as Sir Thomas Roe had found them under the drunken Jahangir; indeed even the *qazi*, Aurangzeb's highest religious adviser, sent to

'A specimen of hell . . . all the hills rise to the sky'—the landscape of Maharashtra, through which Aurangzeb's armies had to drag their guns

[1] 71, V, 393 [2] 75, 375
[3] 26, 342, 256
[4] 71, V, 439; 52, 218 [5] 71, V, 106–7
[6] 53, 288–314; 27, 125;
49, IV, 100–1

Norris in the utmost secrecy for a couple of cases. In the middle of this squalor Aurangzeb himself contrived to maintain a considerable dignity. His lifelong courage, remarkable ever since he had faced a dangerous elephant at the age of fourteen on foot, was still with him; in fact it was all that kept the resources of the empire tied up in this disastrous enterprise. He was now eighty-two, but he still visited the front line and personally inspected the progress of the siege. He received Norris in public audience with the full paraphernalia of the Great Moghul, and was most graciously interested in all the gifts which King William had sent—a far more impressive selection, as it turned out, than King James and Sir Thomas Roe had been able to provide.[6]

Norris gives a most vivid picture of the old man passing through the camp to visit the siege works. He was carried on this occasion in an open litter; 'he was all

237

over white both the dress of his Body & His Turbatt & his beard as white as they'; vast numbers of people crowded to see him, but 'he himselfe tho' carryd openly saw nobody havinge his eyes always affixed upon a Booke he carried in his hands & readinge all ye way he went without ever divertinge to any other object'.[1] The book was almost certainly the Koran—a standard portrait of Aurangzeb as an old man showed him sitting in a window reading it—and his rather ostentatious refusal to be distracted from the holy page fitted precisely the image of himself which he had always tried to cultivate, but which in old age certainly became more and more deeply felt. He now had, in the words of Manucci, a 'craze for being held a saint'.[2]

It was not only in the intractable Deccan that his power was draining away. His long absence from Hindustan had led to an inevitable slackening of authority and growth of corruption in the north. Even at the very centre of Moghul power, in the district round Agra, the local Jat population had become so bold as to plunder Moghul caravans on their way south, and in 1688 they ransacked Akbar's tomb at Sikandra and removed the gold and silver plate and precious carpets.[3] By the end of the reign the caravans had brought south from Delhi and Agra a large proportion of the treasure of Akbar, Jahangir and Shah Jahan, to sink it without trace in the Deccan.[4] Aurangzeb had pledged his empire on the outcome of a type of war which could never be more than inconclusive. Henry Kissinger, adviser to the President of the United States, recently described very succinctly the impasse in which Aurangzeb found himself; in such an encounter, he said, 'the guerilla wins if he does not lose; the conventional army loses if it does not win'.[5]

Aurangzeb, in spite of his resolute refusal to withdraw, seems to have sensed this, and his courage in the face of such relentless futility adds considerable pathos to the end of an otherwise uncharming life. At last the conventional piety which had always filled his letters gives way, under the twin pressures of approaching death and a guilty conscience, to genuine personal anguish. 'I know not to what punishment I shall be doomed', he writes, with unusual simplicity, to one of his sons;[6] and he bewails an old man's lack of close friends and his own particular shortage of good officers in a letter to his third son, Azam, which is almost a poetic lament for the frailty of human affairs:

> My child, my soul, life and prosperity of my life. Behrehmund is sick; Mukhlis Khan, etc. are disgusted; Hammed ed Deen is a cheat; Siadat Khan and Mohammed Ameen Khan, in the advanced guard, are contemptible; Zul Fikir Khan is impetuous; Cheen Kulich Khan is worthless; Firoze Jung is at the head of affairs in equal authority with Umdet ul Mulk; the Mansabdars, great and small, from the dearness of grain, are almost ready to desert; Mirza Sudder ed Deen Mohammed Khan is expert in every business; Sirberah Khan, the Kotwal, is a thief-squeezing pickpocket; Yar Ali Khan and Munaim Khan are unruly jesters; Arshi Khan gets drunk and swills with wine; Muherrim Khan is vicious; the Deccanners are at loggerheads; Abdul Hukk and Multefit Khan are veteran soldiers; Murid Khan, without men, serves as a simple horseman; Meer Khan, the fatherless, is distressed for a coat and turban; Innaiyet Ullah is entirely possessed by the thoughts of his departure; the brother of Munsoor Khan is acting against the accursed Marathas, and you are employed in diffusing liberalities. Akbar is a vagabond in the desert of infamy; Shah Alam and his sons are far distant from the victorious army; Kam Bakhsh is perverse and regardless of what is said to him; your son is obedient to the advice of his illustrious father; I myself am forlorn and destitute, and misery is my ultimate lot.[7]

[1] 53, 295 [2] 49, III, 259
[3] 49, II, 320; 71, V, 293–9
[4] 71, V, 447–8
[5] *The Times*, Aug. 5, 1969, 8
[6] 20, 128 [7] 20, 119–20

That there were no good men left was entirely Aurangzeb's own fault, the result of his obsessive mistrust and refusal to delegate authority.[1] During the reigns of Akbar, Jahangir and Shah Jahan a succession of great generals, confidential ministers, trusted women or royal princes were able to make their mark in history by their achievements on behalf of the empire. In the half century of Aurangzeb's reign, he alone stands out. His only two generals of any stature had already distinguished themselves under Shah Jahan—Mir Jumla, who after driving Shah Shuja out of Bengal died in 1663 while trying to conquer Assam for Aurangzeb, and Jai Singh, who after his victory over Shivaji was nevertheless disgraced by Aurangzeb at the end of a long life of brilliant service because of a subsequent unsuccessful expedition against Bijapur. Even Aurangzeb's own sons and daughters continued to be treated as naughty and dangerous children until well into their fifties and sixties. The record of his treatment of the royal princes is a measure of his ultimate incapacity as leader as well as father. His eldest, Mohammed Sultan, died after sixteen years of imprisonment at the age of thirty-seven. The second, Muazzam, was given the high title Shah Alam and enjoyed some degree of favour until 1687 when he was suspected of embezzlement, was arrested with his sons and was imprisoned for the next eight years, while Aurangzeb arranged for his favourite wife, Nur-un-nissa, to be separately confined and to be deliberately insulted by her eunuchs; the prince was released in 1695 but spent the next twelve years in abject terror of his father until he succeeded him as Bahadur Shah, at the age of sixty-four, in 1707. The third son, Azam, was unique in the family in that he never incurred his father's displeasure to the point of being imprisoned or exiled. The fourth, Akbar, was Aurangzeb's favourite, but after his rebellion of 1681 died in exile in Persia. The youngest, Kam Bakhsh, spent a shorter spell in prison than the others, from 1698 to 1699. Even Aurangzeb's eldest and highly talented daughter, Zeb-un-nissa, a distinguished poet and literary patron, spent the last twenty-one years of her life in the prison of Salimgarh because of her secret correspondence with Akbar during his rebellion.[2] Both Shah Jahan and Aurangzeb had planned their treatment of their sons with one aim in mind, to avoid a repetition of their own rebellion against their fathers. Shah Jahan's solution had been maximum freedom for his favourite, Dara Shukoh, and Aurangzeb's had been minimum freedom for everyone. In achieving the immediate aim Aurangzeb's method was more successful, but the damage it did to the empire was to prove far greater.

In 1705, at the age of eighty-seven, Aurangzeb fell seriously ill at Devapur and began a withdrawal northwards, carried in a palanquin. In January 1706 he reached Ahmednagar, the city from which he had set out twenty-four years earlier for his campaign in the Deccan. Mortality intruded everywhere. During this last year the deaths in his family included one of his daughters, a son-in-law, three adult grandchildren, and his last surviving sister, Gauharara Begam, whose death seemed to affect him even more than any of the others; 'she and I alone were left', he would constantly repeat, 'among the children of Shah Jahan.'[3] Where any other man summons his sons to his death-bed, Aurangzeb, like a dying animal snapping at the vultures, deliberately sent them away. He knew, as the whole of India knew, that chaos would follow his death. Niccolo Manucci, writing now in his own old age in Madras, pointed out that the number of Aurangzeb's living sons, grandsons and great-grandsons of adult age was

[1]**49**, II, 315; **71**, V, 477–8
[2]**71**, III, 49–60 [3]**71**, V, 243–50

Embroidery on a Moghul sash: 17th century

seventeen and commented: 'What an event to behold will be the tragedy following the death of this old man! One only of these princes can succeed, and thereby protect his family; the rest of them will be decapitated, or lose their lives in various other ways. It will be a much worse tragedy than that which happened at the end of King Shahjahan's reign.'[1] Aurangzeb was well aware of this, and in his last months—to judge from his letters and from his will—his thoughts, as he prepared to meet his God, were dominated again by Dara Shukoh. History would repeat itself, but as far away from him as he could contrive. Kam Bakhsh was sent to Bijapur, while Azam—who marched so slowly that he had only gone fifty miles when news reached him of the emperor's death—was dispatched to govern Malwa.[2]

One last wish of Aurangzeb's was answered. He died, as he had always hoped, on a Friday—February 20, 1707—after saying his morning prayers. In his will he left instructions that the four and a half rupees recently earned by the sale of caps which he himself had sewn—a humble and therefore holy pastime—should go towards the expenses of his funeral; that the three hundred and five rupees from the sale of Korans copied out by him should be distributed to holy men on the day of his death; and that his grave should be of the simplest sort, open to the air and with no canopy above it.[3] He was buried at Khuldabad, near Daulatabad, and the grave conforms to his instructions. Its simplicity, after a century of such sumptuous Moghul tombs, reflects as intended the difference between his character and those of his predecessors; but its calculated air of poverty also symbolizes, less intentionally, the comparative value of the legacy which he was handing on to his successors. Aurangzeb was a puritan of overweening ambition, who had been determined to do without the usual pretentious trappings of great power. But in rejecting the symbol he had also, unwittingly, discarded the reality.

On paper, in the year of Aurangzeb's death, the Moghul empire was little more than half way through its history. In the past one hundred and eighty-one years there had been six Great Moghuls, whose achievements, father to son for six generations, can bear comparison with those of the Medici and a handful of other such families in the world's history. In the remaining century and a half of their nominal empire, there would be another eleven Great Moghuls. But Aurangzeb was the last whom the proud title fitted.

[1] 49, IV, 117
[2] 71, V, 255–6; 26, 384–6
[3] 71, V, 256–8, 263–5; 25A, 193–5; 26, 386–7

Epilogue

Manucci's prophecy had been right; only his detailed estimate of the royal carnage was a little high. In the war of succession during which the sixty-four-year-old Shah Alam established himself on his father's throne as the emperor Bahadur Shah, two of Aurangzeb's sons and three of his grandsons were killed. But the longer-term disorders were more serious. Of the next eight Great Moghuls after Aurangzeb, whose combined reigns spanned only the fifty-two years to 1759, four were murdered, one deposed, and only three died peacefully on the throne. And with the violence there entered too a new frivolity and debauchery which makes the family history read like a conventional stage melodrama of the east.

A brutal demonstration of the dynasty's weakness came in 1739, in an event which exactly paralleled the eruption on to Indian soil of their ancestor Timur more than three centuries before. In Persia the decrepit Safavid dynasty, whose decline had mirrored that of the Moghuls, had been displaced in 1736 by Nadir Shah, a Turk from Khurasan. Two years later he invaded India, crossing the Indus at Attock on December 27, 1738. On February 24 he met and easily defeated the army of the panic-stricken Moghul emperor, Mohammed Shah, and on March 20 he entered Delhi. The *khutba* was read in the mosques in his name, just as it had been in Timur's, and as before there was calm for the first day or two in the occupied city. But this time there was no doubt that the people of Delhi themselves provoked the massacre which followed. An argument with some Persian soldiers led to a brawl, which developed in turn into a riot in which nine hundred Persians were killed. Even so Nadir Shah forbad reprisals until he himself had ridden through the streets on the following morning to assess the situation. Certain citizens were unwise enough to throw stones at him from their roofs, and someone even fired a musket which killed an officer by his side. His reply was to order a massacre. During one whole day it continued, and the number of the dead was over thirty thousand. In the evening the Great Moghul begged mercy for his people. Amazingly, Nadir Shah's authority was such that after agreeing to still the whirlwind he was immediately able to do so.

The Persian and his army stayed only long enough to gather their reward. Huge contributions were collected from all the nobles and rich citizens, violence and torture being added where necessary to other forms of encouragement, and the Great Moghul handed over the keys to the imperial treasury. Together with a prodigious assortment of minor jewels Nadir Shah took the peacock throne, which was later broken up; the throne among the present crown jewels in Teheran, which is often called the peacock throne, was built in the early nineteenth century for Fath Ali Shah and bears no relation to Shah Jahan's. Nadir Shah's haul from nobles and emperor combined was sufficient for him to send home from Delhi a decree remitting all taxes in Persia for the next three years. He also took with him a thousand elephants, a hundred masons and two hundred carpenters. The parallel with Timur had been almost uncanny.

Aurangzeb's simple grave at Khuldabad, covered with earth and open to the sky

245

There could have been no more humiliating demonstration of the new status of the Moghul empire than Nadir Shah's brief and expensive intrusion, but the more crucial symptom of real weakness was the number of small independent kingdoms which now established themselves again throughout the land. Even if they still professed allegiance to the emperor they behaved with complete autonomy and impunity, and it was this profusion of principalities which was to help the East India Company in the process of extending its rule steadily throughout the subcontinent.

By the eighteenth century Britain's two earliest European rivals in India, the Portuguese and the Dutch, had largely been superseded by the French; and it was against the French that the East India Company first found itself involved in extensive military operations. The forts which had been founded during the seventeenth century at the company's main settlements, in Bombay, Madras and Calcutta, had been intended only for the defence of trade. But with Britain and France fighting each other in Europe in the War of Austrian Succession, hostilities broke out too, in 1746, between the neighbouring trading posts of the two countries on the east coast of India—between British Madras and French Pondicherry, where even today an otherwise perfectly normal Indian beggar will still approach the traveller murmuring not 'bakhshish' but 'ancien militaire'. The local struggle continued long after the War of Austrian Succession had ended until, in 1761, the British starved Pondicherry into submission.

The Company's first full-scale military intervention in Indian politics had occurred during the same period. It was both accidental and decisive. Bengal, like so many other parts of the Moghul empire, was now in effect an independent hereditary kingdom and in 1756 its young nawab, Siraj-ud-daulah, marched with a large army against Calcutta. The British garrison was soon overwhelmed and one hundred and forty-five men and one woman were locked up for the night in the military jail or 'Black Hole' of Fort William. The room was only eighteen feet square with two small windows, and the month was June, the hottest season in a hot climate. When the door was opened in the morning only twenty-three people, of whom the woman was one, were still alive.

To avenge this horrifying accident and to recapture Calcutta, Clive sailed north from Madras. His army met and easily defeated Siraj-ud-daulah on the field of Plassey in June 1757, and finding himself in control of Bengal Clive put a nominee of his own, Mir Jafar, on the throne as nawab. Making the most of his opportunity he exacted in return vast sums from the grateful nawab, together with the rights to nearly nine hundred square miles of land round Calcutta. Very soon a similar sequence of events led to British control over the Nawab of Oudh, after the battle of Baxar in 1764, and to the granting to the British by the Moghul emperor, Shah Alam, whose forces had been defeated in the same battle, of the right to collect the revenues of Bengal. The pattern was established by which during the following century British force placed amenable rulers on the thrones of India's now numerous principalities, in return for the double benefit of financial considerations and a deciding say in policy.

The Great Moghuls had been virtual puppets in the hands of different factions throughout most of the eighteenth century, and it was a measure of their lack of personal authority that Shah Alam was able to remain on the throne for the last years of his life in spite of the fact that he was brutally blinded by a rebel in 1788:

Cotton painted with European figures, a commodity much in demand for the new trade with Europe: part of a large hanging, Madras region, 17th century

ABOVE *British officers in the late 18th century entertained by an Indian ruler: c. 1820*

BELOW *Sir David Ochterlony, the British Resident in Delhi in the early 19th century, spending an evening in Indian style and risking the displeasure of his ancestors on the wall: c. 1820*

in the days of real Moghul power to deprive a prince of his eyesight had always been regarded as the only sure way, short of assassination, of keeping him off the throne. In 1803 the blind emperor was formally taken under British protection. Deference continued to be paid to him as the Great Moghul, and it was officially he who ruled the empire, but by his side was the British Resident in Delhi to supervise him in his conduct of affairs. The arrangement continued for another fifty-four years, until in 1857 the last Moghul emperor, Bahadur Shah II—whose gentle nature and considerable talents as a poet made him unexpectedly appropriate to the dying fall of his great dynasty—was adopted rather to his reluctance as the symbolic figurehead of the Sepoy Revolt, known to the British as the Indian Mutiny.

The traumatic experience of this mutiny made Parliament in London aware that changes were necessary. By a remarkable process of undisturbed evolution, the government of India was still officially entrusted to the East India Company for whom Sir Thomas Roe, more than two centuries before, had sent back reports on the relative demand in Agra for wine and swords, arras and waistcoats. Every British soldier or administrator in 1857 was still the servant of and paid by the East India Company, just as Clive and Warren Hastings had been. But after the disaster of the mutiny it was felt in London that Parliament, on behalf of the Crown, must take over from the Company official responsibility for Indian affairs.

So Bahadur Shah was exiled to Burma, where he died in 1862. And a greater mogul even than the Timurids, though one whose roots were yet further from the soil of India, added to her existing list of imperial dignities the title *Indiae Imperatrix*. Like each of her predecessors she struck coins in her new name, but she refrained from reading the *khutba*.

Genealogy

r.—reigned
=—married

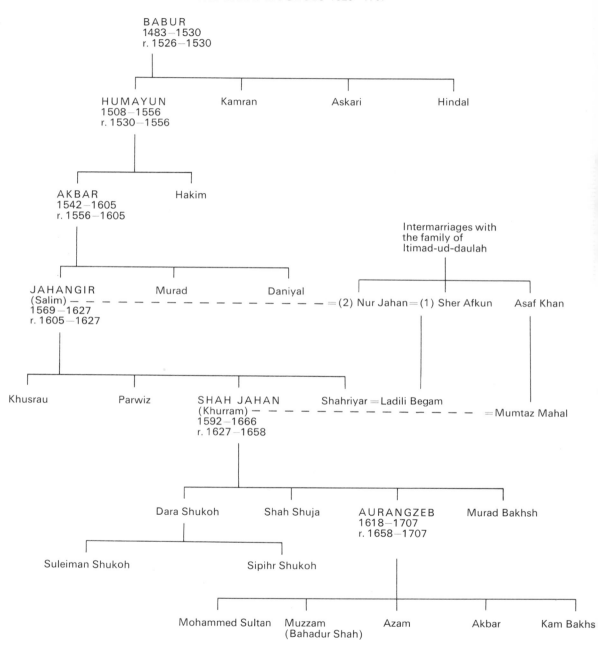

THE GREAT MOGHULS 1526–1707

BABUR
1483–1530
r. 1526–1530

HUMAYUN   Kamran   Askari   Hindal
1508–1556
r. 1530–1556

AKBAR   Hakim
1542–1605
r. 1556–1605

Intermarriages with
the family of
Itimad-ud-daulah

JAHANGIR   Murad   Daniyal   = (2) Nur Jahan = (1) Sher Afkun   Asaf Khan
(Salim) — — — — — — — — — — — — — — — — —
1569–1627
r. 1605–1627

Khusrau   Parwiz   SHAH JAHAN   Shahriyar = Ladili Begam   = Mumtaz Mahal
(Khurram) — — — — — — — — — — — — —
1592–1666
r. 1627–1658

Dara Shukoh   Shah Shuja   AURANGZEB   Murad Bakhsh
                                        1618–1707
                                        r. 1658–1707

Suleiman Shukoh   Sipihr Shukoh

Mohammed Sultan   Muzzam   Azam   Akbar   Kam Bakhs
                   (Bahadur Shah)

Bhara Samarkand Transoxiana Ferghana

Amu Darya (Oxus)

Badakhshan

HINDU KUSH

Kashmir

| The empire at the death of Akbar in 1605 | |
| Extra territory nominally under Moghul control at the death of Aurangzeb in 1707 | |

Kabul
Ghazni
Srinagar
Peshawar
Attock

H I M A L A Y A

dahar
Rohtas
Chenab
Kalanaur
Kangra

M O U N T A I N S

Jhelum
Lahore
Indus
Multan
Sirhind
Sutlej

P u n j a b

Panipat

luchistan
Indus
Hissar Firoz
Delhi
Bhakkar
Bikaner
Jumna
Ganges
Mathura

Jaisalmer
Jaipur (Amber)
Pushkar
Kanauj
Agra
Samugarh
Bhadaur
Gandak

Sehwan
Jodhpur (Marwar)
Ajmer
Fatehpur Sikri
Dholpur
Khanua

Sind
R a j a s t h a n
Gwalior
Khajwah
Jaunpur
Gogra
Patna
Monghyr

Umarkot
Orchha
Allahabad
Benares
Chausa
Ganges
Gaur

Chambal
Chitor (Mewar)
Chanderi
Chunar
Son
Ganges

Rann of Kutch
Udaipur (Mewar)
B i h a r

Patan
Ahmedabad
Dharmat
Hooghly
Calcutta

Gujarat
Malwa
Champaner
Mandu
Bengal

Cambay
Surat
Burhanpur
Balaghat

Diu

Khuldabad
Daulatabad
Orissa

Nasik
Aurangabad

Bombay
Maharashtra
Ahmednagar

Poona

D e c c a n

Bidar

Sangameshwar
Hyderabad (Golconda)
BAY OF BENGAL

Panhala
Bijapur

Goa

Karnatic
Madras

Jinji
Pondicherry

miles
0   100   200   300
0   200   400
kilometres

ARABIAN SEA

1   2   3   4   5   6   7   8   9

Bibliography

This is divided into three parts. Part I lists the Turki and Persian sources which are available in translation. Part II contains the more important accounts of travellers who visited the courts of the Great Moghuls. Part III is a select bibliography of the most useful modern works on the subject. In Parts I and II the material is arranged in roughly chronological order, and in Part III by subject matter.

Footnotes. The footnotes on each page of the text give my sources. They refer to books according to their numbers in this bibliography. So, for example, the reference 4, II, 501–7, 623 would mean pages 501–7 and 623 of Vol. II of the *Babur-nama*. The only exceptions are two journals, the *Journal of the Asiatic Society of Bengal* and the *Memoirs of the Asiatic Society of Bengal*, referred to as JASB and MASB respectively.

I Sources

A few of the works in this section are available in translation only in the form of long extracts in Elliot, H. M., and Dowson, J., *The History of India as told by its own Historians*, London, 1867–77, 7 vols., referred to below as E & D.

1 Sharaf al-Din, *Zafar-nama*. Translated as *The History of Timur-Bec*, London, 1723, 2 vols., from the French edition by Petits de la Croix published the previous year. Sharaf al-Din was a friend of Timur's son, Shah Rukh, and his book is based on an earlier work by Nizam al-Din Shahi which had been written on Timur's orders in 1401–3. It covers the whole of Timur's reign.

2 Ibn Arabshah, *Ajib al-Makdur fi Nawab Timur*. Translated as *Tamerlane, or Timur the Great Amir* by J. H. Sanders, London, 1936. The author was captured at the age of twelve by Timur in Damascus and was sent to Samarkand. His book is a bitterly hostile account of Timur and his conquests, but is full of valuable details, particularly of Samarkand.

3 Khwand Amir, *Habib al-Siyar*. Long extract translated as *Life of Tamerlane, Parts V and VI, A Literal Translation* (Anon.), Bombay, (1900). Khwand Amir wrote this biography long after Timur's death, in the early sixteenth century. It was an abridgment of a larger work written by the author's grandfather at Herat in the second half of the fifteenth century.

4 Babur, *Babur-nama*, tr. Annette Beveridge, London, 1921, 2 vols. Based on notes taken throughout his life, but written mainly between 1526 and 1530 in India, Babur's memoirs cover the period from his accession to the year before his death, i.e. 1494–1529. But losses from the manuscript have resulted in some long gaps. The missing years are 1503–4, 1508–19 and 1520–5.

5 Haidar, *Tarikh-i-Rashidi*. Translated by E. Denison Ross as *A History of the Moguls of Central Asia*, London, 1895. Haidar, born in 1499, was Babur's cousin. He was with Babur in Kabul and on expeditions between 1509 and 1514; he was with Humayun and Kamran at Lahore in 1540; and subsequently he installed himself as the ruler of Kashmir, where he wrote his book in 1541–6. Part I is a history of his own branch of the Mongols, the eastern Chaghatais. Part II is an account of his own life, with many details of Babur and Humayun.

6 Gulbadan, *Humayun-nama*, tr. Annette Beveridge, London (Royal Asiatic Society, Oriental Translation Fund), 1902. Gulbadan was Babur's daughter and was born *c.* 1523. Her book was written on Akbar's orders in about 1587. She deals briefly with her father's life, then in more detail with the reign of Humayun up to the blinding of Kamran. While Humayun and Hamida were fugitives in Sind and Persia, she was with Kamran in Kabul; but her detailed account of their hardships is certainly based on what she heard from Hamida, a close friend in later days at Agra and Fatehpur Sikri.

7 Jauhar, *Tadhkirat al-Waqiat*. Translated by Charles Stewart as *Private Memoirs of the Moghul Emperor Humayun*, London (Oriental Translation Fund), 1832. Throughout Humayun's reign Jauhar was his ewer-bearer—a very close personal servant roughly comparable to a valet or batman. He wrote this account of his master, on Akbar's orders, in 1587.

8 Abdulla, *Tarikh-i-Daudi* (E & D Vol. IV, pp. 434–513). A history, written in Jahangir's reign, of two Afghan dynasties in Delhi—the Lodi, defeated by Babur, and the Sur, defeated by Humayun. The extracts in E & D are useful chiefly for the years immediately before Humayun's return in 1555.

9 Abbas Khan, *Tuzuk-i-Sher-Shahi* (E & D Vol. IV, pp. 301–433). A biography of Sher Shah written by a relation of his in Akbar's service—yet another of the works commissioned by Akbar as

source material for the history of his dynasty. Extracts in E & D end with a section on Sher Shah's administrative reforms.

10 Abul Fazl, *Akbar-nama*, tr. H. Beveridge, Calcutta (Asiatic Society, Bibliotheca Indica), 1907–39, 3 vols. Abul Fazl became Akbar's close adviser and personal friend, and he wrote this continuing chronicle of the reign up to the year of his own death, 1602. Vol. I deals with Timur, Babur, Humayun and the childhood of Akbar; Vols. II and III describe year by year the events of Akbar's reign. An account of the final three years, 1602–5, was added later — based mainly on the *Iqbal-nama* of Mutamid Khan, written *c.* 1620.

11 Abul Fazl, *Ain-i-Akbari*, tr. H. Blochmann and H. S. Jarrett, Calcutta, 1873–94, 3 vols. A gazetteer, almanac, dictionary of science, book of rules and procedures, and statistical digest of Akbar's empire. Compiled by Abul Fazl *c.* 1590. The first work of its kind in India.

12 Asad Beg, *Wikaya* (E & D Vol. VI, pp. 150–74). A personal account of the later years of Akbar's reign. The author was in the service of Abul Fazl for seventeen years, and after Abul Fazl's death was employed directly by Akbar. The extracts in E & D are mainly interesting for details of the assassination of Abul Fazl and of the intrigues round Akbar's deathbed.

13 Badauni, *Muntakhab al-Tawarikh*, tr. G. S. A. Ranking, W. H. Lowe and Sir W. Haig, Calcutta, 1884–1925, 3 vols. The most lively, though slanted, account of Akbar's reign. Written in secret between 1590 and 1596 by an orthodox divine who had been in Akbar's service. Vol. I gives a history of the Muslim rulers of India up to Humayun's death; Vol. II follows the reign of Akbar up to 1596; Vol. III gives biographies of various divines, scholars and poets of Akbar's reign.

14 Nizamuddin Ahmad, *Tabaqat-i-Akbari*, tr. B. De, Calcutta (Bibliotheca Indica No. 225), 1927–39, 3 vols. Written in 1592–3 by an author who was also a soldier and administrator in Akbar's service. Vol. I deals with the Sultans of Delhi; Vol. II with the period from Babur's invasion to 1593; Vol. III with the ruling houses of the various provinces of India.

15 Ferishta, *Gulshan-i-Ibrahimi*. Translated by John Briggs as *History of the Rise of the Mahomedan Power in India, till the year* A.D. *1612*, London, 1829, 4 vols. Written in the first two decades of the seventeenth century by an author who had been in the service of the kings of Ahmednagar and of Bijapur, but who had travelled in the Moghul empire. Vol. II deals with the reigns of Babur, Humayun and Akbar.

16 Jahangir, *Tuzuk-i-Jahangiri*, tr. Alexander Rogers, ed. Henry Beveridge, London (Oriental Translation Fund, New Series, Vols. XIX and XXII), 1909–14, 2 vols. Jahangir began his journal in the year of his accession, 1605, and continued it in his own hand until 1622. Ill health then made him entrust it to his scribe, Mutamid Khan, who

continued it in the first person singular until 1624 and then completed the last three years of the reign in his own *Iqbal-nama*.

16A Mutamid Khan, *Iqbal-nama-i-Jahangiri* (E & D Vol. VI, pp. 400–38). The author was Jahangir's personal scribe. He continued Jahangir's memoirs when the emperor was too ill to write them himself; and on Jahangir's orders he wrote this history of the reign. Extracts in E & D contain details of Jahangir's marriage with Nur Jahan and of Shah Jahan's rebellion, but are particularly useful for the capture and control of Jahangir by Mahabat Khan, of which the author was an eye-witness.

17 Abdul Hamid Lahori, *Padshah-nama* (E & D Vol. VII, pp. 3–72). A book intended to do for Shah Jahan's reign what Abul Fazl's *Akbar-nama* had done for Akbar's. The author, famed for his skill in Abul Fazl's flowery style, was commissioned by Shah Jahan to write it, but old age prevented him from completing more than the first two decades of the reign. Extracts in E & D include the defeat of the Portuguese at Hooghly and the reception of the captives at Agra; the destruction of temples at Benares; and a description of the peacock throne.

18 Inayat Khan, *Shah-Jahan-nama* (E & D Vol. VII, pp. 73–120). The author was in charge of Shah Jahan's library, and his history of the emperor is based on the manuscripts he found there. Extracts in E & D include the founding of Shah Jahan's Delhi; the Kandahar campaigns; and the beginnings of the Moghul alliance with Mir Jumla.

18A Mohammed Salih Kambu, *Amal-i-Salih* (E & D Vol. VII, pp. 123–32). A history of the reign of Shah Jahan by one of the writers at his court. Extracts in E & D are useful for Shah Jahan's illness, Dara's mishandling of the crisis and his attempts to curb Aurangzeb in the Deccan, and the fates of Murad Bakhsh and Suleiman Shukoh.

19 Aurangzeb, *Adab-i-Alamgiri*. Translated by Jonathan Scott in his *Tales, Anecdotes and Letters*, Shrewsbury, 1800, pp. 345–466. A selection of Aurangzeb's letters to his father and other members of his family before and during the War of Succession.

20 Aurangzeb, *Rukaat-i-Alamgiri*, tr. Joseph Earles, Calcutta, 1788. A selection of the emperor's letters, mainly to his sons, grandsons and high officials during the later years of his reign.

21 Aurangzeb, *Rukaat-i-Alamgiri*, tr. J. H. Bilimoria, London, 1908. Another selection from the same original Persian collection of the emperor's letters.

22 Mohammed Kazim, *Alamgir-nama* (E & D Vol. VII, pp. 174–80). The author was a recorder at Aurangzeb's court and was ordered to write an official history of the reign. But after he had presented this account of the first ten years, the emperor forbad any more writing of history. Extracts in E & D include Shah Jahan's illness of

1657, Dara's heresies, and the beginnings of the War of Succession, all from an angle highly favourable to Aurangzeb.

23 Mufazzal Khan, *Tarikh-i-Mufazzali* (E & D Vol. VII, pp. 141–4). A history stretching from the Creation to the tenth year of Aurangzeb's reign. Extracts in E & D are brief and cover in scant detail a variety of incidents between 1627 and 1660.

24 Rai Bhara Mal, *Lubb al-Tawarikh-i-Hind* (E & D Vol. VII, pp. 168–73). The author had been *diwan* to Dara Shukoh, and wrote in the late seventeenth century this history of all the kingdoms of India. The brief extracts in E & D deal exclusively with economics and justice under Shah Jahan.

25 Bakhtawar Khan, *Mirat-i-Alam* (E & D Vol. VII, pp. 145–65). The work is attributed to Bakhtawar Khan, a favourite eunuch of Aurangzeb's, but was probably written by his friend Mohammed Baqa. The work covers the history of the world, but the extracts in E & D consist largely of a panegyric on the piety, humility and wisdom of Aurangzeb.

26 Khafi Khan, *Muntakhab al-Lubab* (E & D Vol. VII, pp. 207–533). The author was a nobleman in the service of Aurangzeb, who, in defiance of the emperor's ban on the writing of history, kept a secret chronicle of events. His book tells the story of the house of Timur, from the time of its founder up to several years after Aurangzeb's death. The extracts in E & D deal first with one isolated incident—the attack on the Europeans at Hooghly in 1632—and then in considerable detail with the whole of Aurangzeb's reign.

26A Mohammed Saki Mustaidd Khan, *Maasir-i-Alamgiri* (E & D Vol. VII, pp. 181–97). A history of Aurangzeb's reign written just after his death by order of his successor, Bahadur Shah. The author was a scribe who had been at Aurangzeb's court for forty years. The extracts in E & D are useful for the destruction of temples, Aurangzeb's relationship with his children, and the details of his death.

27 Anonymous, *Akham-i-Alamgiri*. Translated by Jadunath Sarkar as *Anecdotes of Aurangzib*, Calcutta, 1912. A series of disconnected contemporary anecdotes about Aurangzeb, mostly of a rather popular and unreliable nature. The manuscript includes also the details of Aurangzeb's will.

II Travellers

There are a great many accounts of India in the seventeenth century by travellers who only touched the coastal districts, but who nevertheless included in their accounts the almost obligatory chapter, based on hearsay or other books, about the Great Moghul. The following selection is limited to those travellers who had first-hand experience inside the Moghul empire. Some of the accounts are most easily available in a modern anthology, *Early Travels in India, 1583–1619*, Foster, William (editor), London, 1921, which is referred to below as Foster. I have also included one or two early accounts of Moghul India, written in Europe but based on authentic reports from travellers.

28 Clavijo, Ruy Gonzalez de, *Embassy to the Court of Timur at Samarcand, A.D. 1403–6*, tr. Clements R. Markham, London (Hakluyt Society), 1859. Clavijo left Spain as ambassador to Timur in 1403, and was with the emperor in Samarkand between September and November 1404, during which time he witnessed the victory celebrations for the campaign in Iraq, Syria and Turkey.

29 Sidi Ali Reïs, *Mirat al-Memalik*. Translated by A. Vambery as *The Travels and Adventures of the Turkish Admiral Sidi Ali Reïs*, London, 1899. The author was a Turkish admiral who, after being defeated by the Portuguese at sea, took refuge in India and made his way back to Turkey by land. He was in Delhi when Humayun died in 1556.

30 Monserrate, Father Antony, *Commentary on his Journey to the Court of Akbar*, tr. J. S. Hoyland, London, 1922. One of the three members of the first Jesuit mission to Akbar, Monserrate left a detailed account of his experiences. He was well placed to observe the many facets of the Moghul way of life. In March 1580 he arrived at Fatehpur Sikri and took part in the religious discussions in the *ibadat-khana*. He was appointed tutor to Akbar's son Murad. He accompanied Akbar's camp on the military expedition to Kabul in 1582, and returned to Goa later that year.

31 Fitch, Ralph. Memoirs in Foster, pp. 1–47. Fitch was a member of the first group of English merchants to make the journey to India in search of trade. They reached Fatehpur Sikri in 1584, bearing letters for Akbar from Queen Elizabeth. Fitch leaves a brief but lively account of Fatehpur Sikri and Agra. He went from Agra down the Jumna and Ganges to Bengal, and reached England again in 1591.

32 Du Jarric, Father Pierre, *Akbar and the Jesuits*, tr. C. H. Payne, London, 1926. Written in the first decade of the seventeenth century by a Jesuit priest at Bordeaux, who based his history on the letters, reports and commentaries sent back by Jesuits in India.

33 Guerreiro, Father Fernao, *Jahangir and the Jesuits*, tr. C. H. Payne, London, 1930. Written at much the same time as the previous entry, and from similar authentic sources, but by a Jesuit in Lisbon.

34 Mildenhall, John. A letter in Foster, pp. 54–9. The author was a merchant who, on his own account (though pretending to be an ambassador from Queen Elizabeth) spent two years at Akbar's court, in 1603–5, trying to win trading concessions. He was resolutely opposed by the Jesuits on behalf of Portuguese interests.

35 Hawkins, William. Account in Foster, pp. 70–121. Hawkins commanded a fleet sent out by the East India Company in 1607. He was at Jahangir's court in Agra from 1609 to 1611, but like Mildenhall he made little headway against the

Portuguese. But Jahangir was so pleased by his knowledge of Turkish that he made him a noble at his court with a rank of 400 horse, and married him to an Armenian girl. In 1612 his wife set out with him for England. She reached London a widow, her husband having died on the voyage.

36 Finch, William. Account in Foster, pp. 125–87. Finch was an assistant to Hawkins on the voyage out in 1607, but their paths separated in India. Finch spent most of 1611 in Lahore.

37 Jourdain, John, *Journal*, ed. W. Foster, Cambridge (Hakluyt Society), 1905. Jourdain reached Agra in the service of the East India Company in 1611, when Hawkins was still there. He leaves only a brief description of his five months at court, and is mainly interesting on the bitter rivalries between the Portuguese and English on the west coast.

38 Withington, Nicholas. Account in Foster, pp. 196–233. The author was in Agra and Ajmer in the service of the East India Company in 1614–15.

39 Coryat, Thomas. Letters in Foster, pp. 241–87. Coryat reached India overland and on foot in 1615, on twopence a day. He then walked the length of the imperial trunk road from Lahore through Delhi to Agra, and reached Jahangir's court at Ajmer in July.

40 Roe, Sir Thomas, *The Embassy of Sir Thomas Roe to India, 1615–19*, ed. W. Foster, London, 1926. Roe was England's first official ambassador to the Great Moghul. He was in India from 1615 to 1619, spending most of that time at the court of Jahangir in Ajmer and later in Mandu. His book is a detailed account from a European better placed than any other in the seventeenth century to report on life at the Moghul court.

41 Terry, Edward, *A Voyage to East India*, London, 2nd edition, 1777. Terry was a clergyman who joined Roe at Mandu in February 1617, after Roe's previous chaplain had died. He returned to England with Roe in 1619, and in 1622 he wrote and presented to Prince Charles this account of his travels.

42 Pelsaert, Francis, *Remonstrantie*. Translated by W. H. Moreland as *Jahangir's India*, Cambridge, 1925. Pelsaert was in Agra from 1620 to 1627 as the factor for the Dutch East India Company. His book is a commercial report, designed to help the Company in promoting Dutch trade with India. It concentrates therefore on the details of Indian trade in different commodities, but has some excellent sections on life at Agra.

43 [Pelsaert, Francis], *A Contemporary Dutch Chronicle of Mughal India*, tr. and ed. by Brij Narain and S. R. Sharma, Calcutta, 1957. A rather garbled account of Moghul history in the reigns of Humayun, Akbar and Jahangir, apparently based on a variety of Persian histories which have been ill remembered and combined with hearsay. The editors show that it was the main source for part of De Laet's book (below) and that it was written by Pelsaert.

44 De Laet, Joannes, *The Empire of the Great Mogol*, tr. J. S. Hoyland, Bombay, 1928. De Laet did not go to India but was a director of the Dutch East India Company. His work is both a gazetteer and a history of the Moghul empire from Humayun to Jahangir. It draws on all the sources known in Europe at the time (first published 1631), though most heavily on Pelsaert for the historical section. It is of interest as being Europe's first comprehensive account of the Moghul empire.

45 Mundy, Peter, *Travels in Europe and Asia, 1608–1667*, ed. Sir R. C. Temple, Cambridge (Hakluyt Society), 1907–36, 5 vols. Vol. II contains Mundy's journal of his stay in India from 1628 to 1633. During most of this time he was in Agra, where his visit coincided with the beginning of the Taj Mahal and with much building activity by Shah Jahan in the Red Fort. Mundy is a more perceptive commentator than most travellers of the time, and his journal has an added value in the numerous sketches by himself which illustrate it.

46 Manrique, Sebastien, *Travels*, tr. C. E. Luard and H. Hosten, Oxford (Hakluyt Society), 1927, 2 vols. Manrique was an Augustinian friar who crossed the whole of Hindustan from Orissa to Afghanistan, making even a huge detour down the Indus and through Rajasthan. He reached the Moghul court at Lahore in 1640, and secured the release from prison of one of his order who had been captured at Hooghly.

47 Tavernier, Jean-Baptiste, *Travels in India*, tr. V. Ball, London, 2nd edition, 1925, 2 vols. in one. Tavernier was a French jewel-merchant who made no fewer than five separate journeys from Europe to India between 1638 and 1668. His destination was usually the Deccan, famous for the diamond mines at Golconda. But he was at Agra in 1640 when Shah Jahan was there, and he sold many jewels to Aurangzeb in Delhi in 1665.

48 Bernier, François, *Travels in the Mogul Empire*, tr. Archibald Constable, Westminster, 1891. Bernier was a French physician who spent six years in the Moghul empire, from 1658 to 1664—mainly in Delhi, but also in Kashmir, which he visited with Aurangzeb's camp, and in Bengal. His book is useful, but he is more than usually concerned with criticizing India for failing to conform to the customs of Europe.

49 Manucci, Niccolao, *Storia do Mogor*, tr. William Irvine, London, 1907–8, 4 vols. Manucci was an Italian gunner and quack doctor who landed in India in 1656 and remained there until his death in about 1717. He had an extremely varied series of adventures, including service with several Moghul princes, all of which he describes with great zest. A charlatan by nature, he has often been dismissed as a totally unreliable gossip; but in fact he frequently approaches a rumour with a more healthy scepticism than the better educated Bernier.

50 Thévenot, M. de, *Travels*; in *Indian Travels of Thévenot and Careri*, ed. Surendranath Sen, New Delhi, 1949, pp. 1–152. The author was a young

Frenchman who travelled through the southern part of the Moghul empire in 1666.

51 Martin, François, *Mémoires*, Paris, 1931–4, 3 vols. Martin was the founder of the French city of Pondicherry, where he lived from 1674 to 1693. His very full memoirs provide a view, from the sidelines, of Aurangzeb's long campaigns in the Deccan; and, from the centre, of the growing struggle between the French and the English on the east coast.

52 Careri, J. F. G., *Travels*; in *Indian Travels of Thévenot and Careri*, New Delhi, 1949, pp. 157–276. Careri was an Italian who made a complete tour of the world eastwards in 1693–8. When in India his ambition was to have an audience with the Great Moghul. Aurangzeb was engaged in his interminable struggles in the Deccan. Careri reached the Moghul camp near Bijapur and was granted an interview in 1695.

53 Norris, William, *Journals*; in Das, Harihar, *The Norris Embassy to Aurangzeb*, Calcutta, 1959. Sir William Norris was an ambassador sent out by William III to gain trading concessions from the Great Moghul, like Roe eighty years before. He reached Aurangzeb's camp in 1701, when the aged emperor was besieging the Maratha hill fort of Panhala, and he remained at court for seven months. The book is a historical work by a modern writer, but the author quotes extensively from Norris's unpublished journals.

54 Foster, William, editor, *Letters received by the East India Company from its Servants in the East, 1602–17*, London, 1896–1902, 6 vols. A collection of East India Company documents, which touch frequently on Moghul affairs.

55 Foster, William, and Fawcett, Charles, editors, *The English Factories in India, 1618–1684*, Oxford, 1906–55. A continuation of the above.

III **Modern Works**

BIOGRAPHY AND GENERAL

56 Hookham, Hilda, *Tamburlaine the Conqueror*, London, 1962.

57 Williams, L. F. Rushbrook, *An Empire Builder of the Sixteenth Century: Babur*, London, 1918.

58 Avasthy, Rama Shankar, *The Mughal Emperor Humayun*, Allahabad, 1967.

59 Banerji, S. K. *Humayun Badshah*, London, 1938–41, 2 vols.

60 Prasad, Ishwari, *The Life and Times of Humayun*, Calcutta, 1955.

61 Qanungo, Kalikaranjan, *Sher Shah*, Calcutta, 1921.

62 Smith, Vincent A., *Akbar the Great Mogul*, Oxford, 1917.

63 Srivastava, A. L., *Akbar the Great*, Delhi, 1962, 2 vols.

64 Prasad, Beni, *History of Jahangir*, Allahabad, 1930.

65 Saksena, Banarsi Prasad, *History of Shahjahan of Dilhi*, Allahabad, 1932.

66 Ghauri, Iftikhar Ahmad, *War of Succession between the Sons of Shah Jahan, 1657–1658*, Lahore, 1964.

67 Qanungo,. Kalikaranjan, *Dara Shukoh*, Calcutta, 1935.

68 Sarkar, Jagadish Narayan, *The Life of Mir Jumla*, Calcutta, 1951.

69 Faruki, Zahiruddin, *Aurangzeb and his Times*, Bombay, 1935.

70 Moinul Haq, S., *Prince Awrangzib: a Study*, Karachi, 1962.

71 Sarkar, Jadunath, *History of Aurangzib*, Calcutta, 1912–24, 5 vols.

72 Sarkar, Jadunath, *Studies in Aurangzib's Reign*, Calcutta, 1933.

73 Sarkar, Jadunath, *House of Shivaji*, Calcutta, 1940.

74 Cambridge History of India, Vol. III, *Turks and Afghans*, ed. Sir W. Haig, Cambridge, 1928.

75 Cambridge History of India, Vol. IV, *The Mughul Period*, ed. Sir R. Burn, Cambridge, 1937.

76 Erskine, William, *A History of India under the two first sovereigns of the House of Taimur, Baber and Humayun*, London, 1854, 2 vols.

77 Hodivala, S. H. *Historical Studies in Mughal Numismatics*, Calcutta, 1923.

78 Lane-Poole, Stanley, *The History of the Moghul Emperors of Hindustan illustrated by their coins*, London, 1892.

79 Qureshi, I. H., *The Muslim Community in the Indo-Pakistani Subcontinent*, The Hague, 1963.

80 Rahim, Muhammad Abdur, *History of the Afghans in India*, A.D. *1545–1631*, Karachi, 1961.

80A Sarkar, Jadunath, *Studies in Mughal India*, Calcutta, 2nd edition, 1919.

81 Sharma, G. N. *Mewar and the Mughul Emperors (*A.D. *1526–1707)*, Agra, 2nd edition, 1962.

82 Sharma, S. R., *Mughal Empire in India, 1526–1721*, Bombay, 1934–5, 3 vols.

83 Sharma, S. R., *Studies in Medieval Indian History*, Sholapur, 1956.

84 Srivastava, Ashirbadi Lal, *The Mughul Empire*, Agra, 2nd edition, 1957.

85 Srivastava, A. L., *Medieval Indian Culture*, Agra, 1964.

86 Tod, James, *Annals and Antiquities of Rajasthan*, London, 1920, 3 vols. (1st edition 1829–32).

THE ARTS

87 Arnold, Thomas W., *The Library of A. Chester Beatty: a Catalogue of the Indian Miniatures*, London, 1936, 3 vols.

88 Binyon, Laurence, *The Court Painters of the Grand Moguls*, London, 1921.

89 Brown, Percy, *Indian Painting under the Mughals*, Oxford, 1924.

90 Ettinghausen, Richard, *Paintings of the Sultans and Emperors of India in American Collections*, New Delhi, 1961.

91 Goetz, Hermann, *Bilderatlas zur Kulturgeschichte Indiens in der Grossmoghulzeit*, Berlin, 1930.

92 Smith, Vincent A., *A History of Fine Art in India and Ceylon*, Bombay, 3rd edition, 1962.

93 Stchoukine, Ivan, *La Peinture Indienne à l'époque des Grands Moghols*, Paris, 1929.

94 Stchoukine, Ivan, *Les Peintures des Manuscrits Timurides*, Paris, 1954.

95 Strzygowski, J., editor, *Asiatische Miniaturenmalerei im Anschluss an Wesen und Werden des Mogulmalerei*, Vienna, 1933.

96 Welch, Stuart C., *The Art of Mughul India*, New York, 1963.

97 Brown, Percy, *Indian Architecture (The Islamic Period)*, Bombay, 1942.

98 Havell, E. B., *Indian Architecture*, London, 1913.

99 Nath, R., article 'Taj: Dream in Marble' in the journal *Marg*, Vol. XXII, No. 3 (a special issue devoted to the Taj Mahal), Bombay, June 1969.

100 Smith, Edmund W., *The Mogul architecture of Fatehpur Sikri*, Allahabad, 1894–8, 4 vols.

101 Smith, E. W., *Akbar's Tomb, Sikandarah, near Agra*, Allahabad, 1909.

102 Villiers Stuart, C. M., *Gardens of the Great Mughuls*, London, 1913.

103 Ghani, Muhammad Abdul, *A History of the Persian language and literature at the Moghul Court (Babur to Akbar)*, Allahabad, 1929–30, 3 vols.

104 Aziz, Abdul, and Ahsan, Shakoor, *The Imperial Library of the Mughuls*, Lahore, 1967.

ADMINISTRATION AND THE ARMY

105 Akbar, Muhammad, *The Administration of Justice by the Mughals*, Lahore, 1948.

106 Ali, M. Athar, *The Mughul Nobility under Aurangzeb*, London, 1966.

107 Aziz, Abdul, *The Mansabdari System and the Mughul Army*, Lahore, no date.

108 Ibn Hasan, *The Central Structure of the Mughal Empire*, Lahore, 1967 (1st edition 1936).

109 Irvine, William, *The Army of the Indian Moghuls*, London, 1902.

110 Sangar, Satya Prakesh, *Crime and Punishment in Mughal India*, Delhi, 1967.

111 Sharma, S. R., *Mughal Government and Administration*, Bombay, 1951.

SOCIAL AND ECONOMIC

112 Aziz, Abdul, *The Imperial Treasury of the Indian Mughuls*, Lahore, 1942.

113 Chopra, Pran Nath, *Some Aspects of Society and Culture during the Mughal Age (1526–1707)*, Agra, 2nd edition, 1963.

114 Habib, Irfan, *The Agrarian System of Mughal India (1556–1707)*, Bombay, 1963.

115 Misra, Rekha, *Women in Mughal India (1526–1748 A.D.)*, Delhi, 1965.

116 Moreland, William H., *India at the Death of Akbar: an economic study*, London, 1920.

117 Moreland, W. H., *From Akbar to Aurangzeb: a study in Indian economic history*, London, 1923.

118 Moreland, W. H., *The Agrarian System of Moslem India*, Cambridge, 1929.

119 Sarkar, Jadunath, *The India of Aurangzeb (topography, statistics and roads) compared with the India of Akbar*, Calcutta, 1901.

120 Yasin, Mohammad, *A Social History of Islamic India*, Lucknow, 1958.

RELIGION

121 Krishnamurti, R., *Akbar, the Religious Aspect*, Baroda, 1961.

122 Maclagan, Edward D., *The Jesuits and the Great Mogul*, London, 1932.

123 Modi, Jivanji Jamshedi, *The Parsees at the Court of Akbar*, Bombay, 1903.

124 Roychoudhury, M. L., *The State and Religion in Mughal India*, Calcutta, no date.

125 Roychoudhury, M. L., *The Din-i-Ilahi or the Religion of Akbar*, Calcutta, 1941.

126 Sharma, S. R., *The Religious Policy of the Mughal Emperors*, London, 2nd edition, 1962.

127 Wellesz, Emmy, *Akbar's Religious Thought Reflected in Mogul Painting*, London, 1952.

BIBLIOGRAPHIES

128 Coomaraswamy, Ananda K., *Bibliographies of Indian Art*, Boston, 1925.

129 Marshall, D. N., *Mughals in India: a Bibliographical Survey*, London, 1967.

130 Sharma, S. R., *A Bibliography of Mughal India (1526–1707 A.D.)*, Bombay, 1939.

131 Taraporevala, V. D. D., and Marshall, D. N., *Mughal Bibliography*, Bombay, 1962.

WORKS OF REFERENCE

132 *Cyclopaedia of India*, London, 3rd edition, 1885, 3 vols.

133 *Encyclopedia of Islam*, London, 1913–34, 4 vols.

134 *Encyclopedia of Islam*, New Edition, London, 1960– (in progress).

135 Hughes, T. P., *A Dictionary of Islam*, London, 2nd edition, 1935.

136 *Imperial Gazetteer of India*, Oxford, 1907–9, 25 vols.

137 Murray's *Handbook for Travellers in India, Pakistan, Burma and Ceylon*, (ed. L. F. Rushbrook Williams), London, 21st edition, 1968.

Notes on the Illustrations

We are grateful to the following libraries, museums and private owners for permission to reproduce items in their collections:

	Her Majesty the Queen	Fogg	Fogg Art Museum, Harvard
	His Highness the Nawab of Rampur	Freer	Freer Gallery of Art, Smithsonian Institution, Washington
	His Highness the Maharaja of Alwar	Guimet	Musée Guimet, Paris
	His Highness the Maharaja of Satara	India Office	India Office Library, London
Beatty	Chester Beatty Library, Dublin	Jalan	Private collection of Hira Lall Jalan, Patna
B.M.	British Museum, London	Khuda Bakhsh	Khuda Bakhsh Oriental Public Library, Patna
B.N.	Bibliothèque Nationale, Paris	Moscow	State Museum of Oriental Art, Moscow
Bodleian	Bodleian Library, Oxford		
Bombay	Prince of Wales Museum, Bombay	Nat. Port. Gal.	National Portrait Gallery, London
Boston	Museum of Fine Arts, Boston	Rampur	Raza Library, Rampur
Calico	Calico Museum, Ahmedabad	V & A	Victoria and Albert Museum, London
Delhi	National Museum, Delhi		

The items listed below follow the order of their appearance in the book. The abbreviations used for museums and collections are as in the left-hand column of the above list. Any photographs not by Christina Gascoigne have been credited accordingly.

14 Page from a *Babur-nama*, late 16th c. (B.M. MS. Or. 3714, fol. 491 v.) (Photo B.M.)

16 Detail of page from a *Chingiz-nama*, late 16th c. (Freer, No. 54.31.) (Photo Freer.)

24–5 Detail from a *Babur-nama*, late 16th c. (Moscow.)

30 Page from a *Babur-nama*, late 16th c. (B.M. MS. Or. 3714, fol. 393 r.) (Photo B.M.)

32 Drawing, mid-17th c. (Beatty, MS. 11A, No. IV.)

38 Detail from a *Babur-nama*, late 16th c. (Moscow.)

39 Page from a *Babur-nama*, late 16th c. (Moscow.)

43 Page from an album, c. 1605. (Rampur.)

48 Portrait of Humayun, Delhi, c. 1800. (Freer, No. 39.48 A.v.) (Photo Freer.)

50–1 Detail from an *Akbar-nama*, c. 1590 (V & A, No. 2.1896.I.S.26.117.)

53 Painting of Hamida, 18th c. (By courtesy of His Highness the Maharaja of Alwar.)

56 Turban-box, 16th c. (Bombay.)

59 Painting by Mir Sayyid Ali, c. 1540. (Fogg, No. 1958.75.b. Gift of Louis J. Cartier.) (Photo Fogg.)

61 Painting by Bichitr, c. 1620. (Beatty, MS. 7, fol. 14.)

62 Painting by Mansur, c. 1615. (V & A, No. 137.1921.)

63 Detail from an *Akbar-nama*, late 16th c. (Freer, No. 39.57.) (Photo Freer.)

64 Detail from an *Akbar-nama*, 17th c. (Bodleian, MS. Ouseley Add. 171, fol. 13 v.) (Photo Bodleian.)

71 Shield, said to be 16th c. but possibly 19th c. (Bombay, No. 22.4112.)

72–3 Detail from an *Akbar-nama*, c. 1590. (V & A, No. 2.1896.I.S.65.117.)

76 A drawing from Mundy's journal, 1632. (Bodleian, MS. Rawl. A315, fol. 40 v.) (Photo Bodleian.)

77 A page from a *Tarikh-i-khanadan-i-timuriya*, c. 1590. (Khuda Bakhsh.)

79 A Moghul book-rest, enamelled silver inlaid with gold, 17th c. (Jalan.)

81 Detail from an *Akbar-nama, c.* 1590. (V & A, No. 2.1896.I.S.29.117.)

87 Detail from an *Akbar-nama, c.* 1590. (V & A, No. 2.1896.I.S.24.117.)

91 Two details from an *Akbar-nama, c.* 1590 (V & A, No. 2.1896.I.S.66 and 74.117.)

104 Detail from an *Akbar-nama, c.* 1605. (Beatty, MS. 3, fol. 176 v.)

106 Drawing, *c.* 1605. (India Office, No. Add. Or. 1039.)

111 Painting by Manohar, *c.* 1615. (Bombay, No. 15.280.)

112–13 Detail from an *Akbar-nama, c.* 1590. (V & A, No. 2.1896.I.S.17.117.)

114 Page from an album, *c.* 1620, by Hashim (Jahangir) and Abul Hassan (Christ). (Beatty, MS. 7, No. 12.)

116 Detail from an *Akbar-nama, c.* 1605, by Nar Singh. (Beatty, MS. 3, fol. 263 v.)

116 Page from the Dara Shukoh album; fol. 43. (India Office.) (Photo R. B. Fleming.)

120 Page from an album, early 18th c. (B.M. Oriental Antiquities, No. 1920.9.17.01.) (Photo B.M.)

129 Painting by Bichitr, *c.* 1620. (Freer, No. 42.15A.) (Photo Freer.)

130 Painting by Abul Hassan, *c.* 1620. (Freer, No. 48.19B.) (Photo Freer.)

132 Painting by Mansur, *c.* 1612. (V & A, No. I.M.135.1921.)

133 Painting attributed to Mansur, *c.* 1620. (Boston, No. 14.683.) (Photo Boston.)

134 Drawing, 1618. (Boston, No. 14.678.) (Photo Boston.)

137 Painting, 18th c. (Bodleian, MS. Douce Or. c.4, fol. 29.) (Photo Bodleian.)

139 Gold presentation coin, 1611. (B.M. Dept. of Coins and Medals.)

140 Twelve gold mohurs, *c.* 1620. (B.M. Dept of Coins and Medals.)

142 Oil painting, 17th c. (Nat. Port. Gal.) (Photo Nat. Port. Gal.)

142 Frontispiece to Terry, E., *Voyage to East India*, 1655. (B.M. Printed Books.) (Photo B.M.)

143 Woodcut, from Coryat, T., *Traveller for the English Wits: Greeting from the Court of the Great Moghul*, 1616, fol. A.4. verso. (B.M. Printed Books.) (Photo B.M.)

145 Page from a *Shah-jahan-nama, c.* 1650, fol. 50 v., painted by Bichitr. (Royal Library, Windsor Castle; reproduced by gracious permission of Her Majesty the Queen.) (Photo A. C. Cooper.)

148 Map from Mercator, G., *Atlas sive Cosmographicae Meditationes*, 1613, pp. 346–7. (B.M. Map Room.) (Photo B.M.)

149 Detail from a *Shah-jahan-nama, c.* 1650, fol. 194r., painted by Payag. (Royal Library, Windsor Castle; reproduced by gracious permission of Her Majesty the Queen.) (Photo John Freeman.)

150 Copy of European miniature, early 17th c. (Bodleian, MS. Ouseley Add. 171, fol. 17 v.) (Photo Bodleian.)

151 Miniature of European type, late 17th c. (Beatty, MS. 11A, No. VI.)

153 Painting by Abul Hassan, *c.* 1620. (Beatty, MS. 7, No. 15.)

154–5 Detail from an *Akbar-nama, c.* 1590. (V & A.)

178 LEFT Portrait by Abul Hassan, *c.* 1605 (Guimet, No. 3.676.B.) (Photo Service de Documentation Photographique.)

178 RIGHT Portrait, 17th c. (Delhi, No. 58.58/31.)

186 Painting by Abul Hassan, 1617. (V & A, No. I.M.14. 1925.)

194 Detail from the border of a portrait, mid-17th c. (Beatty, MS. 7, No. 35.)

195 Cameo, mid-17th c. (B.N. Cabinet des Médailles.)

200 Double-page painting from a *Shah-jahan-nama, c.* 1650. (Freer, Nos. 42.17a and 42.18a.) (Photo Freer.)

202–3 Painting, *c.* 1650. (Beatty, MS. 50, fol. 5.)

207 Illustration of a *Dhanasri Ragini*, 18th c. (B.M. MS. Stowe Or. 16, fol. 46 r.) (Photo B.M.)

211 Portrait, *c.* 1650. (Bodleian, MS. Ouseley Add. 173, fol. 17 v.) (Photo Bodleian.)

214 Portrait, *c.* 1660. (B.N., No. Od. 51. fol. 8.) (Photo B.N.)

218 LEFT Portrait, mid-17th c. (Rampur.)

218 RIGHT Portrait, *c.* 1700. (B.N., No. Od. 45.rés.pet.fol.1.) (Photo B.N.)

219 Two pages from the Dara Shukoh album. (India Office.) (Photo R. B. Fleming.)

226 Jewel-encrusted Moghul spoon, 16th c. (V & A, No. I.M.173.1910.)

230 Shivaji's tiger-claws. (By courtesy of His Highness the Maharaja of Satara.)

232 Page from an album, 18th c. (B.M. Oriental Antiquities, No. 1920.9.17.013/24.) (Photo B.M.)

239 Portrait, 18th c. (India Office, No. J.2.2.)

241 Moghul *huqqa* bowl, early 18th c. (Bombay, No. 58.10.)

242 Embroidery on a Moghul sash, 17th c. (Calico.)

247 Part of a painted cotton hanging, Madras-Pulicat school, 17th c. (Calico.)

248 Two paintings, Delhi, *c.* 1820. (India Office, Nos. Add.Or. 1 and 2.)

259

Index

Most of the places mentioned in the text are shown on the map, page 251. The grid reference in brackets after the entry for each place in the index indicates its position on the map.